J. Poyago

KV-514-481

COMPETITION, COOPERATION, RESEARCH AND DEVELOPMENT

Competition, Cooperation, Research and Development

The Economics of Research Joint Ventures

Edited by

Joanna A. Poyago-Theotoky
Lecturer in Economics
University of Nottingham

First published in Great Britain 1997 by
MACMILLAN PRESS LTD
Houndmills, Basingstoke, Hampshire RG21 6XS and London
Companies and representatives throughout the world

A catalogue record for this book is available from the British Library.

ISBN 0–333–65015–8

First published in the United States of America 1997 by
ST. MARTIN'S PRESS, INC.,
Scholarly and Reference Division,
175 Fifth Avenue, New York, N.Y. 10010

ISBN 0–312–17590–6

Library of Congress Cataloging-in-Publication Data
Competition, cooperation, and research and development : the economics
of research joint ventures / edited by Joanna Poyago-Theotoky.
      p.   cm.
Includes bibliographical references and index.
ISBN 0–312–17590–6 (cloth)
   1. Technological innovations—Management.   2. Joint ventures.
   3. Research, Industrial.   4. Competition, International.   5. High
technology industries.   I. Poyago-Theotoky, Joanna, 1961–
HD45.C625 1997
338.7—dc21   97–11685
                                                                    CIP

Selection, editorial matter and Chapter 1 © Joanna A. Poyago-Theotoky 1997
Chapters 2–9 © Macmillan Press Ltd 1997

All rights reserved. No reproduction, copy or transmission of this publication may be made
without written permission.

No paragraph of this publication may be reproduced, copied or transmitted save with
written permission or in accordance with the provisions of the Copyright, Designs and
Patents Act 1988, or under the terms of any licence permitting limited copying issued by
the Copyright Licensing Agency, 90 Tottenham Court Road, London W1P 9HE.

Any person who does any unauthorised act in relation to this publication may be liable to
criminal prosecution and civil claims for damages.

The authors have asserted their rights to be identified as the authors of this work in
accordance with the Copyright, Designs and Patents Act 1988.

This book is printed on paper suitable for recycling and made from fully managed and
sustained forest sources.

10   9   8   7   6   5   4   3   2   1
06   05   04   03   02   01   00   99   98   97

Printed and bound in Great Britain by
Antony Rowe Ltd, Chippenham, Wiltshire

Contents

v

List of Figures

List of Tables

Notes on the Contributors

Raymond De Bondt is Professor of Managerial Economics and Industrial Organization at the Department of Applied Economics of the Catholic University of Leuven, Belgium.

Sumit Joshi is Assistant Professor of Economics at the George Washington University, Washington, DC.

Yannis Katsoulacos is Professor of Economics at the Athens University of Economics and Business and Chairman of the Academic Council of the Centre of Economic Research and Environmental Strategy (CERES), Athens. He has previously taught at the Universities of Bristol, Southampton and the London School of Economics.

Katrien Kesteloot is Associate Professor of Economics at the Catholic University of Leuven.

Lynne Pepall is Associate Professor of Economics at Tufts University and has previously been Assistant Professor at Concordia University and Research Fellow at the European University Institute, Florence, Italy.

Joanna A. Poyago-Theotoky is Lecturer in Economics at the University of Nottingham. She has previously taught at the University of Bristol, England.

Antoine Soubeyran is Professor of Economics at the University of Aix-Marseille II (LEQAM), France.

Rune Stenbacka is Professor of Economics at the Swedish School of Economics and Business Administration, Helsinki, Finland. He has previously served as Director of the Finnish PhD Programme (FPPE) at the University of Helsinki.

Geert Steurs is Assistant Professor at the School of Economics, Sint-Aloysius (Brussels) and Research Fellow at the Department of Applied Economics, Catholic University of Leuven, Belgium.

Mihkel Tombak is Professor of Technology Management and Policy at the Helsinki School of Economics. He has taught at the European Institute of Business Administration (INSEAD), Fontainebleau, France, and at the University of British Columbia, Canada, where he has been the Director of the Advanced Technology Management Programme.

David Ulph is Professor of Economics at University College London and Research Fellow at CEPR (London). Previously, he has taught at the Universities of Stirling, Scotland, and Bristol, England.

Ngo Van Long is Professor of Economics at the University of Montreal, Canada.

Reinhilde Veugelers is Associate Professor at the Catholic University of Leuven, Belgium.

Nicholas Vonortas is Associate Professor of Economics and International Affairs at the George Washington University, Washington, DC.

Changqi Wu is Assistant Professor of Economics at the School of Business and Management, the Hong Kong University of Science and Technology. He has been Research Fellow at the Catholic University of Leuven and the China-Europe Institute in Belgium.

1 Introduction

Joanna A. Poyago-Theotoky

The analysis of innovation has become an important area of research in both theoretical and empirical economics. Innovation is important as it is a major contributory factor to economic growth, as pointed out by Solow (1957) and elaborated upon recently by Grossman and Helpman (1991); it also significantly affects the international competitiveness of a country (see Fagerberg, 1988) and is responsible for the dramatic increase in living standards we have witnessed over the last hundred or so years. Hence, the recent upsurge in theoretical and empirical analysis of several aspects of innovation is not surprising at all. For a comprehensive review of the literature, see Baldwin and Scott (1987), Beath *et al.* (1989, 1991), Cohen and Levin (1988), Kamien and Schwartz (1982) and Reinganum (1988).

The outcome of research activities when successful can be interpreted as a piece of new information or knowledge. However, once produced, that is, discovered, there is no substantial cost in rediscovering it. The cost of finding something new is large but the cost of disseminating this information is relatively negligible; this constitutes an extreme form of scale economy. Thus, information is expensive to produce, cheap to reproduce and difficult to profit from (Arrow, 1962). We can therefore see a problem here, in that if price is to be equated to marginal cost, as would be appropriate from the social point of view, there is no incentive for innovators to undertake research as they cannot recover their costs. There is a conflict between private and social incentives in the provision of new information, since from the social point of view information should be widely disseminated, while from the private point of view wide dissemination involves substantial costs. This is the well-known appropriability problem and its resolution is one of the aims of technology policy. Because of the appropriability problem, or rather the nature of information as a commodity, a certain kind of monopoly power has to be enjoyed by an innovator if there is to be research activity that will lead to innovations. The usual way that society deals with this problem is by granting some intellectual property right in the form of a patent to the successful innovator.[1]

Another difficulty is the problem of the duplication of research effort which is usually identified in discussions of the relationship between market structure and innovation. The logic behind the granting of a patent takes the

1

view that innovation determines market power; however, there is the opposite view that market structure affects innovation, i.e. there is a causal link from market structure to innovation. The reason for this is that if there is high concentration in an industry this will mean that firms enjoy a substantial amount of profit relative to the competitive model benchmark and this profit acts as an incentive to carry out R&D, it is the source of innovation. However, the monopoly position conferred on the innovator is short-lived. The profit the innovator enjoys acts as a signal to other firms/innovators to invest in R&D. Eventually the initial innovator is replaced by another successful firm and so on. This argument is associated with Schumpeter's notion of 'creative destruction' (Schumpeter, 1942). Thus, the more competitive the market becomes the smaller the amount of profit per firm and the weaker the incentive for R&D, generating less R&D output. However, as argued forcibly by Dasgupta (1986) and Dasgupta and Stiglitz (1980a), except in the short run, one should consider both market structure and innovation as being simultaneously and endogenously determined. They both depend on such ingredients as technological opportunities, demand conditions (see Rosenberg, 1974), the nature of the capital system and the legal structure. In such a context the interesting questions to address concern the links between the market outcome and the social optimum; that is, how much R&D each firm is performing individually and how this compares with the social optimum and whether the market in total spends too much on R&D – this latter question refers to the duplication problem.

These questions have been examined recently in the theoretical literature in the context of non-tournament models of innovation. A non-tournament model of innovation is one where the structure of the R&D competition is such that there can be a multitude of winners. Thus there can be a large number of research strategies which are sufficiently different in that they produce outputs which are independently patentable, but sufficiently similar in that these activities yield the same amount of profit and each research path requires the same expenditure on R&D to produce the same level of successful innovation. Thus, in a non-tournament model patents protect a firm's innovation from costless imitation by other firms.

Dasgupta and Stiglitz (1980a) show analytically, in the context of a homogeneous good and process innovation, that firms engage in too little cost reduction from the social point of view (a reflection of the appropriability problem) but, in aggregate, there is excessive duplication of research with too many firms engaged in R&D activities. This latter result is primarily due to the fact that research paths are assumed to be perfect substitutes and the assumption of product homogeneity, as, from the social point of view, one R&D active firm would be optimal. However, when one considers differentiated product markets the picture changes dramatically. According to Katsoulacos and Ulph (1990; 1991), in a differentiated products framework although individual firms underinvest in R&D,[2] aggregate R&D is less than in the social optimum and the market is characterized by insufficient entry (i.e. number of products).[3]

In addition to the appropriability and duplication problems there are other reasons that might lead to additional market failures in the provision of innovation. First, externalities in the form of spillovers of information between firms have to be considered. The existence of spillovers means that some of the research results of one firm may flow to a rival firm without payment so that the incentive to do R&D diminishes as firms hope to free-ride on the research efforts of their competitors.[4] Second, uncertainty is a prevalent feature of technological activity and attitudes to risk become very important especially when one has to consider the finance aspects of R&D. Capital market imperfections coupled with asymmetric information problems might result in excessive risk-aversion towards R&D activities.[5] Third, incomplete information is the norm rather than the exception and this leads to the well-known problems of moral hazard, adverse selection, monitoring difficulties and the like.

Thus it is not at all surprising that a host of policy instruments are being used by governments, in the form of technology and/or industrial policies, with the aim of correcting some of the market imperfections. Such measures might include R&D subsidies,[6] changes in the patent system and licensing,[7] public provision and others.[8] However, a policy that has received considerable attention in the last ten to fifteen years concerns the encouragement of cooperative R&D, at least in the research stage (see, for example, Cecchini, 1988; Jorde and Teece, 1989a, 1989b, 1990; Jacquemin, 1988). Cooperative R&D is perceived as a means to overcome the duplication and free-riding problems mentioned previously, alleviate uncertainty by risk-sharing and boost international competitiveness. However, there is also a downside to these beneficial effects in that collaboration might extend to the product market as well, with detrimental consequences for consumers. Notwithstanding, Jorde and Teece (1989a) and Shapiro and Willig (1990) argue for a favourable treatment of R&D and production cooperation.

There are many different types of cooperation in R&D, for example R&D consortia, Research Joint Ventures (RJVs), R&D agreements and alliances, and so on. For a description of some of these different organizational forms the interested reader should consult Chesnais (1988). Cooperative R&D raises a number of interesting questions that need to be answered at both the theoretical and empirical level, some of which are explored in this book. We next provide a brief summary of each contribution in this volume.

In Chapter 2, Yannis Katsoulacos and David Ulph provide a selective review of technology policy with an emphasis on European policy. The authors focus on a specific set of issues related to a particular type of technology policy, namely the encouragement of technological cooperation amongst competing firms. The main aim of this chapter is to provide an intellectual framework within which one can address questions related to Research Joint Ventures (RJVs) such as information-sharing and research coordination. They provide a brief summary of technology policy as practised in the European Union and consider in some detail the role of the patenting and licensing systems. In discussing the incentives to innovate that agents face in an economy the authors make a clear and important distinction between tournament and non-tournament model of R&D competition. Thus, in a non-tournament model patents protect firms from costless imitation by firms that have not done any R&D themselves but do not protect innovators from successful discoveries by other innovating firms. In contrast, in a tournament model the R&D technology is such that there can only be a single firm that makes a breakthrough: that is, there is only one firm that wins the race to innovate.

The first type of model is most appropriate for discussing whether the market outcome differs from the social optimum (appropriately defined), and in what way, so that appropriate policy measures can be advocated. The second type of model is better suited to discussing issues that deal with the evolution of market structure, namely whether innovation is undertaken by the same successful firm (a case of persistent dominance) or whether there is a successive change in the identity of the innovator (a case of action–reaction or creative destruction). Again, questions of social optimality arise here, as it is usually the case that the market outcome entails overinvestment in R&D, with obvious implications.

Next, Katsoulacos and Ulph concentrate on the way that technological cooperation and its promotion can be used to improve the incentives to carry out R&D, the duplication of research effort and appropriability problems and the amount and extent of information-sharing. In doing this, they argue forcibly that firms both inside and outside a cooperative agreement must be able to choose both the amount of R&D they perform and the extent of information exchange. Thus, information spillovers are being treated as endogenous. This latter choice has important implications for the design of technology policy since it turns out that in certain cases, depending on whether firms operate in the same or different industries and whether the research being pursued is a substitute or a complement for the research undertaken by rivals, it is not always necessary to encourage cooperation as firms may decide to share information fully. In this way, that is by making the spillover endogenous, the authors provide a richer and more realistic framework for the analysis and design of technology policy, in the form of RJVs.

In Chapter 3, Raymond De Bondt and Changqi Wu address in detail the welfare effects of a particular type of R&D cooperation, that is RJV-cartels, in an environment of oligopolistic quantity competition with information spillovers, where firms invest in cost-reducing R&D. Within an RJV-cartel innovative firms cooperate in their R&D investments and share technical information but continue to compete against each other in the product market.[9] The specific questions addressed include the determination of a stable size for a single RJV-cartel and whether consumers benefit from such an RJV-cartel. The size of the RJV-cartel is partly determined by the interplay of voluntary information-sharing amongst cartel members and involuntary industry-wide technological spillovers. Better information-sharing enhances the effective R&D investment of the RJV-cartel, increases members' profitability and leaves outsiders in a disadvantageous position. The authors find that, in general, cooperation in R&D results in higher R&D investment provided that RJV-cartel members improve sufficiently their information-sharing in comparison with non-participants. Moreover, the incentive to be part of an RJV-cartel as expressed by members' profitablity is enhanced. Static welfare, as captured by the sum of consumers' and producers' surplus, increases in line with the size of the RJV-cartel only in industries where spillovers of information are relatively large and the number of firms is small. Otherwise static welfare decreases as the size of the RJV-cartel expands, pointing to the observation that the equilibrium size of the RJV-cartel can be either larger or smaller than the socially optimal size. The policy implications of the analysis in this chapter are that it might be necessary to use corrective measures to close the wedge between the welfare maximizing size and the stable[10] size of the cooperative arrangement. However, it is suggested that an easier way to accomplish this would be to introduce policy measures that would facilitate voluntary information transmission. Throughout the analysis all competing firms are assumed to be innovators so that in order to achieve a cost reduction it is necessary to incur R&D expenditures. It is very often the case that innovators and imitators co-exist in the same industry, especially in the context of product innovations, so that whether a firm is an innovator or an imitator becomes a strategic choice for the firm(s) in question. This is the theme of the next chapter.

Lynne Pepall in Chapter 4, 'Imitative Competition and Public Policy', argues that a firm's choice can be such that the product offered is not very much different from rivals' products. Her analysis is cast within a duopoly model of vertical product differentiation and price competition where consumers' willingness to pay for goods depends on their income and consumers have different income levels. The choice of imitating a competitor's product, although increasing price competition thereby biting on the firm's profits, must be associated with gains coming from reduced costs; that is, the imitator does not have to incur product development costs to the extent of the innovator. This trade-off between reduced costs due to imitation and softer price competition due to increased product differentiation is carefully examined. The main finding is that the incentive to imitate goods in wealthier markets is stronger than the incentive to imitate in poorer markets. The incentive to imitate may be so strong that it deters the innovator from innovating altogether. The associated welfare loss of this type of market failure also increases with the level of wealth. Therefore, wealthier markets face a stronger incentive to solve the problem of imitative competition. To counter this problem two policy measures are considered: tighter patent protection and a cooperative alliance between rival firms. A tight patent policy takes the form of defining the patent breadth in a way that makes it difficult for an imitator to benefit from lower development costs, so that the innovator essentially becomes a monopolist. In contrast, the cooperative alliance solution entails development and marketing of two new products to cover the whole market. Here cooperation allows firms to coordinate their product and pricing strategies, unlike the free market solution. A comparison of social welfare under the three situations of free market, tight patent protection and cooperative alliance proves to be delicate and depends crucially on the relevant range of income distribution. For income distributions that are either relatively poor and heterogeneous, or relatively rich and homogeneous, the policy of tighter patent protection results in higher welfare relative to the cooperative alliance. The latter type of policy performs better for intermediate ranges of income distribution. The results of this chapter, in particular the welfare analysis, may prove useful to the public debate on trade and intellectual property rights.

Given the increased importance of global competition, especially in high-technology industries, and the prevalence of spillovers of information, it would seem appropriate to consider questions relating to the R&D performance of firms in a global context and examine the possible effects of cross-border R&D cooperation in comparison with within-borders cooperation. It would seem that market integration or its absence has a role to play in influencing the effects of R&D alliances. In Chapter 5 Geert Steurs turns his attention to the consequences of national versus international R&D cooperation on R&D investment, production decisions of firms and social welfare. He does so in the presence of both intra-country and international spillovers and compares the case of market integration with the case of segmented markets. His results show that for relatively restricted information spillovers at the international level it is more profitable for the strategic partners when R&D cooperation takes place at the national level and markets are integrated or when cooperation extends across borders and markets are segmented. The position of the non-cooperating firms is less clear-cut but social welfare is generally higher with national R&D cooperation in the presence of market integration.

In recent years there has been an increase in the number of cooperative agreements. Evidence suggests that a growing number of alliances are formed between asymmetric partners. The asymmetries relate to factors such as the nationality of the firms, their size and the size of their home market, the type of product they offer and the nature of product market competition, the degree of spillovers, and so on. Consequently, firms' expected performance and their incentives to engage in alliances as well as the stability thereof will be influenced considerably. Katrien Kesteloot and Reinhilde Veugelers present, in Chapter 6, empirical evidence based on their own database and summarize the scant theoretical literature dealing with the impact of partner asymmetries on the formation and performance of strategic alliances, in particular R&D alliances. Specifically, the authors consider a setting of repeated interaction amongst firms (in a duopoly), where firms cooperate on the choice of R&D expenditure but compete in the product market by choosing output levels. They derive conditions that will guarantee the continued cooperation in R&D, given that there are incentives to cheat on the agreement, especially for the more disadvantaged partner. These conditions are crucially dependent on the relative asymmetry between spillovers of information; substantial asymmetries may render R&D cooperation unprofitable. Relative market size, efficiency in R&D and production costs are also shown to play a role. In general, cooperation will be beneficial for both an advantaged and a disadvantaged firm if both asymmetries affecting them are not too substantial. The literature on cooperation with asymmetric partners is at a developmental stage and this chapter offers some initial insights into a very interesting area that warrants special attention.

In a related context, Ngo Van Long and Antoine Soubeyran, in Chapter 7, make the point that increasing the degree of cost asymmetry within a joint venture in a Cournot oligopoly will always increase firms' combined profit, thus providing a reason for asymmetric contributions. More precisely, if the average unit cost of production is kept constant, an increase in the dispersion of unit costs will leave price and aggregate industry output unchanged, and will raise total industry profits. Thus joint ventures might take place for yet another reason: to increase profitability by requiring partners to contribute in an unequal manner.

The next two chapters look at R&D expenditure and cooperation in dynamic settings, where the passage of time plays an important role. In Chapter 8, Rune Stenbacka and Mihkel Tombak compare two different contractual arrangements, that is, competitive and cartelized RJVs, where participating firms incur investment expenses that will lower the costs of production of all partners. In a competitive RJV firms decide individually on their R&D investment to maximize own discounted profit, whereas in a cartelized RJV firms decide collectively their R&D expenditure to maximize industry profit. The authors study how R&D investments are affected by the degree of commitment implied by these two contractual arrangements. A cartelized RJV results in a higher R&D spending profile and is welfare enhancing. However, when this type of cooperation is not possible or permissible it is always better to abstain from contractual precommitments to a time-dependent profile of R&D expenditure. Being flexible in terms of being able to revise the R&D expenditure profile allows firms to alleviate the free-rider problem associated with a competitive RJV. Note that this aspect is totally absent in a static framework.

Finally, in Chapter 9 on 'Dynamic Cooperation in R&D', Sumit Joshi and Nicholas Vonortas generalize the analysis of static models with process innovation, imperfect appropriability and quantity competition to a dynamic framework of infinite horizon. Their work, in a sense, is a complement to Chapter 8. In each period, firms first spend on R&D and then compete in output; moreover, the stock of knowledge available keeps changing through time as a result of previous R&D investments. They characterize and compare three different cooperative arrangements – 'secretariat RJV', 'operating entity RJV' and 'monopolistic RJV'. The first two refer to RJVs where firms cooperate in R&D but compete later on in the market place: the secretariat RJV does not internalize any spillovers of information, while the operating entity RJV does. Thus these two forms of organization are conceptually similar to the competitive and cartelized RJVs respectively, examined by Stenbacka and Tombak. In a monopolistic RJV firms cooperate both in R&D and output production. The authors confirm a result known from static analysis, namely that the monopolistic RJV results in the highest level of aggregate R&D investment and the secretariat R&D in the lowest. They also provide some preliminary results as to the desirability of each type of RJVs in comparison with non-cooperation. Their stylized model points to the following policy implications: first, that industries with high stocks of technological knowledge benefit from cooperative R&D; second, the more leaky technical knowledge that there is in an industry the better positioned an

RJV is to undertake the relevant research; and third, closer cooperation leads to higher levels of aggregate R&D.

The contributions in this volume are analytical but this in no way should undermine the importance of empirical investigation. It is hoped that the issues raised will generate sufficient interest for empirical research to complement and question the theoretical findings. The topics covered represent a selective attempt at exploring some hitherto neglected but nevertheless important aspects of cooperative R&D.

Notes

1. Kaufer (1988) contains a comprehensive review of the economics of patents and also gives historical details. See also the papers by Beath and Ulph (1990), Gallini (1992), Griliches (1984), Katsoulacos and Ulph (1990, 1991), Klemperer (1990), Levin *et al.* (1987), Scotchmer and Green (1990) and Waterson (1990).
2. As the market becomes larger, equilibrium R&D per firm approaches the socially optimal level.
3. Other related papers include Dasgupta and Stiglitz (1980b), Levin (1978), Loury (1979) and Futia (1980).
4. Theoretical work on spillovers includes the papers by Spence (1984), Katz (1986), D'Aspremont and Jacquemin (1988), Suzumura (1992), Kamien *et al.* (1992), De Bondt and Henriques (1995) on intra-industry spillovers, and Steurs (1994) on inter-industry spillovers. On the empirical side, consider Bernstein and Nadiri (1988, 1989).
5. Bhattacharya and Ritter (1983) discuss some of the finance issues of innovation, but the area certainly needs more researching.
6. R&D subsidies are discussed, for example, by Brander and Spencer (1983a, 1983b), Beath *et al.* (1989), Dixit and Grossman (1986) and Ulph and Winters (1991).
7. On licensing, see Gallini (1984), Gallini and Winter (1985) and Katz and Shapiro (1985, 1986, 1987). See also the Symposium on patents and technology licensing in *Rand Journal of Economics*, Spring 1990.
8. For example, diffusion policies, procurement, education and training policies, the setting of standards, risk-sharing and coordination with other branches of policy such as competition and trade policy.
9. This terminology has been introduced in the literature by Kamien *et al.* (1992).
10. See D'Aspremont *et al.* (1983) for a definition of the concept of stability used.

References

Arrow, K. (1962) 'Economic Welfare and the Allocation of Resources for Inventions', in R. Nelson (ed.), *The Rate and the Direction of Inventive Activity* (Princeton: Princeton University Press).

Baldwin, B.W. and J.T. Scott (1987) *Market Structure and Technological Change* (Chur: Harwood Academic Publishers).

Beath, J., Y. Katsoulacos and D. Ulph (1988) 'Strategic R&D Policy', Discussion Paper No. 88/214, University of Bristol, Department of Economics.

Beath, J., Y. Katsoulacos and D. Ulph (1989) 'The Game-Theoretic Analysis of Innovation: A Survey', *Bulletin of Economic Research*, 42(3), pp. 163–84.

Beath, J., Y. Katsoulacos and D. Ulph (1991) 'Strategic Innovation', In M. Bacharach, M. Dempster and J. Enos (eds), *Mathematical Models in Economics* (Oxford: Oxford University Press).

Beath, J. and D. Ulph (1990) 'The Trade-off between Static and Dynamic Efficiency in a Non-Tournament Model of Innovation', Discussion Paper No. 90/286, University of Bristol, Department of Economics.

Bernstein, J.I. and M.I. Nadiri (1988) 'Interindustry R&D Spillovers, Rates of Return, and Production in High-Tech Industries', *American Economic Review*, 78 (Papers and Proceedings), pp. 429–34.

Bernstein, J.I. and M.I. Nadiri (1989) 'Research and Development and Intraindustry Spillovers: An Empirical Application of Dynamic Duality', *Review of Economic Studies*, 56, pp. 249–69.

Bhattacharya, S. and J. Ritter (1983) 'Innovation and Communication: Signalling with Partial Disclosure', *Review of Economic Studies*, 50, pp. 331–46.

Brander, B.J. and J.A. Spencer (1983a) 'Strategic Commitment with R&D: The Symmetric Case', *Bell Journal of Economics*, 14, pp. 225–35.

Brander, B.J. and J.A. Spencer (1983b) 'International R&D Rivalry and Industrial Strategy', *Review of Economic Studies*, 50, pp. 707–22.

Cecchini, P.A. (1988) *The European Challenge: 1992* (Aldershot: Wildwood House for the Commission of the European Communities).

Chesnais, F. (1988) 'Technical Cooperation Agreements between Firms', *STI Review*, 4 (December), pp. 52–119.

Cohen, W. and R. Levin (1988) 'Empirical Studies of Innovation and Market Structure', in R. Schmalensee and R. Willig (eds), *Handbook of Industrial Organization* (Amsterdam: North-Holland).

D'Aspremont, C. and A. Jacquemin (1988) 'Cooperative and Noncooperative R&D in a Duopoly with Spillovers', *American Economic Review*, 78, pp. 1133–7.

D'Aspremont, C., A. Jacquemin, J. Gabszewicz and J. Weymark (1983) 'On the Stability of Collusive Price Leadership', *Canadian Journal of Economics*, 16(1), pp. 17–25.

Dasgupta, P. (1986) 'The Theory of Technological Competition', in J. Stiglitz and F. Mathewson (eds), *New Developments in the Analysis of Market Structure* (Cambridge, Mass.: MIT Press).

Dasgupta, P. and J. Stiglitz (1980a) 'Industrial Structure and the Nature of Innovative Activity', *Economic Journal*, 90, pp. 266–93.

Dasgupta, P. and J. Stiglitz (1980b) 'Uncertainty, Industrial Structure and the Speed of R&D', *Bell Journal of Economics*, 11, pp. 1–28.

De Bondt, R. and I. Henriques (1995) 'Strategic Investment with Asymmetric Spillovers', *Canadian Journal of Economics*, 28(3), pp. 656–74.

Dixit, A. and G. Grossman (1986) 'Targeted Export Promotion with Several Oligopolistic Industries', *European Economic Review*, 30, pp. 233–49.

Fagerberg, J. (1988) 'International Competitiveness', *Economic Journal*, 98, pp. 355–74.

Futia, C. (1980) 'Schumpeterian Competition', *Quarterly Journal of Economics*, 93, pp. 675–95.

Gallini, N. (1984) 'Deterrence through Market Sharing: A Strategic Incentive for Licensing', *American Economic Review*, 74, pp. 931–41.

Gallini, N. (1992) 'Patent Policy and Costly Imitation', *Rand Journal of Economics*, 23, pp. 52–63.

Gallini, N. and R. Winter (1985) 'Licensing in the Theory of Innovation', *RAND Journal of Economics*, 16, pp. 237–52.

Griliches, Z. (ed.) (1984) *R&D, Patents, and Productivity* (Chicago: Chicago University Press).

Grossman, G. and E. Helpman (1991) *Innovation and Growth in the Global Economy* (Cambridge, Mass.: MIT Press).

Jacquemin, A. (1988) 'Cooperative Agreements in R&D and European Antitrust Policy', *European Economic Review*, 32, pp. 551–60.

Jorde, T. and D. Teece (1989a) 'Innovation, Cooperation, and Antitrust: Balancing Competition and Cooperation', *High Technology Law Journal*, 4, pp. 1–113.

Jorde, T. and D. Teece (1989b) 'Acceptable Cooperation Among Competitors in the Face of Growing International Competition', *Antitrust Law Journal*, 58, pp. 529–56.

Jorde, T. and D. Teece (1990) 'Innovation and Cooperation: Implications for Competition and Antitrust', *Journal of Economics Perspectives*, 4(3), pp. 75–96.

Kamien, M. and N. Schwartz (1982) *Market Structure and Innovation* (Cambridge: Cambridge University Press).

Kamien, M., E. Muller and I. Zang (1992) 'Research Joint Ventures and R&D Cartels', *American Economic Review*, 82, pp. 1293–306.

Katsoulacos, Y. and D. Ulph (1990) 'Social Welfare Losses under Product Differentiation and R&D Rivalry', Discussion Paper No. 90/285, University of Bristol, Department of Economics.

Katsoulacos, Y. and D. Ulph (1991) 'R&D Rivalry under Product Differentiation: Market Equilibria and Social Optimum', Discussion Paper, University of Liverpool.

Katz, M. (1986) 'An Analysis of Cooperative Research and Development', *RAND Journal of Economics*, 17(Winter), pp. 527–43.

Katz, M. and C. Shapiro (1985) 'On the Licensing of Innovations', *RAND Journal of Economics*, 16, pp. 504–20.

Katz, M. and C. Shapiro (1986) 'How to License Intangible Property', *Quarterly Journal of Economics*, 101, pp. 567–90.

Katz, M. and C. Shapiro (1987) 'R&D Rivalry with Licensing and Imitation', *American Economic Review*, 77, pp. 402–21.

Kaufer, E. (1988) *The Economics of the Patent System* (Chur: Harwood Academic Publishers).

Klemperer, P. (1990) 'How Broad Should the Scope of Patent Protection Be?', *Rand, Journal of Economics*, 21, pp. 113–30.

Levin, R. (1978) 'Technical Change, Barriers to Entry and Market Structure', *Economica*, 45, pp. 347–61.

Levin, R., A.K. Klevorick, R.R. Nelson and S.G. Winter (1987) 'Appropriating the Returns from Industrial Research and Development', *Brookings Papers on Economic Activity*, 3, pp. 783–820.

Loury, G. (1979) 'Market Structure and Innovation', *Quarterly Journal of Economics*, 93, pp. 395–410.

Reinganum, J. (1988) 'The Timing of Innovation: Research, Development and Diffusion', in R. Schmalensee and R. Willig (eds), *Handbook of Industrial Organization* (Amsterdam: North-Holland).

Rosenberg, N. (1974) 'Science, Innovation and Economic Growth', *Economic Journal*, 84, pp. 90–108.

Schumpeter, J. (1942) *Capitalism, Socialism and Democracy* (New York: Harper).

Scotchmer, S. and J. Green (1990) 'Novelty and Disclosure in Patent Law', *Rand Journal of Economics*, 21, pp. 131–46.

Shapiro, C. and R. Willig (1990) 'On the Antitrust Treatment of Production Research Joint Ventures', *Journal of Economic Perspectives*, 4(3), pp. 113–30.

Solow, R. (1957), 'Technical Change and the Aggregate Production Function', *Review of Economics and Statistics*, 39, pp. 312–20.

Spence, M. (1984) 'Cost Reduction, Competition and Industrial Performance', *Econometrica*, 52, pp. 101–22.

Steurs, G. (1994) 'Spillovers and Cooperation in Research and Development', PhD thesis, Katholieke Universiteit Leuven, 252 pp.

Suzumura, K. (1992) 'Cooperative and Non-cooperative R&D in an Oligopoly with Spillovers', *American Economic Review*, 82, pp. 1307–20.

Ulph, D. and L.A. Winters (1991) 'Strategic Manpower Policy and International Trade', Discussion Paper No. 91/311, University of Bristol, Department of Economics.

Waterson, M. (1990) 'The Economics of Product Patents', *American Economic Review*, 80, pp. 860–69.

2 Technology Policy: A Selective Review with Emphasis on European Policy and the Role of RJVs

Yannis Katsoulacos and David Ulph

2.1 INTRODUCTION

Technology policy can be thought of as a specific set of industrial policies that aim to improve the ability of firms to compete by promoting technological improvements through the generation, diffusion and adoption of process, product and organizational innovations. In recent years technology policy has moved to the forefront of the discussion of industrial policy within the European Commission, the United States and Japan.

There are many types of policy that come under the heading of technology policy, each of which has been, and continues to be the subject of extensive theoretical and empirical analysis. We do not intend to offer a comprehensive survey of this literature. Instead we want to focus the central part of this chapter on the economic analysis of a specific set of issues that arise in connection with a particular type of technology policy, that of *promoting technological cooperation*, and to report on some recent work that we have been undertaking in this area. This particular type of technology policy has underlined the Commission of the European Union's attempts to improve competitiveness and cohesion (or integration) for a very long time. A short review of the history of this policy in Europe is also provided in the next subsection.

However, in order to provide some kind of intellectual framework within which we can see why it might be also of some theoretical interest to focus on this particular set of technology policy issues, we will begin by examining the fundamental rationale for technology policy. This will lead us to a brief discussion in sections 2.2 and 2.3 of a number of different technology policies, before coming to the specific set of issues on which we wish to undertake a more detailed analysis in section 2.4. Concluding remarks are offered in section 2.5.

The starting point for providing a rationale for technology policy lies in the well-understood market failure associated with the problems of appropriating the gains from knowledge. These problems arise from the public good nature of knowledge of being expensive to produce but relatively cheap to disseminate.

The difficulty to which this gives rise is that in the absence of any intervention firms see too low a return to any R&D they undertake and we get too slow a pace of innovation.

The fundamental resource allocation problem is therefore to find a mechanism that rewards the creator of knowledge with a return that reflects the value of that knowledge to society, while making the knowledge as widely available in society as fast as possible.

Now of course we know from the work of Cohen and Levinthal (1989) that while knowledge may be relatively cheap to disseminate it is not always cheap for firms to exploit the knowledge they gain from another source, and that part of the R&D that some firms do is undertaken in order to enable them to exploit any findings they obtain from other sources. This does not however alter the fundamental resource allocation problem which is that the originator of the discovery does not obtain the full return, and so incentives to undertake R&D are too low.

Technology Policy in Practice

There are many types of policy that come under the heading 'technology policy'. Specifically, policy intervention in technology activities can be categorized into three major categories (see also Itoh *et al.*, 1991):

1. Setting up of a legal framework such as a licensing system and copyrights to protect intellectual property.
2. Government-sponsored R&D and other new technology promotion activities, through the network of universities and national research institutes. Also creating the necessary infrastructure and establishing links between research and production.
3. Direct policies to foster and assist private sector R&D, based on various types of subsidies, interest rate reductions, tax reductions and exemptions. A particularly important dimension of such policies in recent years (both theoretically and at the level of the practice of technology policy) is the assistance and promotion of the formation of associations or cooperations between firms – for example, cooperations as research joint ventures (RJVs).

Since the 1960s, developments in Community R&D policies have been largely determined by industrial policy concerns. Industrial policy concerns were expressed through technological gap arguments and called for an encouragement of European competitiveness which was crystallized in the Single European Act (SEA).

From the very beginning there was emphasis on *cooperative efforts* across European countries. As far back as January 1972 in the First European Conference on Scientific and Technological Research, held in Brussels in the presence of delegates from 19 European countries, seven cooperation agreements were signed concerning data-processing, telecommunications, metallurgy and environmental pollution. The Commission would provide for the coordination of the collaboration. Thus, COST (Cooperation in Science and Technology) was set up as a framework for Community concerted action programmes the execution of which is financed by the participating countries.

The concept of a Common Policy in Science and Technology appeared in the early 1970s. On 14 July 1972 the Commission sent the Council a package of proposals to set up an early organization for a Common Science and Technology Policy. According to this, opportunities for a Common Policy lie on:

1. Sharing the costs of large installation facilities in basic research as well as coordinating basic research programmes of common interest.
2. Defining R&D programmes linked with industrial objectives in major technologies (aeronautics, space, telecommunications, data processing).
3. Linking R&D and industrial policies to the creation of a Common Market in order to ensure the coordination needed for industrial success.

Nevertheless little changed during the 1970s. From 1977, however, Commissioner Davignon was bringing a new dynamism in industrial policies. In May 1977 he introduced what was later named the Davignon Plan, a very interventionist plan based on the European Coal and Steel Community (ECSC) Treaty to save the Community's steel industry from the crisis in which it had found itself. In 1979 he also initiated the direct formulation by the Commission of a European industrial network in micro-electronics which was institutionalized in ESPRIT and was seen as providing a Community dimension in science and technology policy.

Thus, during the 1980s the common industrial base climbed again up the agenda. In 1981 in its 5th Medium Term Economic Policy Programme the Commission emphasized the introduction of a policy for industrial innovation and technology based on the Internal Market. This line of approach led to the Commission's White Paper on the completion of the Internal Market which was put forward to the European Council in Milan in June 1985. This was complemented by the Commission's Memorandum 'Towards a European Technology Community'.

The Technology Community was endorsed by the European Council together with the completion of the Internal Market. According to the Memorandum,

the fundamental objective is to strengthen the technological bases of European industry and to develop its international competitiveness. To serve this objective, the Technology Community must have the remit and the resources to carry out certain actions in the interests of the Community: to conduct technology research and development with the participation, which may vary from one programme to another, of Member States' firms and research centres, and to carry out horizontal or back-up measures in support of the coordination of national programmes in order to take advantage of synergies.

Three types of technological research and development projects are envisaged. First, projects in generic technologies which aim at inducing industrial firms to *join force and cooperate* with universities, research centres and public authorities for a mastery up to the development stage of technologies whose specific applications will spread throughout the industrial fabric, modernizing processes or giving rise to new products. Second, development and exploitation of joint facilities for basic research purposes. Third, strategic programmes which are technology intensive, or major talent and resource mobilizing programmes whose specific purpose could be a field of general interest.

All these programmes became incorporated into the, now famous; Framework Programmes run by the Commission since 1992/3. Each framework programme provides for the coordination of national and Community policies. It is a collective response to collectively identified needs. 'The adoption of such a framework programme and its periodic review would give all Member States the opportunity to establish in every field whether Europe has an adequate S-T base and whether the resources deployed will enable its industry to meet outside competition.'

Within the framework programmes in order to increase the *efficiency of cooperation*, methods are envisaged which: (1) draw together for each project those partners who wish to participate on the basis of a clear perception of the costs and benefits of their cooperation; (2) lead to the establishment of industrial consortia and organization of inter-governmental cooperation in such a way as to harness the best available skills; (3) rely on a European network of research establishments and universities in regular touch with each other and able to act as centre for generating research and technology and disseminating the results; and (4) allow for participation of partners from non-Community countries.

2.2 THE PATENT AND LICENSING SYSTEMS

The first and most obvious component of technology policy as a way of solving the resource allocation problem mentioned above is to increase the return to R&D through the creation of a legal framework for the protection of intellectual property rights through patents, licences, copyright, etc.

This is a huge topic in its own right, but to set some of the later discussion in context we need to say something about the effectiveness of such a system.

Let us begin by examining the impact of *a pure patent system*. We can think of this as a system that gives a firm that discovers an idea the exclusive right to use it. Suppose, for the moment, that this were completely effective – patents last for ever, and are never breached. To see how far this goes towards solving the resource allocation problem, it is useful to consider two contrasting cases.

The first is that in which there are many different research paths which firms in a given industry can pursue towards making some new discovery – a lower-cost technology or a higher-quality product. These paths are sufficiently similar that a given amount of R&D spent on one research path will bring about the same amount of cost reduction/quality improvement as on any other research path. In that sense the paths are perfect substitutes. However, they are sufficiently different that a discovery made on one path can be patented whether or not firms have made discoveries on other research paths.

Thus while patents protect firms from costless imitation by firms that have undertaken no R&D they cannot protect firms from successful discovery by other innovators. This type of model is what is known in the literature as a *non-tournament* model of R&D competition (see, for example, Beath *et al.*, 1995).

To see what happens in this model, consider first the case where R&D leads to cost-reductions, where competition in the output market takes the form of Cournot competition, but where, in choosing their R&D, firms act in a non-strategic fashion, choosing R&D and output simultaneously. This means that the gains firms see from R&D is simply the reduction in its costs for producing a given output. Then firms will spend on R&D up to the point where the marginal gain from an additional amount of R&D equals the marginal cost. The marginal gain will be directly proportional to a firm's output.

Since all these R&D paths are perfect substitutes, the social optimum would essentially involve having a single firm undertake all the R&D and setting output at the point where price equals marginal cost. The level of R&D chosen by this firm would again be where the marginal benefit equals the marginal cost, but here the marginal benefit would be proportional to total industry output. Thus compared to the social optimum, the market fails for two reasons:

1. Each firm undertakes too little R&D, because its own output is too low: in part this is because it produces only a fraction of industry output; and in part it is because industry output is itself too low since imperfect competition drives price above marginal cost.
2. The second market failure is that too many firms engage in R&D – there is excessive duplication of R&D effort.

If firms act strategically – choosing R&D before output – then they have a stronger incentive to innovate than was suggested by the above model, because they now calculate that an additional advantage of lowering their own costs is that they will grab market share from their rivals' output thus further driving up profits. This is the *strategic investment effect*, and, as we have indicated, this reinforces the conventional cost-minimizing calculation. However, in a wide class of cases, the private incentives of firms to undertake R&D will still be below the social optimum, thus maintaining the general conclusion from *non-tournament* models that the market fails by needlessly duplicating R&D while achieving too little in the way of cost reduction/ product improvement.

A second kind of model arises when there is effectively only a single research path that firms can pursue. Now, given the assumed perfect patent protection, whoever first makes the discovery on the research path becomes the sole firm that can exploit the new technology/new product. In this case R&D competition takes the form of a race to be the first to innovate. The sharpest contrast with the *non-tournament* models comes in the case where the R&D technology is such that there can only ever be a single firm that wins the race to innovate. The class of models of R&D competition that this produces is what is known as *tournament models* (see, for example, Beath *et al.*, 1995).

In these tournament models the main calculation that determines the amount of R&D that each firm does is that by spending a little more on R&D then it might become the successful innovator and thereby prevent any of its rivals from becoming the successful innovator. Thus the firm compares the marginal cost of an additional amount of R&D with the marginal gain from getting forever the stream of profits that accrues to a successful innovator as distinct from getting *forever* the stream of profits associated with a non-innovating firm. In other words, what determines the incentive to innovate is what is known as the *competitive threat* – the difference between *the present value* of a firm's profits if it becomes the sole innovator and the profits it would make if some other firm became the sole innovator.

Notice that if the real rate of interest was 5 per cent then this would mean that the competitive threat would be 20 times the difference between the *flow* rate of profits of a successful innovator and a firm that failed to innovate.

Now, from the point of view of society, it does not matter who makes the discovery, as long as someone does, provided they share it with everyone else. If we assume diminishing returns to R&D effort, then the social optimum in the case of *tournament* models of R&D competition would be characterized by having many firms undertake R&D but having whoever makes the discovery share it with everyone else. This arrangement is efficient since, for a given total expenditure on R&D, it maximizes the probability that any single firm, and hence every firm, gets the new technology or product.

An immediate implication is that in the case of pure *tournament* R&D models there is no needless duplication of R&D effort.

To see whether markets obtain the optimum amount of R&D effort, notice that the optimum amount of R&D to do involves balancing off the gains to society from bringing forward the likely date of discovery by one period against the costs of the additional amount of R&D necessary to do this. Thus in the social optimum the incentive to do R&D for any one firm is determined by the difference between the *flow* rate of social surplus (per firm) associated with having the new technology/product available to all firms, and the flow rate of social surplus (per firm) associated with having the existing technology/product in place.

While in general the difference between the flow rate of social surplus per firm from having the new technology/product available and the flow rate of surplus per firm from having the old technology/product around will be larger than the difference between the flow rate of profits to a firm that succeeds in innovating and the flow rate of profits of a firm that fails to innovate, the difference in surplus will in general be nothing like 20 times the difference in profit, and it is this latter figure that is reflected in the *competitive threat* that drives the innovative decisions of firms in the market.

Thus the general conclusion from *tournament models* is that markets fail by giving excessively large incentives to firms to innovate, and consequently firms overinvest in R&D.

We see, then, that by giving exclusive rights of development to the discoverer of an idea a pure patent system is an unsatisfactory way of solving the fundamental resource allocation problem. For, in the case of *non-tournament* models where there can be many winners, each firm sees only their own fraction of the gain from having a new technology/product available to society and so underinvests in R&D while at the same time duplicating the efforts of all other firms to introduce effectively the same new technology or product; whereas in the case of *tournament* models where there can be just a single winner, firms devote all their efforts to the socially irrelevant issue of determining the particular identity of the winner, and this leads them to overinvest in R&D.

The reason why patents are unsatisfactory is that there are two separate aspects to the resource allocation problem which we have to get right *simultaneously*:

1. we have to get the right level of R&D expenditure;
2. we have to get the right amount of sharing of the R&D discoveries.

In an attempt to solve the appropriability problem, patents completely rule out any sharing of the R&D discoveries, and, precisely because they get this aspect of the resource allocation problem wrong, they also get the level of R&D wrong. Before discussing how we might improve on the resource allocation brought about by the pure patent system let us just note a number of points.

First note that the underinvestment in R&D that occurs in the case of non-tournament models arises even when, as we have assumed, patents are completely effective, and there are no unintentional leakages or spillovers of R&D from one firm to another. So the underinvestment problem is not an externality problem.

However, patents are not completely effective, in part at least because they are not of infinite duration. It is often thought that this is desirable, because while it exacerbates the underinvestment problem by further reducing the returns to innovators and so generates greater *dynamic* inefficiency, the reduction in patent life brings about greater *static* efficiency because it allows non-innovating firms to get access to the new technology/product earlier and this extra competition drives price down towards its competitive level. A finite patent life is thought to be optimal because it trades off this greater static efficiency against a loss of dynamic efficiency.

However, this is only true in a special class of models, and some recent work (Beath and Ulph, 1990; Katsoulacos and Ulph, 1994a) has shown that with *non-tournament* models there may be no trade-off between static and dynamic efficiency, and that the optimum patent life may be infinite.

When competition takes the form of a *tournament* then having finite-life patents or some other form of spillover can ameliorate the overinvestment problem generated by patents. Indeed in the extreme case where spillovers are very large the model can turn into that of a *waiting game* where each firm sits back waiting for the other to spend money on making the discovery.

The second point we want to make about the pure patent system is that the excessive duplication that arises in the non-tournament model depends on the assumption that we are dealing with process innovation. In some recent work by Katsoulacos and Ulph (1993) it has been shown that with product innovation the needless duplication loss arises when R&D leads to the discovery of generic products, but not in the case of specific products.

Turning back to the question of how we might improve on a pure patent system, the core of the problem is that because the utilization of an idea is confined to the firm that discovers it, firms do not perceive the wider gains to others from the discovery of an idea.

One way in which it might be thought that we could improve on a pure patent system would be by supplementing it by a licensing system whereby a firm that discovers an idea makes it available by agreement to other firms in return for some payment.

Most of the formal analysis of licensing has been conducted in the context of models which have much of the structure of *tournament models* (see also Beath *et al.*, 1995).

To see what happens here consider the case where firms make a decision about whether or not to license their discovery only after the discovery has been made – that is, we have *ex-post* licensing. As in the existing literature, we will focus solely on the case of process innovation where R&D lowers costs of production, and output in the product market is determined as a Cournot equilibrium. For the moment, we will assume that there are only two firms in the industry.

Suppose that a firm has won the patent race, then the firm that has made the discovery has to consider whether it will be better off by letting the other firm get access to the new low-cost technology it has discovered (in return for a fee) than by remaining as the sole firm with access to the new technology. The non-innovating firm has to decide whether it would be better off with access to the new technology and paying the licence fee rather than remaining as the high-cost firm. For licensing to occur it is necessary that industry profits are greater when both firms have access to the new technology than when only the innovating firm has such access. This in turn will only occur if the costs with the new technology are not too far below those with the existing technology.

Thus licensing may not always occur, even though there would be clear gains to society from increasing competition by giving both firms access to the new technology.

If licensing does occur, and then we consider how this affects the incentives of firms to innovate, we see that licensing increases profits both if the firm succeeds in discovering the new technology and if it fails to discover it. What this does to the competitive threat depends on the licence fee, and hence on the bargaining strengths of the licensor and the licensee. If the licensor has the greater bargaining power then licensing will increase the *competitive threat* thus further exacerbating the overinvestment problem to which tournament models are prone.

Turning to the use of licences in *non-tournament* models, let us continue to focus on the case of process innovation, Cournot equilibrium in the product market and duopoly.

Now in order to get round both the problem of excessive duplication and the underinvestment problem what we seem to require is an *ex-ante* licensing agreement. That is, one firm negotiates with the other an ex-ante agreement whereby in return for a licence fee it alone undertakes any R&D that is to be done, agreeing in advance that it will certainly license any technology it discovers to the other firm.

In the initial agreement, firms bargain over the amount of R&D to be done and the licence fee. Since the fee is independent of any R&D that is actually done, the two firms would always agree to undertake the efficient level of R&D – that which maximizes *industry* profits net of R&D costs.

Once again there are two components to the incentive to reduce costs. The first is output, and here the output that is relevant is total industry output rather than output per firm. This is precisely what ought to appear if we want R&D to be socially efficient.

However, the second term that enters the firm's R&D calculation is the *strategic investment incentive*. The problem is that this is now negative rather than positive; since lowering costs through R&D means lowering both its own costs *and* the costs of its rival the net effect is to expand rather than contract its rival's. Therefore such an *ex-ante* licensing agreement will still result in underinvestment in R&D. So while in principle licensing may go some way towards correcting the resource allocation problems associated with a pure patenting system, it does not fully resolve them. This is because licenses are still rather restricted in the way in which they share out the R&D discoveries.

Specifically there are a number of problems with licensing.

1. In the case of *ex-post* licensing, it may not always occur.
2. When we move outside the rather simple framework considered here, *ex-ante* licensing is clearly subject to severe problems of informational asymmetry.
3. When we move beyond the case of duopoly then how much one licensee is willing to pay for a licence depends on how many other firms the licensor is going to license, and there are complex issues in designing mechanisms to address this problem.
4. In a more complex framework where we are dealing with a sequence of ongoing innovations, licensing one discovery may affect the licensee's ability to compete against the licensor in future R&D races.

It may not be too surprising therefore to find that while licensing is undoubtedly a significant phenomenon, nevertheless most of the patents held by corporations are used exclusively by those corporations.

2.3 PUBLIC OR GOVERNMENT-SPONSORED R&D, SPILLOVERS AND SMEs

For the second major type of policy intervention mentioned in the Introduction, R&D activity undertaken directly or indirectly by the government through public research institutions, there are two main shortcomings. First, the efficiency of the R&D activity itself may be impeded since the institutions involved in the R&D are not profit motivated and there is nothing to ensure that the R&D activity is carried out at the socially minimum cost. A lack of profit motive, in conjunction with a moral hazard problem, can give rise to a particularly high degree of inefficiency in the case of R&D activities involving uncertainty.

A second equally important issue in relation to public R&D is how to optimize the use of the discoveries resulting from it, given that public organizations, such as universities, are not involved in the commercial exploitation of the discoveries that are the outcome of their research efforts.

More generally the research laboratories of universities and other public R&D institutes provide a source of innovation – generating knowledge that is available to private enterprises for commercial exploitation. Jaffe (1989) and Acs, Audretsch and Feldman (1992), for example, found that the knowledge created in university laboratories 'spills over' to contribute to the generation of commercial innovations by private enterprises. Similarly, Link and Rees (1990) surveyed 209 innovating firms to examine the relationship between firm size and university research. They found that, in fact, large firms are more active in university-based research. However small-and medium-sized enterprises apparently are better able to exploit their university-based associations and generate innovations. Link and Rees conclude that, contrary to the conventional wisdom, diseconomies of scale to the 'inherent bureaucratization process which inhibits both innovative activity and the speed with which new inventions move through the corporate system towards the market' (Link and Rees, 1990, p. 25).

In relation to this last point it is worth noting here that the recent wave of studies documenting the extent to which innovative activity occurs outside of the largest corporations poses something of a paradox to the traditional model of the knowledge production function. That small enterprises are the engine of innovation activity in certain industries despite an obvious lack of formal R&D activities raises the question, 'Where do small firms get their innovation producing inputs?'

In a series of recent papers Audretsch and his collaborators argue that, while the model of the knowledge production function may be valid, the relevant unit of observation may be somewhat broader than at the level of an individual enterprise, and may span both a product and spatial dimension. Placing the knowledge production function in such a context allows for the possibility of what we term 'knowledge spillovers', where the investment in R&D made by private and public firms, as well as universities, spills over for economic exploitation by third-party firms.

While a link between R&D spillovers from universities to small firms has already been identified in the United States, until recently it was not known whether such research externalities also existed in Europe. The results of a paper by Audretsch and Vivarelli (1994) suggest that not only do such R&D spillovers exist but *they are much stronger for small firms than for their larger counterparts.*

They use a modified version of the knowledge production function that is estimated using a new longitudinal data base comprising 15 Italian regions over the period 1978–86. Each observation spans all economic activity within the relevant region and is divided by resident population to control for the relative size of different Italian regions.

Innovative activity is measured as the number of patents within the region in the relevant year. There are two main sources of innovation-generating knowledge included in the model. The first is expenditures on R&D by both private and public firms. The second is the expenditures on research expended by universities.

Based on the pooled, cross-section results, the authors find that while R&D inputs, both from private and public firms as well as universities, contribute to the generation of innovative output, the spillovers from universities are apparently more important for small firm innovation than for their larger counterparts. Not only does this confirm similar findings for the United States, but it also suggests that an environment with a high endowment of knowledge-based workers and skilled engineers is particularly conducive to the innovative activity of small firms.

In another recent paper by Acs, Audretsch and Feldman (1993a) the authors use US data that allow them to utilize another measure of innovative activity – the number of innovations recorded by the US Small Business Administration in each manufacturing industry. Because each innovation is recorded subsequent to its introduction in the market, the resulting data base provides a more direct measure of innovative activity than do patent counts. That is, the innovation data base includes inventions that were not patented but were ultimately introduced into the market and excludes inventions that were patented but never proved to be economically viable enough to appear in the market.

What is very important is that the findings from this study provide even greater support for the predictions mentioned above using patient data. Jaffe's (1989) arguments that spillovers are facilitated by geographic proximity of universities and industries is re-confirmed and strengthened, as is the prediction that small firms exploit better spillovers from university research. Indeed, the elasticity of innovative activity with respect to university research is about 50 per cent greater for small firms than for large corporations.

The major policy implication of the literature just briefly surveyed is that an extremely important dimension of technology policy must be to:

1. Identify the actual mechanisms and linkages facilitating R&D spillovers from non-corporate research activities to the corporate sector that induce enhanced innovative activity in the latter especially for smaller firms. Such mechanisms range from formal programmes facilitating technology transfer to informal transmission of knowledge via the mobility of knowledge workers and skilled engineers.
2. Promote the establishment of missing links and mechanisms and support existing ones.
3. Promote the geographic coincidence (clustering) of universities, research laboratories and new firms.

2.4 PROMOTION OF TECHNOLOGICAL COOPERATION

A research joint venture is just a cooperative arrangement between firms whereby they take certain R&D decisions cooperatively so as to maximize joint profits. The distinction between this and licensing is that any sharing of information is done free of charge and by cooperative agreement, and all R&D decisions are taken by cooperative agreement.

In particular, we want to focus on a policy that takes the form of a subsidy to information-sharing (or result-sharing) research joint-ventures (RJVs). This type of policy is becoming particularly common in the European Commission, where it takes the specific form of a 50 per cent R&D subsidy to RJVs that agree to share the results of their R&D. Notice that there are two parts to the policy: the allowance of cooperative R&D arrangements between firms, and the subsidy to R&D.

In order to examine the rationale for such a policy we need to understand what incentives firms may or may not have to share information in the absence of any policy, and then how their decisions would be affected by the presence of this policy.

Now while there has been a significant amount of work done on RJVs in recent years, virtually all of it operates in a framework in which there is a given R&D spillover that operates when firms act non-cooperatively outside the RJV and another given (though possibly different) spillover parameter that operates when firms operate cooperatively within the RJV (see, for example, D'Aspremont and Jacquemin, 1988; Katz, 1986; Suzumura, 1992). The problem with these models is that they essentially conflate the decision on the amount of R&D to do with that of the optimal sharing of R&D.

As we have stressed, to solve the underlying resource allocation problem we need to separately but simultaneously solve the problem of how much R&D to do and how much R&D to share. To make progress in analyzing how well RJVs perform this task it is therefore necessary to have a framework in which, inside and outside the RJV, firms choose both the amount of R&D to do, and their spillover parameter. That is, rather than treat the spillover parameter as exogenous, we need to model it as endogenous.

It is precisely this exercise that we have been involved in, in some recent work we have been doing (Katsoulacos and Ulph, 1994b), a summary of which is given in the Appendix to this chapter. Before setting out some of the details of our findings, it is important to note that as soon as we start operating in a model in which spillovers are endogenous then it is important to make some distinctions which are not always made in the literature.

Some Crucial Distinctions

In the first place it is necessary to be clear about the nature of the spillover. We usually think of spillovers as arising through one firm's acquiring information about the research discoveries of the other. There are two factors that will bear on the extent of this spillover: the amount of information acquired (quantity of information), and the usefulness of that information to the acquiring firm (quality of information). In principle both of these facets of the spillover are under the firms' control, so when, as here, we think of these spillovers being endogenously determined by firms, we need to be clear about what is being chosen. We will show that this matters by focusing on two polar cases. The first is that of a pure *information-sharing* spillover where it is the quantity of information that passes between firms that is being chosen. Here we implicitly assume that there is no scope for choosing the research design and that information produced by each firm's research is of use to the other. The second is that where firms choose their *research design* in order to control the quality of information acquired by the other firm. In this case we implicitly assume that firms have no control over the quantity of information that passes between them.

Second we show that it matters whether the spillover arises between firms that are operating in the *same industry* or in *different industries* since this will crucially affect the private incentives to give potentially beneficial spillovers to another firm. If firms operate in completely separate industries then each has nothing to lose from having the other firm benefit from a spillover from itself, whereas if they are in the same industry then, if one firm alone has made a discovery, it can be damaging to have its rival receive a beneficial spillover.

Third it is important to distinguish between the case where the research that is being undertaken by one firm is a *substitute* or a *complement* for that undertaken by the other. Again this affects our understanding of the incentives to create spillovers. For the *substitute* case is where firms are essentially undertaking exactly the same research, and will consequently make the same discovery. Thus if *both* firms make a discovery then neither can benefit from any spillover, though one firm can benefit from the other's when it has not itself discovered. When research is *complementary*, then one firm's discovery can be of benefit to the other, and is indeed likely to be most beneficial when they have both made a discovery. Notice that this distinction relates to the previous one in that if firms are operating in completely different industries they will not be undertaking substitute research whilst if they are operating in the same industry they may be undertaking substitute or complementary research.

Finally it is important to distinguish between *cooperation* and *information sharing/coordinating research design*. Just because firms choose to cooperate (maximize joint profits) it does not necessarily mean that they will choose to share information or coordinate research design – and we will show that there are cases where indeed cooperation does not induce information sharing/research coordination. Equally, the fact that firms choose not to cooperate does not mean that they will not share information or coordinate their research, and again we will show that full research coordination can arise even when firms do not cooperate.

The Model and Discussion of Two Important Cases

To analyze what happens when we endogenize the spillover parameter, we follow the existing literature by focusing on the case where there are just two firms that might potentially form an RJV. We allow these firms to be located either in the *same* industry, or in *different* industries. We allow firms to be pursuing either *complementary* or *substitute* research. Finally we examine three types of equilibria. In the *non-cooperative equilibrium* firms choose their R&D and spillover parameters independently. In the *cooperative* equilibrium firms choose their R&D and spillover parameters to maximize joint profits, but there is no subsidy to R&D. Third we consider the *social optimum*. Here a social planner chooses the R&D levels and spillover parameters to maximize social surplus. We can thus explore what market failures arise in terms of both the amount of R&D that is undertaken and the extent of information sharing/research design coordination. We can examine how far these would be corrected by simply allowing cooperative arrangements without any subsidy.

Another feature of our model is that we focus on output spillovers rather than input spillovers. We do this by assuming that when a firm chooses its R&D this determines the probability of making a discovery, and this probability is completely independent of the amount of R&D done by the other firm. However, the profits a firm makes contingent on whether it has or has not discovered, and on whether the other firm has or has not discovered, depend on the spillovers that arise between them.

Notice that since we allow the possibility that either both firms simultaneously make a discovery or that one alone makes a discovery, our model is a mixture of a tournament and a non-tournament model.

Now given the number of distinctions we have indicated need to be made, a full discussion of policy within this framework would be very space-consuming, so let us just concentrate on two diametrically opposite cases.

Case 1:   Same Industry; Substitute Research; Information-Sharing

This case is characterised by the following assumptions:

As far as firms profits are concerned, then, if both firms make a discovery, because they have effectively discovered exactly the same thing, each firm's profits are completely unaffected by any spillover it may give to the rival firm, or any spillover it may receive from a rival firm.

If one firm alone discovers, then its profits are a strictly decreasing function of any spillover it gives to its rival since this helps the rival compete against it in the same industry. On the other hand this firm's profits are unaffected by any spillover from the other firm since it has not made any discovery.

For the firm that fails to make a discovery, its profits are strictly increasing in any spillover it receives from its rival, but again are unaffected by any spillover it itself makes.

We make the natural assumption that a firm's profits are highest if it alone makes a discovery and gives no spillover to its rival; that a firm's profits if both discover are greater than if neither discovers (so firms are not just competing for market share); and that a firm's profits are lowest if the other firm alone discovers but gives no spillover.

We assume that when one firm alone discovers and when spillovers are at a maximum then each firm's profits are exactly the same as if both firms had discovered.

As far as society is concerned, we make the natural assumption that total surplus is larger if both firms make a discovery than if neither firm makes a discovery. If one firm alone makes a discovery but gives no spillover to its rival, then social surplus is lower than if both firms discover together. Social surplus is strictly increasing in the spillover given by the firm making the discovery.

To see the implications of these assumptions let us consider the various equilibria.

(i) Non-Cooperative Equilibrium

Since spillovers take the form of information-sharing then in the non-cooperative equilibrium, firms first of all choose their R&D and then decide the size of their spillover.

Given our assumptions, it is clear that in the non-cooperative equilibrium spillovers will always be zero, since each firm's profits will be strictly decreasing in its own spillover.

(ii) Cooperative Equilibrium

If we turn to the cooperative equilibrium *in the absence of any subsidy*, then it is clear that firms will agree to share information if and only if industry profits when both firms have access to the discovery are higher than they would be if one firm alone has access to the discovery. Note that, not surprisingly, this is precisely the same condition as is required for ex-post licensing to occur.

Notice also that if no information is shared then we have a case where cooperation does not automatically lead to full information-sharing.

Further notice that firms will always be better off in this cooperative equilibrium than in the non-cooperative equilibrium. So, as long as R&D cooperation is allowed, firms will choose to cooperate – even in the absence of a subsidy.

What is the *implication for policy*?

Note first of all that, given our assumptions, the social optimum involves full information-sharing.

If the cooperative equilibrium also involves full information-sharing, then obviously if firms can get an R&D subsidy provided they share information, they will always apply for the subsidy. Is the R&D subsidy warranted?

It is easy to show that in the cooperative equilibrium in the absence of subsidy R&D is below the socially optimal level since firms are motivated by profit rather than surplus. Hence an R&D subsidy is warranted. Indeed in the special case of process innovation and linear demands, a 50 per cent subsidy is exactly the right one to apply.

In this case then the policy of subsidizing R&D cooperation achieves the full social optimum.

It is worth noting that getting the R&D decision right here involves the question of how many firms should do R&D and how much each should do. For if the optimum level of R&D is high then, if two firms undertake it, there is a high probability that both will discover and hence effectively duplicate research. Under some circumstances it will be better to have this R&D done by a single firm. Provided the R&D subsidy gets the overall incentive right then the cooperative equilibrium will get both the number of firms doing R&D and R&D per firm right.

The more interesting case arises when the cooperative equilibrium involves no information-sharing. Here in deciding whether to apply for the subsidy, conditional on agreeing to share information, firms have to decide whether the loss from having to share information exceeds the gain from the subsidy. If they do decide to apply for the subsidy then – assuming again that we have linear demand curves – the 50 per cent subsidy will achieve the optimum.

However, if it is not worth applying for the subsidy, then the government by insisting that firms share information cannot achieve the social optimum. For if it raises the subsidy to induce correct information-sharing then it distorts the R&D decision.

So while this policy may *achieve the social optimum there is certainly no guarantee of this.*

Now let us turn to the case which is diametrically opposite to that we have just considered.

Case 2: Different Industries, Complementary Research, Research Coordination

The characteristics of this case are as follows.

First if both firms make a discovery, then each firm's profits are an increasing function of the spillover received from the other firm (because the research is complementary) but completely unaffected by its own spillover parameter – because firms are operating in different industries and so helping the other firm does not damage their own profits.

If one firm alone makes a discovery then its profits are unaffected by any spillover it gives to its rival – again because the firms are in different industries – and are also unaffected by any spillover from the other firm since it has not made any discovery.

We allow the possibility that a firm that has made no discovery may potentially benefit from a discovery by the other firm, but we assume that the benefit a firm receives from the other firm's discovery is greatest when it itself has discovered. From the point of view of society we have to examine the surplus arising in each industry.

If both firms innovate, then surplus in each industry is an increasing function of the spillover received from the other industry.

If one firm alone innovates then surplus in that industry is unaffected by any spillover, whereas we again allow the possibility that surplus in the industry which fails to innovate can increase in the spillover from the innovating industry. Finally because the spillover takes the form of research coordination, in the non-cooperative equilibrium firms have to choose their spillover before their R&D.

The implications of these assumptions are as follows.

(i) Non-Cooperative Equilibrium

The non-cooperative equilibrium involves full research coordination. The reason is that if one firm increases its spillover, this increases the value of R&D to the rival firm, which will therefore increase its R&D thus increasing the benefit the first firm receives from any spillover from its rival.

So here we have a case where full coordination can occur without any cooperation.

(ii) Cooperative Equilibrium

Once again firms will always choose to cooperate if they can, and so the cooperative equilibrium will involve full research coordination.

It is therefore clear that if a subsidy is available to firms conditional on full information-sharing firms will always claim it.

Social Optimum and Policy Implications

Now it is obvious that the social optimum will involve full research coordination, so the question that arises is whether this subsidy is justified since firms would have fully coordinated even in the non-cooperative equilibrium.

The subsidy would be justified if firms were underinvesting in R&D in the cooperative equilibrium.

It is hard to say whether in general firms do underinvest. One case where we can be more definite is where there is process innovation; firms are monopolists in their own industry; and demand curves are linear. Then firms do indeed underinvest, and the optimal subsidy required to correct this is now one-third. So note that a 50 per cent subsidy will lead to overinvestment.

So we see then that a policy of providing a 50 per cent subsidy to R&D provided firms agree to share information can lead to the social optimum, though it will not always do so.

In many cases the policy works not because it induces any additional information-sharing, because there are quite strong private incentives for this, but because it induces, improved R&D performance. However the policy can prove effective in inducing additional information-sharing in cases where the license system would not work.

Incidentally it is worth noting that most of the joint ventures that have actually been supported by the European Commission's policy are indeed between firms in different industries pursuing complementary research.

2.5 CONCLUDING REMARKS

Let us now try to draw together some of results mentioned above and make some suggestions for future research.

While our analysis of research joint ventures with endogenous spillovers has yielded some useful insights, it is still very preliminary.

As with licensing, future research needs to address seriously issues to do with how the cooperative arrangements can be enforced in the face of informational asymmetries, and where the number of firms among whom cooperation takes place is also endogenized. We also need to examine what happens in a more dynamic context where there may be a sequence of innovations to be undertaken. In addition we need to examine what happens when there are both input and output spillovers, and where firms may be restricted to cooperating on spillovers but not on R&D.

In terms of the fundamental resource allocation problem with which we started, it is clear that we still do not have a policy tool which completely resolves the problem of inducing the right amount of R&D spending both within and between firms while at the same time encouraging firms to undertake the right amount of sharing.

APPENDIX: THE MODELLING FRAMEWORK

In this Appendix we describe briefly the endogenous spillovers framework that we have used to derive the results discussed in Section 2.4.

We consider a two-firm framework. Firms sell a substitute good and also invest in R&D (using identical research paths) to make a discovery.

We assume that innovations (or discoveries) generate spillovers and we use $\delta = (\delta_1, \delta_2)$ to indicate the spillover parameters where δ_i, $i = 1, 2$, $0 \leq \delta_i \leq 1$ is the spillover parameter for firm i's discovery.

The R&D Process

R&D is a stochastic process with the amount of R&D chosen by each firm determining the probability that it will make a discovery. Each firm's probability of discovery is independent of that of the other firm, so there is a chance that both will discover, that each alone will discover, and that neither will discover. This is true whether firms operate in a cooperative or non-cooperative R&D environment.

Throughout we use the probability of discovery as the choice variable and model the R&D technology through a cost function, $c(p)$, giving the amount a firm has to spend on R&D to achieve a probability p. We assume that $c(0) = 0$, $c'(0) = 0$; $\forall p, 0 < p < 1$, $c'(p) > 0$; $c''(p) > 0$ $c(p)$, $c'(p) \to \infty$ as $p \to 1$.

The first part of the assumption guarantees that as long as the innovation is profitable a firm will choose to spend a positive amount on R&D, while the latter part guarantees that no firm would end up innovating for sure.

Basic Assumptions and the Objective Function of the Firms

Let $s = t, w, l, o$ be the state of world depending on the outcome of the innovation race. We will indicate the profit realised by firm i in state s as follows:

π_i^t – profits of i if both firms discover
$\pi_i^w(\delta)$ – profits of i if it alone discovers
$\pi_i^l(\delta)$ – profits of i if the other firm alone discovers
π_i^o – profits of i if neither firm discovers

We will assume symmetry between firms (so whenever it is convenient we will drop subscripts). The basic constructs for the individual firms can be expressed through the following assumptions on their profit functions:

Assumption 1: As indicated above profits if both firms discover are independent of spillovers, and equal to π^t, reflecting the assumption that firms undertake identical research and produce homogeneous products so that, since the discoveries are effectively identical, each firm neither gains nor loses from any spillover. Of course, profits each firm makes if no one discovers are also independent of spillovers and equal to π^0.

Assumption 2: Profits from winning, $\pi^w(\delta)$ are strictly decreasing in δ whilst profit from losing, $\pi^l(\delta)$ are strictly increasing in δ.

Assumption 3: We assume that

$$\pi^w(0) > \pi^l > \pi^0 > \pi^l(0) \tag{2.1}$$

The archetypal non-cooperative model is that in which the objective function of firm 1 is:

$$V_1 = p_1 p_2 \pi_1^l + p_1(1 - p_2)\pi_1^w + p_2(1 - p_1)\pi_1^l + \\ (1 - p_1)(1 - p_2)\pi_1^0 - c(p_1) \tag{2.2}$$

There is an analogous function for firm 2. Let:

$$A = (\pi_1^l - \pi_1^l), B = (\pi_1^w - \pi_1^0), C = (\pi_2^l - \pi_2^l), D = (\pi_2^w - \pi_2^0) \tag{2.3}$$

Then the first-order conditions for each of the two firms are:

$$Ap_2 + B(1 - p_2) = c'(p_1) \tag{2.4}$$

$$Cp_1 + D(1 - p_1) = c'(p_2) \tag{2.5}$$

A detailed interpretation of these conditions is given in Katsoulacos and Ulph (1994b). It is straightforward to show that given our assumptions on $c(p)$ the model has a unique stable solution.

The Market Equilibrium and Socially Optimal R&D and Spillover Levels

The Non-Cooperative Equilibrium

Thinking here of a case where the spillover takes the form of post-innovation *information-sharing*, the non-cooperative equilibrium takes the form of a two-stage game in which firms first choose their R&D and then, when they have made a discovery, decide how much of the information they have discovered to reveal. In the case where one firm alone makes a discovery, it is clear from the specification of profits that since the discovering firm's profits are strictly decreasing in its own spillover, it will choose to reveal nothing. In the case where both firms make a discovery, since they have both discovered effectively the same thing, they have nothing to gain or lose from any information revelation so we can again take the spillover parameter to be zero. Thus we have:

Result 1: The non-cooperative equilibrium spillover parameters will be zero.[1]

Let us therefore turn to the first stage of the game – the choice of R&D. It is easy to check that when the spillover parameters are both zero then $A = C = \pi^l - \pi^l(0)$, while $B = D = \pi^w(0) - \pi^0$. Therefore the symmetric non-cooperative equilibrium value of p is given by

$$p[\pi^t - \pi^t(0)] + (1 - p)[\pi^w(0) - \pi^0] = c'(p) \tag{2.6}$$

For later purposes, it helps to write this as

$$[\pi^w(0) - \pi^0] + p[\pi^t + \pi^0 - \pi^w(0) - \pi(0)] = c'(p) \tag{2.7}$$

The Cooperative Equilibrium

If firms form an RJV then p and δ will be chosen to maximize expected profits per firm, i.e. so as to maximize

$$\bar{V}(p, \delta) = p^2\pi^t + p(1 - p)[\pi^w(\delta) + \pi^l(\delta)] + (1 - p)^2\pi^0 - c(p) \tag{2.8}$$

We can see immediately that:

Result 2: If total industry profit when just one firm innovates (the term in square brackets) is increasing in δ then the cooperative equilibrium value of $\delta = 1.^2$ The cooperative equilibrium value of p if Result 2 holds is given by:

$$2(1 - p)(\pi^t - \pi^0) = c'(p) \tag{2.9}$$

Result 3: In the opposite case, that is, where total industry profit is decreasing in δ when just one firm innovates, then the cooperative equilibrium value of $\delta = 0$, and the cooperative equilibrium value of p is given by:

$$(\pi^w(0) + \pi^l(0) - 2\pi^0) + 2p[\pi^t + \pi^0 - (\pi^w(0) + \pi^l(0))] = c'(p) \tag{2.10}$$

Result 3 illustrates a case where *research cooperation does not lead to any information revelation.*

The Joint Social Optimum in p and δ

The problem is to choose p and δ to maximize total expected surplus given by

$$W(p, \delta) = p^2S^t + 2p(1 - p)S^s(\delta) + (1 - p)^2S^0 - 2c(p) \tag{2.11}$$

where we make the following assumptions:

Assumption 4: Analogously with profits, S^t, the total surplus in the industry if both firms innovate and S^0 the total surplus in the industry if neither firm innovates, are independent of spillovers.

Assumption 5: The total surplus in the industry if a single firm innovates and gives a spillover δ to its rival, $S^s(\delta)$ is strictly increasing in δ.

Assumption 6: We assume

$$S^t > S^0; \quad S^t > S^s(0);$$
$$S^t > 2\pi^t; \quad S^0 > 2\pi^0; \quad S^s(0) > \pi^w(0) + \pi^l(0)$$

Hence total surplus is higher when both firms innovate than is the case either in the absence of any innovation, or in the case where one firm alone innovates (and there is no spillover). Also total surplus always exceeds total profits. Given that

$S^t > S^s(0)$, $S^s(\delta)$ is strictly increasing in δ and so therefore is expected social surplus. Thus we have:

Result 4: It is socially optimal to engage in maximum information revelation (the socially optimal value of $\delta = 1$).

With $\delta = 1$, from (2.11), the socially optimal value of p is defined by the first-order condition:

$$(1 - p)(S^t - S^0) = c'(p) \tag{2.12}$$

where we have used the fact that $S^s(1) = S^t$.

There are clearly two distinct distortions that the market may produce that might justify policy intervention. First, the market may under cooperation generate less than optimal information revelation (a value of δ that is less than unity). Secondly, even when there is maximum information revelation under cooperation, the amount of R&D and hence probability of success may be less than at the socially optimal level.

Consider first the case where total industry profit when one firm innovates is increasing in δ, so under cooperation firms *will* choose maximum information revelation ($\delta = 1$) and the only market distortion can come from suboptimal p. In this case equilibrium p is given by (2.9) which can be rewritten in the presence of a subsidy h as:

$$(1 - p)(\pi^t - \pi^0) = c'(p)(1 - h) \tag{2.13}$$

Comparing (2.13) with (2.12) we see that with $h = 0$ optimum p will be greater (equal, smaller) than equilibrium p if $S^t - S^0$ is greater (equal, smaller) than $2(\pi^t - \pi^0)$. So we have:

Result 5: If total industry profit when one firm innovates is increasing in δ, in the linear demand case where $S^t - S^0 = 4(\pi^t - \pi^0)$, the social optimum is greater than the equilibrium value of p and the optimum subsidy is positive – indeed it should be 50 per cent.

On the other hand, if total industry profit is decreasing in δ then the cooperative equilibrium value of $\delta = 0$, and the cooperative equilibrium value of p is given by (2.10). So the market is now generating the wrong amount of information revelation and, as a comparison of (2.10) and (2.12) shows, the cooperative equilibrium value of p will in general be different from the optimum value of p, $\hat{p}$, through at this level of generality it is impossible to say whether p is greater than or less than $\hat{p}$. That is, there are now two market failures, and as intuition also suggests, it may not be possible to correct them and achieve the optimum outcome with the single instrument of an R&D subsidy.

Notes

1. As is shown in Katsoulacos and Ulph (1994b) this need not hold under more general assumptions concerning research path and product substitutability.
2. Sufficient conditions for this are given in Katsoulacos and Ulph (1994b).

References

Acs, Zoltan J. and David B. Audretsch (1987) 'Innovation, Market Structure and Firm Size', *Review of Economics and Statistics*, 69(4) (November) pp. 567–75.

Acs, Zoltan J. and David B. Audretsch (1988) 'Innovation in Large and Small Firms: An Empirical Analysis', *American Economic Review*, 78(4) (September) pp. 678–90.

Acs, Zoltan J. and David B. Audretsch (1990) *Innovation and Small Firms* (Cambridge, MA: MIT Press).

Acs, Zoltan J. and David B. Audtretsch (1993a) 'Innovation and Technological Change: The New Learning', in Gary D. Libecap (ed.), *Advances in the Study of Enterpreneurship Innovation and Growth*, vol. 6 (Greenwich, Conn.: JAI Press) 109–42.

Acs, Zoltan J. and David B. Audretsch (eds) (1993b) *Small Firms and Entrepreneurship: An East–West Perspective* (Cambridge University Press).

Acs, Zoltan J., David B. Audretsch and Maryann P. Feldman (1992) 'Real Effects of Academic Research: Comment', *American Economic Review*, 81(3) (March).

Acs, Zoltan J., David B. Audretsch and Maryann P. Feldman (1993a) 'Innovation and R&D Spillovers', *CEPR Discussion Paper* no. 865, December.

Acs, Zoltan J., David B. Audretsch and Maryann P. Feldman (1993b) 'R&D Spillovers and Recipient Firm Size', *Review of Economics and Statistics*, 99.

Audretsch, D.B. and Marco Vivarelli (1994) 'Small Firms and Spillovers: Evidence From Italy', *CEPR Discussion Paper* no. 927, March.

Beath, J. and D. Ulph (1990) 'The Trade-off between Static and Dynamic Efficiency in a Non-Tournament Model of Innovation', Discussion Paper No. 90/286, Dept. of Economics, University of Bristol.

Beath, J., Y. Katsoulacos and D. Ulph (1995) 'Game Theoretic Approaches', in P. Stoneman (ed.), '*Handbook of the Economics of Innovation and Technological Change* (Oxford: Basil Blackwell).

Cohen, W. and D. Levinthal (1989) 'Innovation and Learning: The Two Faces of R&D', *Economic Journal*, 99 pp. 569–96.

Commission of the European Communities (1990) *Industrial Policy in an Open and Competitive Environment*, COM (90)556.

D'Aspremont, C. and A. Jacquemin (1988) 'Cooperative and Non-Cooperative R&D in a Duopoly with Spillovers', *American Economic Review*, 78, pp. 1133–7.

Itoh, M. *et al.* (1991) *Economic Analysis of Industrial Policy* (San Diego, California: Academic Press).

Jaffe, Adam B. (1986) 'Technological Opportunity and Spillovers of R&D: Evidence from Firms' Patents, Profits and Market Value', *American Economic Review*, 76 (December) pp. 984–1001.

Jaffe, Adam B. (1989) 'Real Effects of Academic Research', *American Economic Review*, 79(5) (December) pp. 957–70.

Katsoulacos, Y. and D. Ulph (1993) 'Market R&D Allocations When Research Paths Are Product Specific', *Scandinavian Journal of Economics*, vol. 95, no. 3.

Katsoulacos, Y. and D. Ulph (1994a) 'Evaluating Welfare Losses Under R&D Rivalry and Product Differentiation', *CEPR Discussion Paper* No. 992.

Katsoulacos, Y. and D. Ulph (1994b) 'Information Revelation, R&D Cooperation and Technology Policy', mimeo, Athens University of Economics and Business.

Katz, M. (1986) 'An Analysis of Cooperative Research and Development', *RAND Journal of Economics*, 17 (Winter) pp. 527–43.

Link, Albert N. and John Rees (1990) 'Firm Size, University Based Research, and the Returns to R&D', *Small Business Economics*, 2(1), pp. 25–32.

Stoneman, P. (1987) *Economic Analysis of Technology Policy* (Oxford University Press).

Suzumura, K. (1992) 'Cooperative and Non-cooperative R&D in an Oligopoly with Spillovers', *American Economic Review.*

3 Research Joint Venture Cartels and Welfare

Raymond De Bondt and Changqi Wu

3.1 INTRODUCTION

Cooperative arrangements in R&D among otherwise competing firms have evolved as a response to the externalities that accompany such strategic investment activities. The modes of cooperation differ in several ways but particularly in the extent that they allow a more useful information-sharing and a better coordination of efforts. Sometimes firms continue to compete and simply share more information. In other cases they only coordinate efforts, and in still other instances they realize both a better coordination of investments and a better sharing of information.

It has been shown in symmetric industry settings that coordinated efforts tend to result in an increase in investment efforts and static welfare if (and only if) spillovers in R&D are important (D'Aspremont and Jacquemin, 1988).[1] But a research joint venture (RJV) cartel that coordinates efforts and succeeds in perfect (or better) information-sharing may well yield the highest technological improvements and static welfare (Kamien et al., 1992).

In reality cooperative arrangements tend to involve only some of the suppliers. One relevant industry organization is that of a group of firms cooperating while other rivals continue to compete.[2] This chapter argues that in such a setting, even though better information-sharing and coordination improves static welfare, the size of an RJV cartel is likely to differ from the size that maximizes static welfare. Only in industries with high spillovers and few firms can market forces be trusted to generate a welfare-maximizing RJV cartel. In other industries, public policy instruments may be needed to correct the size of the cartel in order to maximize static welfare.

The framework employed here describes an industry with technological spillovers in which some firms form a cartel to coordinate strategic R&D investments and to enhance information exchange between the members, while they continue to compete against non-participating rivals. Our findings can be related to the recent studies in Katz (1986), Combs (1993) and Poyago-Theotoky (1995), who have found that the Nash-equilibrium size of an RJV is usually smaller than the socially optimal one. We show that the equilibrium size of an RJV cartel can be either larger or smaller than the socially optimal one, depending on the industry-wide spillovers, degree of information-sharing among the cooperative firms, and market structure. In a subsequent section implications for investment levels, profits, and static welfare are also detailed.

3.2   A STRATEGIC INVESTMENT FRAMEWORK

Consider an industry consisting of n firms, indexed $i = 1,2, \ldots n$, competing non-cooperatively in the product market. For simplicity, it is assumed that these n firms face a linear demand function and produce homogenous products

$$p = a - Q$$

where the market size parameter is $a > 0$ and the industry output $Q = q_1 + \ldots + q_n$.

The initial unit cost for all the firms is denoted by c and $a > c$. Firms engage in cost-reducing innovation before production starts. Among these n firms, k firms participate in an R&D cooperation. The remaining $n - k$ firms, acting as outsiders, decide their own R&D investment non-cooperatively by taking into account the R&D investments of all other firms. When $k = 1$, all firms conduct their research non-cooperatively. When $k = n$, industry-wide R&D cooperation prevails. While this configuration imposes asymmetry on the two groups of firms, all firms within each group are identical.

The actual unit production costs, excluding the R&D expenses, are expressed as the differences between initial unit costs c and the effective cost reductions determined in the R&D stage

$$c_i^c = c - \left(x_i^c + \beta \sum_{\substack{s=1 \\ s \neq i}}^{n} x_s + \varepsilon \sum_{\substack{t=1 \\ t \neq i}}^{k} x_t^c \right) \qquad i = 1, \ldots, k \qquad (3.1)$$

$$c_j^f = c - \left(x_j^f + \beta \sum_{\substack{s=1 \\ s \neq j}}^{n} x_s \right) \qquad j = k+1, \ldots, n \qquad (3.2)$$

where all c_i and $c_j \geq 0$, $0 \leq \beta \leq \beta + \varepsilon \leq 1$, $\varepsilon \geq 0$. Superscripts c and f identify whether a firm participates in the R&D cooperation or remains on the fringe. The R&D investment, $x_i \geq 0$, represents the individual R&D investment of firm i in its cost-reducing effort.

The unit production costs are not affected by output level. For the members of the R&D cooperation, their effective cost reduction includes their own R&D investment, the R&D spillovers from all other firms, and technical information obtained from other participants of the cooperative agreement. Unlike the members of the cartel, fringe firms can only benefit from industry-wide spillovers.

The spillover parameter β represents the degree of involuntary industry-wide spillovers or information leakage. The causes of information leakage may include reverse engineering, exchanges between the research scientists and business, and scientific publications. This leakage is assumed to be symmetric and reciprocal.

The information-sharing parameter ε captures the notion of a better technology-sharing among the participants in the R&D cooperation. Its magnitude can be thought of as depending on the internal organizational features of the cartel.[3] Borrowing terminology from Kamien *et al.* (1992), the case of $\varepsilon = 0$ applies to an R&D cartel in which the participating firms maximize their joint profits by coordinating their R&D investments without information-sharing. However, when the cooperative firms can share technical information perfectly they belong to an RJV cartel ($\varepsilon = 1 - \beta$). In this chapter this term is also used to designate coordination of investments together with improved, but not perfect, information-sharing among the cooperating firms ($0 < \varepsilon < 1 - \beta$).

Another interpretation for the asymmetry in information-sharing is the difference in firms' abilities to absorb information. The industry-wide spillovers β can be understood as the general knowledge that is absorbed by all firms. The information-sharing parameter ε results because the group of cooperating firms possesses specific assets allowing them to absorb more than others and to gain information advantages in the R&D stage.

The net profit (payoff) function of firm i is defined as the difference between its gross profit function $\pi_i = (P - c_i)q_i$ and its R&D costs

$$V_i = \pi_i - g(x_i) \tag{3.3}$$

where the R&D cost function, $g(x_i) = (\Gamma/2)x_i^2$, is quadratic in R&D investment, implying diminishing returns in R&D. The parameter Γ, $\Gamma > 0$, is inversely related to the industry-wide R&D efficiency.

The game proceeds as follows.[4] In the first stage, all firms, by perfectly foreseeing what will happen in the second stage, simultaneously choose the R&D investment levels, x_i, which determine their unit production costs. The participants in the R&D cooperation coordinate their R&D efforts to maximize their joint profit; the firms that act as outsiders maximize their own profits. When production costs are known, all firms choose their output in a Cournot–Nash way and then compete in the product market. Details of the resulting equilibrium values are given in Appendix 1.

3.3   R&D INVESTMENTS

The differences in equilibrium R&D investments of members of the RJV cartel and outsiders crucially depend on the magnitude of the industry spillovers and the information-sharing in the cartel. In Appendix 2 it is verified that:

Proposition 1: *With large spillovers β ($>1/2$), the cooperative firms always invest more in R&D than their outside rivals. Also with small spillovers β ($<1/2$) they make larger R&D efforts than outsiders, provided that the RJV sufficiently improves on information-sharing.* (See Figure 3.1.)

A sufficient condition for the cooperative investment x^c to exceed the effort level x^f of the outsider in sectors with small industry spillovers is

$$\varepsilon \geq \frac{1 - 2\beta}{n - k + 1} \qquad \beta < 1/2 \tag{3.4}$$

(see Appendix 2). This sufficient condition is satisfied and $x^c > x^f$ in an RJV cartel with perfect information-sharing ($\varepsilon = 1 - \beta$). But also for less than perfect information-sharing, the RJV cartel may spend more than the outsiders.

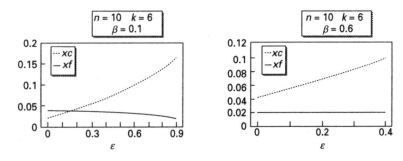

Figure 3.1 Individual R&D efforts as a function of spillovers and information-sharing

This characterization of the asymmetric effort levels of RJV cartel members and outsiders is reminiscent of earlier reported findings that efforts with industry-wide cooperation are larger (smaller) than those with competition if and only if industry spillovers are large (small). But this last well-known tendency is driven by the fact that with small (large) spillovers the R&D reaction curves are downward (upward) sloping (De Bondt and Veugelers, 1991; Vonortas, 1994).

Here, however, the RJV members may spend more on R&D even though their investments are strategic substitutes *vis-à-vis* the efforts of the outsiders. The intuition is that with better information-sharing in the cartel, the unit costs are lower and output is higher than they would be otherwise. This tends to increase the profitability of a further decrease in unit costs and consequently it stimulates the cost-reducing efforts of RJV members.

3.4 PROFITABILITY OF THE RJV CARTEL

Obviously a key question is whether firms are willing to join and stay with the RJV cartel. Following D'Aspremont *et al.* (1983), the cartel coalition is considered to be stable if both internal and external stability conditions are met.[5] The *internal stability* condition states that no insider has an incentive to leave. This means that for $k \geq 2$:

$$V^c(k) \geq V^f(k-1) \tag{3.5}$$

where $V^c(k)$ and $V^f(k)$ are the profits of the cooperative firms and outsiders respectively, and k denotes the number of firms in the RJV cartel.

The cooperation is *externally stable* if for $k \leq (n-1)$:

$$V^f(k) \geq V^c(k+1) \tag{3.6}$$

so that no outsider has an incentive to join. By convention, the industry-wide cooperation ($k = n$) is externally stable and the competitive setting ($k = 1$) is internally stable. A stable RJV of size k^*, $2 \leq k^* \leq (n-1)$, satisfies both $V^c(k^*) \geq V^f(k^*-1)$ and $V^f(k^*) \geq V^c(k^*+1)$. The present setting, although simple, because of the quadratic payoffs, still appears to be too complicated to produce an analytical solution. By means of numerical simulation, however, it is possible to detect a number of tendencies.

The case in which cooperation results only in coordinated investments and no better information transfer ($\varepsilon = 0$) can be characterized as an R&D cartel (Kamien *et al.*, 1992). In such a setting it can be shown that the profits of outsider firms are higher than those of cartel members, while levels of profits

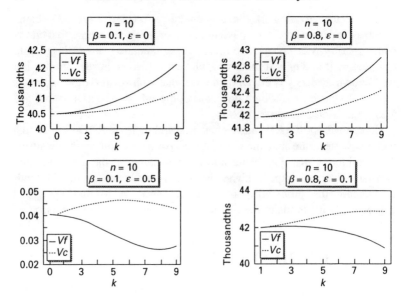

Figure 3.2 Profitability of RJV cartel and competitive fringe

for both tend to increase as the size k of the cartel increases (see Appendix 3 and Figure 3.2). The intuitive explanation for why outsiders perform better is that, with low industry spillovers, they benefit from the lower R&D levels of the cartel. This is similar to effects that apply to an output cartel and fringe firms (see Salant *et al.*, 1983).[6] With large spillovers, outsiders enjoy a free ride on the larger investment levels and knowledge transfer of the cartel members; also in this case they perform better than cartel members (Figure 3.2).

It is hard to envisage how such an R&D cartel would come about, since it is more profitable for firms to sit back and wait until others cooperate. One interpretation may be that external circumstances – for example, participation in a government-sponsored project – can result in the coalition of size k. The question then is whether that coalition will remain stable if they coordinate their cost-reducing investments. Extensive computer simulations[7] indicate that with small spillovers only very small sizes of $k = 2$ or 3 are stable. With large spillovers and sufficiently high R&D efficiency it appears that two cartel sizes are stable, i.e., one which comprises all firms in the industry, and another with only a few firms.[8]

In an RJV cartel, information-sharing is improved ($0 < \varepsilon \leq 1 - \beta$), and simulations[9] indicate that sharing tends to produce large stable coalition sizes (see Table 3.1). It is interesting to note how important the presence of the

Table 3.1   Size of the stable RJV cartel

$n = 5$, $a-c = 10$, $\Gamma = 10$

$\beta\backslash\varepsilon$	0.00	0.01	0.02	0.03	0.04	0.05	0.06	0.07	0.08	0.09	0.10
0.00	2	3	3	3	4	4	4	4	5	5	5
0.10	2	3	3	4	4	5	5	5	5	5	5
0.20	2	3	4	5	5	5	5	5	5	5	5
0.30	2	4	5	5	5	5	5	5	5	5	5
0.40	2	5	5	5	5	5	5	5	5	5	5
0.50	*	5	5	5	5	5	5	5	5	5	5
0.60	3	5	5	5	5	5	5	5	5	5	5
0.70	3	4	5	5	5	5	5	5	5	5	5
0.80	3	3	4	4	5	5	5	5	5	5	5
0.90	3	3	3	3	4	4	5	5	5	5	5
0.95	3	3	3	3	3	4					
0.96	3	3	3	3	3						
0.97	3	3	3	3							
0.98	3	3	3								
0.99	3	3									
1.00	3										

*each cartel size is stable solution

$n = 10$, $a-c = 10$, $\Gamma = 10$

$\beta\backslash\varepsilon$	0.00	0.01	0.02	0.03	0.04	0.05	0.06	0.07	0.08	0.09	0.10
0.00	2	4	5	6	7	8	9	9	9	10	10
0.10	2	5	6	8	9	9	10	10	10	10	10
0.20	2	6	8	10	10	10	10	10	10	10	10
0.30	2	9	10	10	10	10	10	10	10	10	10
0.40	2	10	10	10	10	10	10	10	10	10	10
0.50	*	10	10	10	10	10	10	10	10	10	10
0.60	3	10	10	10	10	10	10	10	10	10	10
0.70	3	10	10	10	10	10	10	10	10	10	10
0.80	3	4	8	10	10	10	10	10	10	10	10
0.90	3	3	4	6	10	10	10	10	10	10	10
0.95	3	3	4	5	7	10					
0.96	3	3	4	4	6						
0.97	3	3	4	4							
0.98	3	3	3								
0.99	3	3									
1.00	3										

Research Joint Venture Cartels and Welfare

Table 3.1 *cont.*

$n = 20$, $a - c = 10$, $\Gamma = 30$

$\beta\backslash\varepsilon$	0.00	0.01	0.02	0.03	0.04	0.05	0.06	0.07	0.08	0.09	0.10
0.00	2	9	13	16	17	18	19	19	20	20	20
0.10	2	11	16	18	19	20	20	20	20	20	20
0.20	2	16	19	20	20	20	20	20	20	20	20
0.30	2	20	20	20	20	20	20	20	20	20	20
0.40	2	20	20	20	20	20	20	20	20	20	20
0.50	*	20	20	20	20	20	20	20	20	20	20
0.60	3	20	20	20	20	20	20	20	20	20	20
0.70	3	20	20	20	20	20	20	20	20	20	20
0.80	3	12	20	20	20	20	20	20	20	20	20
0.90	3	5	20	20	20	20	20	20	20	20	20
0.95	3	4	7	20	20	20					
0.96	3	4	6	20	20						
0.97	3	4	6	20							
0.98	3	4	5								
0.99	3	3									
1.00	3										

information-sharing parameter is for the stability of the RJV size. In the illustrated parameter ranges, industry-wide cooperation quickly becomes stable when the information-sharing parameter is still relatively small, $\varepsilon < 0.1$. The basic reason is that the improvement in information-sharing results in higher profits for member firms (see also Baumol, 1992, and Figure 3.2). In addition it tends to also increase the profitability of further increases in these strategic investment activities, as explained above. This in turn improves the competitive position of the RJV *vis-à-vis* the outsiders, and everybody prefers to be a member of the RJV. Table 3.1 also shows that, when the degree of information-sharing is small but constant, the closer the rate of spillovers moves toward the critical value of 1/2, the larger the size of the industry-wide stable cartel. Intuitively speaking, a firm must consider the positive and negative implications on its profit before deciding to join or leave an RJV cartel. Information-sharing benefits only the cartel members. For the same benefit of information-sharing and small β ($\beta < 1/2$), the strategic investment effect dominates. A firm needs to reduce its R&D investment to internalize the strategic investment effect. Joining the cartel may hurt its profit. As a result, the larger the beta, the lower the negative strategic investment effect and the larger the relative gain by joining the cartel. It leads to a large size of stable RJV cartel. With large spillovers ($\beta > 1/2$), free-riding becomes an important incentive. The larger the spillover rate, the more a firm can benefit from free-riding by staying out of the cartel, therefore the smaller the stable size of the RJV cartel. From a different perspective, the closer the spillover rate moves toward the critical value of 1/2, the smaller is the degree of information-sharing required to reach the industry-wide stable RJV cartel.

The employed stability conditions assume a free membership, but clearly the RJV cartel may have incentives to limit membership in order to maximize the profits per member.[10] In the present framework these tendencies are strongest when industry spillovers and the improvements in information-sharing are modest (see also Poyago-Theotoky, 1995).

3.5 WELFARE IMPLICATIONS

Even though the RJV cartel may improve innovative investment efforts, it still remains to be seen whether or not the size of the RJV cartel is appropriate from the viewpoint of static welfare. Static welfare W, by definition, is the sum of consumer surplus and producer surplus, and can be written as

$$W = Q^2/2 + \sum_{i=1}^{n} V_i \qquad (3.7)$$

with Q the total industry output and V_i the profit of industry member i. The complex expression of this welfare function in terms of spillovers, information-sharing and size of cooperation again prevents an analytical characterization. But extensive numerical simulations clearly reveal a number of inferences, provided R&D efficiency is not too high (Γ is sufficiently high, so that all investment and profit levels are positive and second-order conditions are met).

A first result concerns the effect of the larger cartel spillovers:

Proposition 2: *Better information-sharing in the RJV cartel results in a higher consumer surplus and higher static welfare.* (See Figure 3.3.)

While this result is perhaps not surprising, it is not trivial either, since it is the net effect of two opposing tendencies. On the one hand the innovative investment activities and the profitability of the RJV cartel tend to increase,

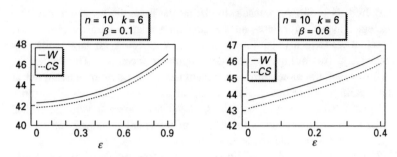

Figure 3.3 Impact of information-sharing on consumer surplus and static welfare

as information-sharing among the members captured by ε increases. But the opposite tendency applies for outsiders. They reduce their investment levels, and their profitability also diminishes as the RJV members improve on their information-sharing. The positive effects on the investment and profitability of the RJV dominate in the present setting, and consumer surplus and static welfare benefit from the enhanced spillovers within the RJV.

The relation between static welfare and the size of the R&D cartel that only coordinates efforts without additional information-sharing ($\varepsilon = 0$) is given in Figure 3.4. Welfare decreases (increases) with the size of the R&D

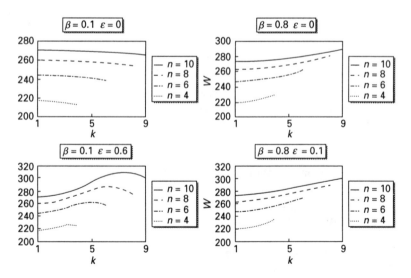

Figure 3.4 Static welfare and the size (k) of the RJV cartel ($a-c = 10$, $\Gamma = 20$)

cartel if industry spillovers are small (< 1/2) (large (> 1/2)). If $\beta = 1/2$, welfare is independent of the size of the cartel.

But this inference is strongly dependent on the absence of additional information-sharing. Simulations suggest that in an RJV cartel that allows better information-sharing ($0 < \varepsilon \leq 1 - \beta$) a different pattern emerges, as summarized by:

Proposition 3: *In industries with a small number of firms and large industry spillovers, consumer surplus and static welfare tend to increase as the size of the RJV cartel increases.*

In other settings with more numerous suppliers and smaller industry spillovers, consumer surplus and static welfare first increase and then decrease as the size of the RJV cartel increases.

Numerical analysis suggests that the indicated pattern of static welfare closely resembles the pattern of consumer surplus. In essence it reflects the investment and resulting output of the RJV cartel members. As the size of the RJV cartel increases, the tendency for cartel members to restrict output begins to dominate incentives to expand resulting from better information–sharing. For some large cartel sizes outsiders may in response operate with larger output,[11] but this is not sufficient to compensate for the decrease in the RJV cartel members' output. Consequently a tendency exists for consumer surplus and static welfare to decrease as well. All of this tends to have especially strong effects in industries with many firms and low industry spillovers. In other settings larger cartel sizes improve static welfare.

These tendencies are reminiscent of earlier findings that in some cases innovative activities are highest in industries with an intermediate degree of rivalry, while in others a monopoly may be most conductive to technological change (Kamien and Schwartz, 1976; De Bondt *et al.*, 1992). Even though his discussion of technology-sharing cartels is sympathetic towards such modes of cooperation, Baumol (1992) notes after a discussion of the welfare gains:

Still, none of this is certain ... if innovation is undertaken by firms purely for its competitive advantage a cartel may adopt a truce committing all of its members to reduce R&D outlays severely or eliminate them altogether. The cartel can, then, harm welfare by discouraging innovation. (p. 136)

The findings reported here highlight circumstances in which this is most likely to happen for an RJV cartel: large membership in industries with smaller spillovers and moderate enhancement of information flows.[12]

These results contradict what is reported by Poyago-Theotoky (1995). She states that the equilibrium size of an RJV cartel is less than the optimum size which requires all firms to participate in a cooperative agreement. Poyago-Theotoky's model is very similar to our model, but it defines social surplus as the payoff of the innovative firms. Including consumer surplus in the welfare calculations, however, would not change the direction of the results. The main difference lies in the different type of RJV considered, and the different values of spillovers and information-sharing parameters in the RJV. We consider an RJV cartel to be stable when both its external and internal stability conditions specified in D'Aspremont *et al.* (1983) are satisfied, while Poyago-Theotoky (1995) considers the stable size of an RJV as the size that maximizes its individual members' profits and she assumes that the existing members are able to block the entry of new firms. Our findings also differ from those of Combs (1993) who considers a model with uncertain outcome of innovation and free-entry in an RJV. The probability of success in innovation of a firm depends on the size of RJV in which the innovative firms share information. A firm can benefit by participating in the RJV, which increases its chance of success in innovation, but must consider the consequence of the increased competition in the product market. Combs argues, on the basis of simulation, that the equilibrium size of cooperation never exceeds the size which maximizes total surplus.

The possible reduction in output of the RJV members also tends to result in a decrease in the profit of any cartel member. Hence RJV members have an incentive to limit membership. The simulations indicate that if the RJV cartel with perfect information-sharing were to maximize the profits per member, it would maintain a size smaller than the size that maximizes consumer surplus and static welfare. For less than perfect information-sharing, the cartel may comprise all companies in the industry; this is larger than the more limited size that maximizes welfare. This result strongly suggests that any welfare analysis of stable coalitions in R&D will depend strongly on the properties of information-sharing.

3.6 CONCLUSIONS

Most of the analytical work to date suggests that pre-competitive R&D improves on consumer surplus and static welfare if and only if industry spillovers are large. This chapter qualifies this inference for industries in which a research joint venture cartel both coordinates investments and improves information-sharing. Consumer surplus and static welfare tend to increase and then decrease as the size of the cartel increases, especially in industries with many rivals and smaller spillovers. This result applies even though better information-sharing in the RJV cartel results in a larger consumer surplus and increased static welfare.

Although public policy instruments may be called in to correct the wedge between the welfare maximizing size and the stable size of R&D cooperation, it seems that an easier route would be to attempt to stimulate policies that facilitate voluntary information transfers.[13] Our analysis indicates that transfers of this type tend to improve the profitability of the RJV members, albeit at the expense of outsiders. These redistribution effects may result in political support of RJV members for government programmes that improve information-sharing, while at the same time non-participating fringe firms may argue for an adapted special treatment.

Extensions of the analysis may test for robustness of findings with other cost and demand specifications. In addition the assumption of a constant spillover parameter β and information-sharing parameter ε can be relaxed, since one could expect for example such transfer effects to diminish as the number of transmitting and recipient firms increases. A full endogenization of stable coalitions, taking into account possibilities for better information-sharing that is also at least partly endogenous, still needs to be accomplished. Firms may, in addition, through their internal organizational architecture and their choice of product characteristics, influence spillovers. The impact of these aspects on profitability and welfare in asymmetric industry settings also awaits further clarification.

APPENDIX 1

A two-stage setting is presented. In the second stage all firms compete }à la Cournot–Nash. In the first stage they choose the level of R&D investment that reduces the constant unit cost of production. The first-order conditions are:

$$\frac{\delta \pi_i}{\delta q_i} = a - c_i - 2q_i - \sum_{\substack{j=1 \\ j \neq i}}^{n} qj = 0 \qquad i = 1, \ldots, n \tag{3A.1}$$

which implies $\pi_i = q_i^2$.

After substituting c_i by equations (3.1) and (3.2) of the text into (3A.1) and solving for q_i and q_j, the Nash equilibrium outputs in the product market follow:

$$q_i^c = Z + (A - D)x_i^c + B \sum_{\substack{s=1 \\ s \neq i}}^{n} x_s + (C - D) \sum_{\substack{t=1 \\ t \neq i}}^{k} x_t^c \qquad i = 1, \ldots, k \tag{3A.2}$$

$$q_j^f = Z + Ax_j^f + B \sum_{\substack{s=1 \\ s \neq i}}^{n} x_s - D \sum_{t=1}^{k} x_t^c \qquad j = k+1, \ldots, n \qquad (3A.3)$$

where

$$A \equiv \frac{n - (n-1)\beta}{n+1}, \quad B \equiv \frac{2\beta - 1}{n+1}, \quad C \equiv \frac{(n+1)\varepsilon}{n+1}, \quad D \equiv \frac{(k-1)\varepsilon}{n+1}, \quad Z \equiv \frac{a-c}{n+1}$$

Subsequently, the payoff for member insiders of the RJV cartel V_i^c and for outsiders V_i^f can be written as

$$V_i^c = [Z + (A - D)x_i^c + B \sum_{\substack{s=1 \\ s \neq i}}^{n} x_s + (C - D) \sum_{\substack{t=1 \\ t \neq i}}^{k} x_t^c]^2 - \Gamma(x_i^c)^2/2 \qquad (3A.4)$$

$$V_j^f = \left[Z + Ax_j^f + B \sum_{\substack{s=1 \\ s \neq i}}^{n} x_s - D \sum_{t=1}^{k} x_t^c \right]^2 - \Gamma(x_j^f)^2/2 \qquad (3A.5)$$

The investment strategies in the first R&D stage satisfy:

$$\frac{\delta \sum_{i=1}^{k} V_i^c}{\delta x_i^c} = ZS + [S^2 - \Gamma']x^c + (n-k)BSx^f = 0 \qquad (3A.6)$$

$$\frac{\delta V_j^f}{\delta x_j^f} = ZA + kA(B - D)x^c + [A^2 + (n-k-1)AB - \Gamma']x^f = 0 \qquad (3A.7)$$

in which $\Gamma' \equiv \Gamma/2$ and $S \equiv A + (k-1)(B + C) - kD > 0$

Second-order conditions require $\Gamma' > S^2$ and $\Gamma' > A^2 + (n-k-1)AB$.

The best response functions of the RJV cartel members and outsiders in the R&D stage are respectively:

$$x^c = \frac{ZS + (n-k)BSx^f}{\Gamma' - S^2} \qquad (3.A8)$$

$$x^f = \frac{ZA + kA(B - D)x^c}{\Gamma' - A^2 - (n-k-1)AB} \qquad (3A.9)$$

Equations (3A.8) and (3A.9) reveal the nature of strategic interactions among the rival firms. The best response functions of the RJV firms and outsiders all slope downward when $0 \leq \beta < 1/2$ and the R&D investments of rival firms are strategic substitutes. When spillovers are large ($\beta > 1/2$), the outcomes are not so clear-cut. Although the best response function of the RJV members still slopes upward, the slope of the best response function for the outsiders is determined by B and D, which depends on β and ε. The best response function of the outsiders is downward sloping when $\varepsilon > (2\beta - 1)/(k - 1)$ and is upward sloping otherwise. Hence, it becomes possible for the slopes of the best response functions to have opposite signs. If this happens, we cannot simply characterize the interactions as strategic substitutes or complements. Such an outcome is more likely when k and/or ε become larger.[14]

The R&D investments follow from solving equations (3A.8) and (3A.9)

$$x^c = \frac{ZS[A(B - A) + \Gamma']}{T} \tag{3A.10}$$

$$x^f = \frac{ZA\{S[B - A - (k - 1)C] + \Gamma'\}}{T} \tag{3A.11}$$

where $T \equiv S^2 - \Gamma')[A^2 + (n - k - 1)AB - \Gamma'] - (n - k)kABS(B - D) > 0$, because $ZS[A(A - B) + \Gamma'] > 0$ and because of the positivity requirement of the R&D investment.

The equilibrium profits of the RJV members V^c and of the outsiders V^f can be computed as

$$V^c = \left(\frac{\Gamma'}{S^2} - 1\right)(x^c)^2 \tag{3A.12}$$

$$V^f = \left(\frac{\Gamma'}{A^2} - 1\right)(x^f)2 \tag{3A.13}$$

APPENDIX 2

Starting from the R&D investment levels defined in equations (3A.10) and (3A.11) it is possible to verify that $(x^c - x^f)$, has the same sign as

$$(k - 1)ACS + (S - A)\Gamma' \tag{3A.14}$$

The first term in expression (3A.14) is greater than (equal to) zero when the information-sharing parameter ε is positive (zero) because of C as defined in (3A.3). The second term has the same sign as $[2\beta - 1 + (n - k + 1)\varepsilon]$. When $\beta > 1/2$, it is clear that $(S - A)$ is positive and $x^c > x^f$. When $\beta > 1/2$, the positivity of $(S - A)$ requires that

$$\varepsilon \geq (1 - 2\beta)/(n - k + 1)$$

which is the sufficient condition (3.4) for $x^c > x^f$.

APPENDIX 3

From the definition of the profits of the RJV cartel members and outsiders given above by (3A.12) and (3A.13) with $\varepsilon = 0$ and thus $C = D = 0$, it is possible to verify that $(V^f - V^c) > 0$ for $\beta \neq 1/2$ and $V^f = V^c$ for $\beta = 1/2$. Tedious manipulation reveals

$$\text{sign}(V^f - V^c) = \text{sign}(k - 1)B^2[(k + 1)\Gamma' + ((k + 1)A + \\ (k - 1)B(B - A)))] \tag{3A.15}$$

The result for $\beta = 1/2$ follows immediately since it means that $B = 0$. The expression between square brackets can be rewritten as:

$$[(k + 1)(\Gamma' + A(B - A) + (k - 1)B(B - A)] > 0 \text{ for } \beta < 1/2,$$

since for such small spillovers $B < 0$. Use is also made of the positivity of A and $(\Gamma' + A(B - A))]$ which is needed in any case to assure positive investments and profits.

For $\beta > 1/2$ and $B > 0$ it is likewise possible to use the restriction $(\Gamma' + S(B - A)) > 0$ which follows from $x^f > 0$ and (3A.11), to give

$$0 < [\Gamma' + (A + (k - 1)B)(B - A)] = [(k + 1)\Gamma' + ((k + 1)A +$$
$$(k + 1)(k - 1)B)(B - A)] < (k + 1)\Gamma' + (A + (k - 1)B)(B - A)]$$

noting $S = (A + (k - 1)B) > 0$, $(A - B) < 0$ and $k \geq 2$.

The stated dependence of profits on k follows in part from

$$\text{sign}(\delta V^c/\delta k) = \text{sign } B^2[k(n - k)AB + (k - 1)(\Gamma' - S^2)] > 0 \text{ for } \beta > 1/2 \tag{3A.16}$$

$$\text{sign}(\delta V^f/\delta k) = \text{sign } B^2[((B - A)A + \Gamma')k + ((B - A)S + \Gamma')(k - 1)] > 0 \tag{3A.17}$$

for $\beta \neq 1/2$. The first inequality (3A.16) uses $B > 0$ for $\beta > 1/2$ and $(\Gamma' - S^2) > 0$ by second-order condition. Simulations indicate that $(\delta V^c/\delta k)$ may be negative for small k in industries with very small β and low Γ. The second inequality (3A.17) again uses restrictions that are necessary for the positivity of investment and profits.

Notes

1. On the relation with first- and second-best welfare levels, see Suzumura (1992). For a discussion of policy issues, see Jorde and Teece (1990), Shapiro and Willig (1990) and Geroski (1993).
2. For results on symmetric cooperative clusters, see Kamien and Zang (1993). On the endogenization of R&D coalitions, see Bloch (1991) and Yi and Shin (1992).
3. Less than perfect information-sharing may arise in the real world because of technical difficulties, differences in company culture and organization, and strategic factors. In many situations despite the efforts of participating firms to improve information flow, perfect information-sharing may not occur.
4. In this chapter, we look at the Nash-equilibrium R&D organization and do not consider how these firms reach the equilibrium. The latter has been modelled explicitly as a participation stage or a membership stage. (See Katz, 1986, and Combs, 1993.)
5. See Veugelers and Kesteloot (1994) and Kesteloot and Veugelers (1993) for somewhat different approaches to stability in a duopoly setting.
6. There is a sequel to this observation; see, e.g., Farrell and Shapiro (1990), Martin (1990) and Shaffer (1993).
7. Details are available from the authors.

8. These tendencies are reminiscent of findings by Donsimoni *et al.* (1986) concerning price leadership cartels. Using a similar analytical definition of a stable cartel they showed that unique stable sizes exist, as long as firms are not too cost-efficient relative to the market demand. If they are efficient then two cartel sizes exist, one of which comprises all industry members.

9. It is checked that for the parameter values chosen for Γ, all second-order conditions are satisfied.

10. Yi and Shin (1992) discuss both open- and closed-membership R&D coalitions with reciprocal spillovers, but they do not look at improved information-sharing.

11. This discussion is based on additional simulations, the details of which are available from the authors.

12. Another concern is that the RJV cartel may use the agreement to facilitate cartel-like production.

13. Contrary to popular belief, the amount of direct R&D subsidies provided to private firms by the Japanese government is much smaller in relative as well as absolute terms than that in both the European Community and the United States. R&D policies in Japan are characterized by the encouragement and coordination of R&D collaboration among large Japanese firms (see Suzumura and Goto, 1993).

14. When slopes of the best response curves differ, De Bondt and Henriques (1995) show that a Stackelberg equilibrium, where the firm with upward sloping best-response curve (in our case, the cooperative firms) acts as a leader, may produce a superior solution to a Cournot – Nash equilibrium in the sense that all firms are better off.

References

Baumol, W. (1992) 'Horizontal Collusion and Innovation', *Economic Journal*, 102, pp. 129–37.

Bloch, F. (1991) 'Endogenous Structures of Association in Oligopolies', Working Paper, Brown University.

Combs, K.L. (1993) 'The Role of Information Sharing in Cooperative Research and Development', *International Journal of Industrial Organization*, 11, pp. 451–602.

D'Aspremont, C. and A. Jacquemin (1988) 'Cooperative and Noncooperative R&D in Duopoly with Spillovers', *American Economic Review*, 78, pp. 1133–7.

D'Aspremont, C., A. Jacquemin, J. Gabszewicz and J. Weymark (1983) 'On the Stability of Collusive Price Leadership', *Canadian Journal of Economics*, 16(1), pp. 17–25.

De Bondt, R. and I. Henriques (1995) 'Strategic Investment with Asymmetric Spillovers', *Canadian Journal of Economics*, 28(3), pp. 656–74.

De Bondt, R., P. Slaets and B. Cassiman (1992) 'The Degree of Spillovers and the Number of Rivals for Maximum Effective R&D', *International Journal of Industrial Organization*, 10, pp. 35–54.

De Bondt, R. and R. Veugelers (1991) 'Strategic Investment with Spillovers', *European Journal of Political Economy*, 7, pp. 345–66.

Donsimoni, M.-P., N.S. Economides and H.M. Polemarchakis (1986) 'Stable Cartel', *International Economic Review*, 27(2), pp. 317–27.

Farrell, J. and C. Shapiro (1990) 'Horizontal Mergers: An Equilibrium Analysis', *American Economic Review*, 80, pp. 107–27.

Geroski, P. (1993) 'Antitrust Policy towards Co-operative R&D Ventures', *Oxford Review of Economic Policy*, 9, pp. 58–71.

Jorde, T. and D. Teece (1990) 'Innovation and Cooperation: Implications for Competition and Antitrust', *Journal of Economic Perspectives*, 4, pp. 75–96.

Kamien, M., E. Muller and I. Zang (1992) 'Research Joint Ventures and R&D Cartel', *American Economic Review*, 82, pp. 1293–306.

Kamien, M.I. and N.L. Schwartz (1976) 'On the Degree of Rivalry for Maximum Innovative Activity', *Quarterly Journal of Economics*, 90, pp. 245–60.

Kamien, M.I. and I. Zang (1993) 'Competing Research Joint Ventures', *Journal of Economics and Management Strategy*, 2, pp. 23–40.

Katz, M.L. (1986) 'An Analysis of Cooperative Research and Development', *The Rand Journal of Economics*, 17, pp. 527–43.

Kesteloot, K. and R. Veugelers (1993) 'Stable R&D Cooperation with Spillovers', Working Paper, K.U. Leuven.

Martin, S. (1990) 'Fringe Size and Cartel Stability', Working Paper 90/13, European University Institute.

Poyago-Theotoky, J. (1995) 'Equilibrium and Optimal Size of A Research Joint Venture in an Oligopoly with Spillovers', *Journal of Industrial Economics*, 43(2), pp. 205–26.

Salant, S., W. Switzer and R. Reynolds (1983) 'Losses from Horizontal Merger: The Effect of an Exogenous Change in Industry Structure on Cournot-Nash Equilibrium', *Quarterly Journal of Economics*, 98, pp. 185–99.

Shaffer, S. (1993) 'Stable Cartels with a Cournot Fringe', Working paper No. 93–8, Economic Research Division, Federal Reserve Bank of Philadelphia.

Shapiro, C. and R. Willig (1990) 'On the Antitrust Treatment of Production Joint Ventures', *Journal of Economic Perspectives*, 4, pp. 113–30.

Suzumura, K. (1992) 'Cooperative and Non-cooperative R&D in an Oligopoly with Spillovers', *American Economic Review*, 82(5), pp. 1307–20.

Suzumura, K. and A. Goto (1993) 'Collaborative Research and Development: Economic Analysis in the Light of Japanese Experience', Working Paper.

Veugelers, R. and Kesteloot, K. (1994) 'The Design of Stable Joint Ventures', *European Economic Review*, 38(9), pp. 1799–815.

Vonortas, N. (1994) 'Inter-Firm Cooperation with Imperfectly Appropriable Research', *International Journal of Industrial Organization*, 12(3), pp. 413–35.

Yi, S.-S. and H. Shin (1992) 'Endogenous Formation of Coalitions in Oligopoly: I. Theory, II. Applications to Cooperative Research and Development', Dartmouth College.

4 Imitative Competition and Public Policy*

Lynne Pepall

4.1 INTRODUCTION

Policy debate on imitative competition and its negative impact on innovation and trade figured strongly in the recent Uruguay round of GATT negotiations. Inventors and entrepreneurs in 'high technology' sectors such as information technology and telecommunications, as well as representatives from the more traditional sectors of fashion and music recording, were calling for tighter patent and copyright regulation to protect their product designs from imitators. Yet at the same time policy-makers were eager to foster more competition and trade in these sectors. The discussions were further compounded by the observation that the innovators tended to come from the richer countries and the imitators from poorer countries. As a result, rules on tightening trade-related intellectual property rights and strengthening the market power of innovators could be seen to exacerbate wealth differences among the rich and the poor countries.

The question of how public policy affects innovative activity and welfare is a complex one. There is a recent and growing theoretical literature on this topic (Gilbert and Shapiro, 1990; Scotchmer and Green, 1990; Klemperer, 1990; Pepall and Richards, 1994; Pepall, 1997) and in the context of international trade, welfare and intellectual property rights (Helpman, 1993; Diwan and Rodrik, 1991; Deardorff, 1992; Chin and Grossman, 1990). In these analyses, the late entrant firms are always assumed to be 'copy-cat' imitators who perfectly duplicate the innovator's product. Moreover, the poorer countries are assumed to be the imitators and the rich countries are assumed to be the innovators.

Imitation is, however, a product strategy, and as such should be analyzed in terms of the degree to which a firm *chooses* to differentiate its product from an already existing one. A classic theme in industrial organization is that a firm does have an incentive to differentiate *maximally* its product from another firm's because the closer two goods are, or the more substitutable are the two goods, the more intense is the price competition between them. When a firm chooses to imitate another firm's product there must be, therefore, some offsetting gain from closer differentiation such as reduced costs. Indeed in the software, music and fashion industries a firm's costs are substantially lower the more closely it copies an already marketed product.

The trade-off between reducing costs and imitation, on the one hand, and softening price competition and differentiation, on the other, is the important focus of this chapter. The trade-off is analyzed in a stylized model of innovation and imitation. There are two firms. The first firm is the innovator who 'opens' a new product market. In doing so, the firm incurs a sunk product development cost. A second firm subsequently enters the market. This firm is the potential imitator. The second firm also incurs a sunk entry cost but its cost is lower the more closely it copies the innovator's product. Against this second-mover advantage, there is the drawback that the more similar are the two products, the more intense is the price competition.

The trade-off for the potential imitator between imitation and differentiation is affected by consumer demand, and in particular by the degree of consumer heterogeneity in the market. Consumers are assumed to differ only by their level of income. There is an important relationship between the incentive to imitate and the distribution of consumer income. In the model the incentive to imitate goods in wealthier markets is much stronger than the incentive to imitate in poorer markets. This result is quite relevant to the policy debate on trade and intellectual property rights, where much of the pirated goods produced in poorer countries are targeted for sale in wealthy countries.[1]

I consider two possible policy responses to the problem of imitative competition. The first is tightening patent protection which restricts the product strategy of the late entrant firm. The second is a cooperative joint venture or alliance between the innovator and its rival. Welfare in the unrestricted market model provides a useful benchmark against which to compare the welfare effect of the two different policy responses to imitative competition.

4.2   A MODEL OF INNOVATION AND POTENTIAL IMITATION

The innovator and the potential imitator play a two-stage non-cooperative game. In the first stage, the innovator chooses whether or not to introduce a new good, and if so, what quality of new good to market. The innovator anticipates the subsequent entry of a rival firm who will also choose the quality of product to market. Quality is measured according to a vertical model of product differentiation. This assumption allows the set of potential new goods to be *ranked* by a scalar index θ. All consumers prefer a more highly ranked good or a higher quality of good. I assume that the set of possible qualities is such that $\theta \in [1,2]$.

Although consumers have identical preferences, they differ in their income, denoted by Y. Each consumer buys either one unit of a new good θ at a price p, or buys nothing at all. Consumer preferences are represented by the following utility function:[2]

$$U = \begin{cases} u(Y - p) + \theta, & \text{if buy} \\ u(Y), & \text{if does not buy} \end{cases} \tag{4.1}$$

If p is assumed small relative to Y, then a first-order Taylor expansion implies that the surplus from purchasing one unit of the good can be approximated by $-u'(Y)p + \theta$. Define the parameter $\omega \equiv 1/u'(Y)$ to be the inverse of the consumer's marginal utility of income. The function u is assumed to be concave so that wealthier consumers have a higher value of ω. Moreover, the distribution of consumer income over $[\underline{Y}, \overline{Y}]$ is assumed to be such that ω is uniformly distributed between $\omega \geq 0$ and $\bar{\omega} = \underline{\omega} + 1$. The density of the distribution of ω is assumed to be one.

An important feature of vertical product differentiated markets is that only a finite number of products are sustainable in a market equilibrium.[3] This number depends on the degree of heterogeneity among the consumers in this market. The greater the degree of heterogeneity the greater the number of products that can be sustained. Heterogeneity in the market depends on the distribution of consumer income. Heterogeneity is measured by the ratio of ω for the richest consumer to that of the poorest, $\bar{\omega}/\underline{\omega}$, and it *decreases* as $\bar{\omega}$ *increases*. Markets which are wealthier have a more homogeneous distribution of income and therefore sustain a *fewer* number of products.

The innovator incurs a sunk cost, F, to 'open' the new market. The unit cost of production is constant for each quality of good, and is set equal to zero. This assumed relationship between cost and quality is appropriate to such markets as computer software, music and film, where significant costs are incurred in designing and producing the prototype. The cost of manufacturing or replicating the product is much less important and does not depend on the talent input used in producing the prototype. The quality choice of the innovator is denoted by θ^I. The potential imitator enters second, and has the second-mover advantage that it can choose to expend less on development costs and imitate the innovator's product. This advantage is captured by the assumption that the second firm's sunk cost for marketing a new product of quality θ^i is $F(\theta^I - \theta^i)^2$. The 'closer' – where closeness is defined by the distance metric $|\theta^I - \theta^i|$ – is its product to the innovator's the less costly it is to enter the market.

In the second period of the game the firms compete in prices for consumers. I want to specify the model so that (i) the firms' price strategies in the second period are a Nash equilibrium for any qualities of product chosen in the first period, and (ii) at most *two* qualities can be sustained in equilibrium. To ensure that conditions (i) and (ii) hold in any market outcome I assume that $\bar{\omega} \equiv 1/u'(Y)$, the inverse of the marginal utility of the most wealthy consumer, is such that $4/3 \leq \bar{\omega} < 2$.

In the second period, suppose that two new products θ_1, θ_2, with $\theta_2 > \theta_1$, are marketed at prices p_1 and p_2. Define consumer ω_2, where $\omega_2 \equiv 1/u'(Y_2)$, to be the consumer who is indifferent between good 1 at price p_1 and good 2 at price p_2. Consumer ω_2 satisfies the equation: $\omega_2 = \dfrac{p_2 - p_1}{\theta_2 - \theta_1}$. Now define consumer ω_1, where similarly $\omega_1 \equiv 1/u'(Y_1)$, to be the consumer with income level Y_1, such that this consumer is indifferent between buying good 1 at price p_1 and not buying any new good at all. Consumer ω_1 satisfies $\omega_1 = p_1/\theta_1$. Any consumer $\omega > \omega_2$ strictly prefers good 2 at price p_2 to good 1 at price p_1, and any consumer ω, such that $\omega_1 < \omega < \omega_2$, strictly prefers good 1 at price p_1 to good 2 at price p_2. Therefore, the demand structure for the two goods is as follows:

$$Q_2(p_1, p_2) = \bar{\omega} - \omega_2$$

$$Q_1(p_1, p_2) = \begin{cases} \omega_2 - \omega_1 & \underline{\omega} < \omega_1 \\ \omega_2 - \underline{\omega} & \underline{\omega} \geq \omega_1 \end{cases} \tag{4.2}$$

In the second period each firm chooses a price for its good that maximizes its profit. An equilibrium is defined by a set of Nash equilibrium prices (p_1^*, p_2^*), where $p_i^* \equiv \text{argmax}\{p_i Q_i (p_i, p_j^*)\}$ for $i, j = 1,2, i \neq j$.

Because the product market is a 'natural' duopoly,[4] for any pair of goods (θ_1, θ_2), the market share of each of the two goods is positive, $Q_1 > 0$, $Q_2 > 0$, and the entire market is served, $\underline{\omega} \geq \omega_1$, or $Q_1 + Q_2 = 1$. If a third good θ_3 is marketed, then second period price competition for consumers will lead to positive market shares for only the top two preferred goods, and the least preferred good will be squeezed from the market.

For any pair of feasible goods θ_1, θ_2, where $\Delta\theta \equiv \theta_2 - \theta_1 \geq 0$, the second period equilibrium prices are:

$$p_1^* = (2 - \bar{\omega})(\Delta\theta)/3 \qquad p_2^* = (\bar{\omega} + 1)(\Delta\theta)/3$$

with market shares:

$$Q_1^* = (2 - \bar{\omega})/3 \qquad Q_2^* = (\bar{\omega} + 1)/3 \tag{4.3}$$

and revenues:

$$R_1^* = \frac{(2 - \bar{\omega})^2}{9}(\Delta\theta) \qquad R_2^* = \frac{(\bar{\omega} + 1)^2}{9}(\Delta\theta)$$

The firm marketing the higher quality θ_2 sets a higher price, gains a larger market share, and earns a higher revenue than the firm with the lower quality θ_1. Furthermore, the higher is $\bar{\omega}$, or the more homogeneous and wealthy is the distribution of consumers, the *more* profitable is the higher quality. Indeed when $\bar{\omega}$ approaches its upper bound of 2, the lower quality has almost zero market share. This result is important for understanding why the incentive to imitate is stronger in wealthier countries.

Price competition is tougher the 'closer', or the less differentiated, are the two goods. Price competition gives both firms the incentive to differentiate their products. However, in this game, the late entrant firm also has an incentive to imitate, or not to differentiate. The second entrant's sunk costs decline the more 'closely' it imitates the innovator.

4.3   ENTRY AND POTENTIAL IMITATION

In the first stage of the game the firms sequentially choose quality. The innovator moves first and chooses to market a product θ^I at cost F. When the firm makes its choice it correctly anticipates the entry of a rival firm. The potential imitator's product choice θ^i costs $K(\theta^I - \theta^i)^2$ to bring to market.

Consider the profit-maximizing response θ^{i*} of the potential imitator, to any choice θ^I of the innovator. The late entrant has two possible strategies from which to choose. It can choose either strategy (*H*) and market a higher quality $\theta^i > \theta^I$, or strategy (*L*) and market a quality $\theta^i < \theta^I$.

If the second firm adopts strategy (*H*), then its profit-maximizing quality satisfies:

$$\theta^{i*} = \text{argmax}\{\Pi^i(\theta^I, \theta^i) = (\bar{\omega} + 1)^2(\theta^i - \theta^I)/9 - K(\theta^i - \theta^I)^2\}$$

which implies:

$$\theta^{i*} = \min\left\{\theta^I + \frac{(\bar{\omega} + 1)^2}{18F}, 2\right\} \qquad (4.4)$$

Define the term $I(\bar{\omega}) \equiv (\bar{\omega} + 1)^2/18$. When the innovator chooses a quality $\theta^I < 2 - I(\bar{\omega})/F$, then the potential imitator's optimal strategy is to choose a product θ^{i*} that is not maximally differentiated. The firm has an incentive, in this case, to imitate or to move 'closer' to the innovator's product. On the other hand, if the innovator chooses $\theta^I \geq 2 - I(\bar{\omega})/F$, then, the late entrant's optimal strategy is to choose the maximally differentiated quality. For relatively small values of the development cost, $0 < F < I(\bar{\omega})$, the innovator's choice $\theta^I > 2 - I(\bar{\omega})/F$ and so the late entrant firm chooses the most differentiated quality under strategy (H).

Suppose that instead the late entrant chooses strategy (L) and markets a new good $\theta^{i*} < \theta^I$. Its best response under strategy (L) is to choose

$$\theta^{i*} = \text{argmax}\{\Pi^{i}(\theta^I, \theta^i) = (2 - \bar{\omega})^2(\theta^I - \theta^i)/9 - F(\theta^I - \theta^i)^2\}$$

whose solution is:

$$\theta^{*i} = \max\left\{ 1, \ \theta^I - \frac{(2 - \bar{\omega})^2}{18F} \right\} \tag{4.5}$$

Define the term $M(\bar{\omega}) \equiv (2 - \bar{\omega})^2/18$. If the innovator chooses $\theta^I > 1 + M(\bar{\omega})/F$, then the late entrant will choose a good that is not maximally differentiated. The firm has an incentive to imitate in this case. For relatively low values of F where $0 < F < M(\bar{\omega})$, $\theta^I < 1 + M(\bar{\omega})/F$, and so the late entrant always chooses the most differentiated good under strategy L.

The profitability of the late entrant adopting strategy (H), $\theta^i > \theta^I$, or strategy (L), $\theta^i < \theta^I$, must be compared for *any quality* θ^I. This comparison underlies the derivation of the late entrant's best response function which describes the late entrant's most profitable quality choice θ^{i*} as a function, $r^i(\theta^I)$, of the innovator's quality θ^I. After deriving $\theta^{i*} = r^i(\theta^I)$ the innovator then chooses θ^{I*} to maximize profit as given by $\Pi^I[\theta^I, r(\theta^I)]$. The equilibrium outcome $(\theta^{I*}, \theta^{i*})$ is derived in the Appendix. There I show that:

For $0 < F \leq M(\bar{\omega})$ $\theta^{I*} = 2,$ $\theta^{i*} = 1$

For $M(\bar{\omega}) < F \leq F^1(\bar{\omega})$ $\theta^{I*} = 2,$ $\theta^{i*} = 2 - M(\bar{\omega})/F$

Not surprisingly, the degree to which the late entrant has an incentive to imitate depends upon the sunk cost F to market a new product. Three cases can be distinguished. The first case occurs when the innovator firm's sunk cost is sufficiently large so that the late entrant has a strong incentive to imitate and as a result the subsequent price competition makes it unprofitable for the innovator to innovate in the first place. The new product market is, therefore, not opened. This case occurs when $F > F^1(\bar{\omega}) \equiv [2I(\bar{\omega})M(\bar{\omega})]^{1/2}$.

The second case holds for relatively large sunk costs $F^1(\bar{\omega}) \geq F > M(\bar{\omega})$. In this case the innovator does find it profitable to open the market and introduce the *highest* quality of good which is $\theta^{I*} = 2$. The late entrant imitates this product and chooses the good $\theta^{i*} = 2M(\bar{\omega})/F$, which is less than maximally differentiated from the innovator's product.

The last case holds for relatively low sunk costs $0 < F \leq M(\bar{\omega})$. Again the innovator chooses the *highest* quality of good, $\theta^{I*} = 2$, but in this case the late entrant's best response is to maximally differentiate and produce $\theta^{i*} = 1$.

The model suggests that the pattern of innovation and imitation in a non-regulated market has the following features. The first is that innovation is more likely to occur in markets where there is more heterogeneity in wealth. Innovation occurs only if the innovator's sunk cost $F \leq F^1(\bar{\omega})$, and $F^1(\bar{\omega})$ is a decreasing function of $\bar{\omega}$. Wealthier markets have a higher $\bar{\omega}$, and hence, a more homogeneous distribution of wealth, and as a result imitative competition in these markets makes innovation less profitable.

Second, copycat imitation is more likely in markets with a more homogeneous distribution of income, or higher $\bar{\omega}$. When the innovator *does* enter and chooses the *highest* quality good $\theta^{I*} = 2$, the rival enters and chooses $\theta^{i*} = 2 - M(\bar{\omega})/F$, where the function $M(\bar{\omega})$ is also decreasing in $\bar{\omega}$. The rival more closely imitates the innovator the wealthier, or the less heterogeneous, are the consumers.

The intuition behind this result is that the wealthier are the consumers the stronger is their preference for quality. Since the innovator always markets the highest quality good, a rival firm will find it worthwhile in high income markets to produce a similarly ranked product despite the more intense price competition that this brings. This result is supported by the empirical evidence that a substantial share of the pirated goods produced in poorer countries are intended for export to richer countries.

Welfare, defined as the sum of consumer surplus and firm profits, also depends on both the level of sunk cost F and the distribution of income as measured by the parameter $\bar{\omega}$. For a given level of sunk cost F, welfare is increasing in $\bar{\omega}$. Wealthier markets benefit more from the innovation. Moreover, since $F^1(\bar{\omega})$ is decreasing in $\bar{\omega}$, the potential welfare loss from the failure to innovate is also increasing in $\bar{\omega}$. Wealthier markets have a stronger incentive to solve the market failure problem in the non-regulated market.

4.4 POLICY RESPONSES TO IMITATIVE COMPETITION

Two different policy responses to the problem of imitative competition are discussed in this section. The first is a *tight* patent policy. Tight refers to defining patent breadth in such a way as to prevent a late entrant from benefiting from lower product development costs. Here, a tight patent policy means that if the innovator patents a good $\theta^I < 2$, then the second entrant firm is restricted from entering the market. When $\theta^I < 2$ there is no feasible product which does not benefit, through lower development costs, from the first firm's innovation.

The innovator has, under a tight patent policy, an incentive to market one good $\theta^I = 2 - \varepsilon$ and remain a monopolist in market. The innovator's monopoly profit is maximum when the firm markets only *one* product, not two, and *does not* serve the entire market. Serving consumers with a lower willingness to pay constrains the price that the innovator can set to those consumers with a high willingness to pay. As a monopolist the innovator will have an incentive to open new markets and market the most preferred good when the product development cost F is less than $F^2(\bar{\omega}) = \bar{\omega}^2/2$.

The monopoly outcome under tighter patent policy is different from a cooperative alliance between the first and second firm. This is the second policy response to imitative competition. In a cooperative alliance the first and second entrant firm create an alliance in order to cooperate in the development and marketing of *two* new products to serve the entire market. Alliances, unlike mergers or the monopoly case, are designed to facilitate more products being marketed by more firms in the new market. Of course, the joint firm profit in the cooperative solution is lower therefore than that attained in the monopoly outcome.

Under a cooperative alliance the firms jointly decide to market the goods θ_1, θ_2, and incur development costs, F and $F(\Delta\theta)^2$. The essential difference between the cooperative and the free market solution is that cooperation between the firms allows them to coordinate their product strategies and their pricing strategies. For any two new goods, θ_1, θ_2, the firms choose p_1^c, p_2^c, to maximize joint revenue defined by $p_1 D_1 + p_2 D_2$, where the demands for the two goods are defined by $D_1 = (\omega_2 - \underline{\omega})$ and $D_2 = (\bar{\omega} - \omega_2)$ for $\omega_2 \leq \bar{\omega}$.

The solution to this problem is such that for the entire market to be served the low quality good θ_1 is marketed at the least wealthy consumer's reservation price, $p_1^c = \underline{\omega}\theta_1 = (\bar{\omega} - 1)\theta_1$, and the high quality good is marketed at price $p_2^c = (\bar{\omega} - 1)\theta_1 + \bar{\omega}(\Delta\theta)/2$. At these prices, the two goods, θ_1, θ_2, have market shares $1 - \bar{\omega}/2, \bar{\omega}/2$, respectively.

The profit-maximizing product strategy, θ_1^c, θ_2^c, is found by maximizing the revenue of marketing the two new goods at prices p_1^c, p_2^c, less the sunk marketing costs. For sunk costs less than the critical threshold, $F^3(\bar{\omega})$, the product strategy is as follows:

$$F^3(\bar{\omega}) \geq F > 9M(\bar{\omega})/4 \qquad \theta_1^c = 2 - 9M(\bar{\omega})/4F \qquad \theta_2^c = 2$$

$$0 < F \le 9M(\bar{\omega})/4 \qquad \theta_1^c = 1 \qquad \theta_2^c = 2$$

where the threshold sunk cost under cooperation, $F^3(\bar{\omega})$, is found by setting the joint firm profit under the cooperative venture equal to zero.

In the free market solution maximal product differentiation occurs when sunk costs are very low and satisfy $0 < F \le M(\bar{\omega})$. However, under a cooperative alliance, this range of development costs, and even higher, leads to maximal differentiation of products. Similarly for higher values of F there is more differentiation under a cooperative alliance than under a free market solution. This is, of course, because the incentive to differentiate and soften price competition is stronger in the cooperative solution than in the market solution.

Policy prescriptions for imitative competition need to be based on the maximum potential welfare attainable under the three policies: free market, tight patent or cooperative alliance. Maximum potential welfare under a particular policy is found by adding up welfare over the range of development costs for which innovation occurs. In the case of the free market regime, or no policy response to imitative competition, maximum welfare W^f is defined over the range $0 \le F \le F^1(\bar{\omega})$, whereas in the case of a tight patent policy maximum welfare W^m is defined over $0 \le F < F^2(\bar{\omega})$, and under a policy of cooperative alliance maximum welfare W^c is defined over $0 \le F \le F^3(\bar{\omega})$. Observe that $F^2(\bar{\omega}) > F^3(\bar{\omega}) > F^1(\bar{\omega})$.

The total welfare under each policy is derived in the Appendix. The following is a summary of the welfare comparisons. For all possible income distributions, which are summarized by the range of the ratio of ω of the richest consumer to ω of the poorest, or $2 \le \bar{\omega}/ \le \underline{\omega} \le 4$, social welfare is lowest under the free market regime, or no policy case. For income distributions that are either rather poor, and heterogeneous, $3.3 \le \bar{\omega}/\underline{\omega} \le 4$, or rather rich and homogeneous, $2 \le \bar{\omega}/\underline{\omega} \le 2.4$, welfare is higher under tight patent policy or monopoly. However, for income distributions in the middle as described by $2.4 < \bar{\omega}/\underline{\omega} < 3.3$, welfare is higher under the policy of cooperative alliance. This result holds because under tight patent policy firm profit is higher, and hence more products are likely to be introduced. This benefits the 'rich' markets who strongly value new products and 'poor' markets where the increase in firm monopoly profit is more important to overall welfare than the decreased consumer surplus under monopoly.

4.5 CONCLUSION

This stylized model of imitative competition has revealed a number of insights which are hopefully relevant to public policy debate on intellectual property rights. First, the incentive to imitate is stronger in markets which are wealthier, and as a result have a more homogeneous distribution of income. Indeed the innovator may be deterred from entering new product markets for relatively wealthy consumers unless the firm can enter under a tight patent policy or under a cooperative alliance with the late entrant rival. A second and related point is that the welfare gain from solving the problem of imitative competition increases with the level of wealth of the consumers. However, the preferred policy prescription depends upon the range of the distribution of consumer income. For income distributions that are either relatively poor and heterogeneous, or relatively rich and homogeneous, a policy of tight patent law that protects the innovator's profitability yields higher welfare than a policy of cooperative alliance. Cooperative alliances yield higher welfare under intermediate ranges of income distribution. There, the increased consumer surplus from two, rather than one good being marketed is more important than the surplus obtained from increasing the range of marketable innovations under tight patent policy.

APPENDIX

Optimal Product Choice, θ^{i*}, θ^{I*} in a Free Market

Consider the profit-maximizing response θ^{i*} to any product choice decision θ^I of the innovator where $1 \leq \theta^I \leq 2$. The potential imitator can choose strategy (H) and $\theta^i \geq \theta^I$, or strategy (L) and $\theta^i < \theta^I$. Under strategy (H), θ^{i*} maximizes profit:

$$\Pi^i(\theta^I, \theta^i) = (\bar{\omega} + 1)^2(\theta^i - \theta^I)/9 - F(\theta^i - \theta^I)^2$$

The solution is:

$$\theta^{i*} = \min\left\{\theta^I + \frac{I(\bar{\omega})}{F}, 2\right\} \tag{4A.1}$$

where $I(\bar{\omega}) \equiv (\bar{\omega} + 1)^2/18$. The solution in (4A.1) implies that:

$$\text{For } \theta \leq \theta^I \leq 2 - I(\bar{\omega})/F \qquad \theta^{i*} = \theta^I + I(\bar{\omega})/F \qquad \Pi^i = (\bar{\omega} + 1)^4/324F \tag{4A.2}$$

$$\text{For } 2 - I(\bar{\omega})/F < \theta^I < 2 \qquad \theta^{i*} = 2 \qquad \Pi^i = (\bar{\omega} + 1)^2(2 - \theta^I) \\ /9 - F(2 - \theta^I)^2 \tag{4A.3}$$

Suppose the firm chooses $\theta^i < \theta^I$. Under strategy (L) θ^{i*} maximizes:

$$\Pi^i(\theta^I, \theta^i) = (2 - \bar{\omega})^2(\theta^I - \theta^i)/9 - F(\theta^I - \theta^i)^2$$

The solution in this case is:

$$\theta^{i*} = \max\left\{1, \theta^I - \frac{M(\bar{\omega})}{F}\right\} \qquad (4A.4)$$

where $M(\bar{\omega}) \equiv (2 - \bar{\omega})^2/18$. The solution in (4.5) implies the following about the profitability of choosing $\theta^{i*} < \theta^I$:

> For $1 < \theta^I \le 1 + M(\bar{\omega})/F$ $\quad \theta^{i*} = 1$ $\quad \Pi^i = (2 - \bar{\omega})^2(\theta^I - 1)/9 - F(\theta^I - 1)2$
>
> $\qquad (4A.5)$
>
> For $1 + M(\bar{\omega})/F < \theta^I \le 2$ $\quad \theta^{i*} = \theta^I - M(\bar{\omega})/F$ $\quad \Pi^i = (2 - \bar{\omega})^2/324F$
>
> $\qquad (4A.6)$

To compare the profitability of strategy H and L, it is convenient to define $\theta_1 = 2 - I(\bar{\omega})/F$ and $\theta_2 = 1 + M(\bar{\omega})/F$. There are several cases to consider.

> *CASE 1*: $I(\bar{\omega}) + M(\bar{\omega}) < F \le F^1(\bar{\omega}) \Rightarrow 1 < \theta_2 < \theta_1 < 2$
>
> For $1 \le \theta^I < \theta_2$ $\quad \Pi^i$ in (4A.2) > Π^i in (4A.5) $\Rightarrow \theta^{i*} = \theta^I + I(\bar{\omega})/F$
>
> For $\theta_2 < \theta^I < \theta_1$ $\quad \Pi^i$ in (4A.2) > Π^i in (4A.6) $\Rightarrow \theta^{i*} = \theta^I + I(\bar{\omega})/F$
>
> For $\theta^1 < \theta^I \le \hat{\theta}$ $\quad \Pi^i$ in (4A.3) $\ge \Pi^i$ in (4A.6) $\Rightarrow \theta^{i*} = 2$
>
> For $\hat{\theta} < \theta^I \le 2$ $\quad \Pi^i$ in (4A.3) < Π^i in (4A.6) $\Rightarrow \theta^{i*} = \theta^I - M(\bar{\omega})/F$

Given the late entrant's reaction function for this case, the innovator's profit is the same and equal to $\Pi^I = 2M(\omega)I(\omega)/F - F$ for any $1 \le \theta^{I*} \le 2$.

> *CASE 2*: $I(\bar{\omega}) < F \le I(\bar{\omega}) + M(\bar{\omega}) \Rightarrow 1 < \theta_1 < \theta_2 < 2$
>
> For $1 \le \theta^I < \theta_1$ $\quad \Pi^i$ in (4A.2) > Π^i in (4A.5) $\Rightarrow \theta^{i*} = \theta^I + I(\bar{\omega})/F$
>
> For $\theta_1 \le \theta^I < \theta_2$ $\quad \Pi^i$ in (4A.3) > Π^i in (4A.6) $\Rightarrow \theta^{i*} = 2$
>
> For $\theta_2 \le \theta^I \le \hat{\theta}$ $\quad \Pi^i$ in (4A.3) $\ge \Pi^i$ in (4A.6) $\Rightarrow \theta^{i*} = 2$
>
> For $\hat{\theta} < \theta^I \le 2$ $\quad \Pi^i$ in (4A.3) < Π^i in (4A.6) $\Rightarrow \theta^{i*} = \theta^I - M(\bar{\omega})/F$

Given the late entrant's reaction function for this case the innovator's profit is greatest, and equal to $\Pi^I = 2I(\bar{\omega})M(\bar{\omega})/F - F$, when it chooses $1 \le \theta^{I*} < \theta_1$, or $\hat{\theta} < \theta^{I*} \le 2$.

> *CASE 3*: $M(\bar{\omega}) < F \le I(\bar{\omega}) \Rightarrow \theta_1 < 1 < \theta_2 < 2$
>
> For $1 \le \theta^I < \hat{\theta}$ $\quad \Pi^i$ in (4A.3) > Π^i in (4A.5) $\Rightarrow \theta^{i*} = 2$
>
> For $\hat{\theta} \le \theta^I \le \theta_2$ $\quad \Pi^i$ in (4A.3) $\le \Pi^i$ in (4A.5) $\Rightarrow \theta^{i*} = 1$
>
> For $\theta_2 < \theta^I \le 2$ $\quad \Pi^i$ in (4A.3) < Π^i in (4A.6) $\Rightarrow \theta^{i*} = \theta^I - M(\bar{\omega})/F$

Given the late entrant's reaction function for this case the innovator's profit is maximized and equal to $\Pi^I = 2I(\bar{\omega})M(\bar{\omega})/F - F$, when it chooses $\theta_2 \le \theta^{I*} \le 2$.

CASE 4 : $0 < F \leq M(\bar{\omega}) \Rightarrow \theta_1 < 1 < 2 < \theta_2$

For $1 \leq \theta^I < \hat{\theta}$ Π^i in (4A.3) $\geq \Pi^i$ in (4A.5) $\Rightarrow \theta^{i*} = 2$

For $\hat{\theta} < \theta^I \leq 2$ Π^i in (4A.3) $< \Pi^i$ in (4A.5) $\Rightarrow \theta^{i*} = 1$

Given the late entrant's reaction function for this case the innovator's profit is maximized and equal to $\Pi^I = 2I(\bar{\omega}) - F$ when it chooses $\theta^{I*} = 2$.

Observe that in Cases 1, 2 and 3, there is not a unique solution. However, whereas the innovator's profit is maximized and is the same for a subset of quality choices, the late entrant's profit is not the same over the same interval. Indeed if the innovator markets the most highly ranked good $\theta = 2$, it minimizes the profit of the late entrant. This coupled with the 'finiteness' property of a vertically differentiated product market gives the innovator the incentive to market the most preferred good $\theta = 2$. Hence, for the cases such that $M(\bar{\omega}) < F \leq \bar{F}^1(\bar{\omega})$, the innovator chooses $\theta^{I*} = 2$, and this implies that the late entrant chooses $\theta^{i*} = 2 - M(\bar{\omega})/F$. Firm profits are: $\Pi^I = 2I(\bar{\omega})M(\bar{\omega})/F - F$ and $\Pi^i = M(\bar{\omega})^2/F$.

Welfare Comparisons

Define CS_1 to be the consumer surplus from buying at price p_1 the good θ_1, and CS_2 to be the consumer surplus from buying good θ_2 at p_2, where $\theta_2 > \theta_1$.

CASE 1: The Free Market

(1A) : $0 < F \leq M(\bar{\omega})$

$$CS_1^f = \int\limits_{\underline{\omega}}^{\omega_2} [\hat{\omega} - (2 - \bar{\omega})/3]d\hat{\omega}   \quad CS_2^f = \int\limits_{\omega_2}^{\bar{\omega}} [2\hat{\omega} - (\bar{\omega} + 1)/3]d\hat{\omega}$$

$$\Pi_1^f = 2M(\bar{\omega}) - F   \quad \Pi_2^f = 2I(\bar{\omega}) - F$$

Maximum Welfare for (1A): $W_{1A}^f = \int\limits_{0}^{M(\bar{\omega})} (CS_1^f + CS_2^f + \Pi_1^f + \Pi_2^f)dF$

$$= \int\limits_{0}^{M(\bar{\omega})} [92(2\bar{\omega} - 1) - 36F +$$

$$5\bar{\omega}^2 - 14\bar{\omega} + 8]/18dF$$

(2A): $M(\bar{\omega} < F \leq \bar{F}^1(\bar{\omega})$

$$CS_1^f = \int\limits_{\bar{\omega}}^{\omega_2} \{\hat{\omega}[2 - M(\bar{\omega})/F] - (2 - \bar{\omega})M(\bar{\omega})/3F\}d\hat{\omega}$$

$$CS_2^f = \int\limits_{\omega_2}^{\bar{\omega}} [2\hat{\omega} - (\bar{\omega} + 1)M(\bar{\omega})/F]d\hat{\omega}$$

$$\Pi_1^f = M(\bar{\omega})^2/F \qquad \Pi_2^f = 2I(\bar{\omega})M(\bar{\omega}) - F$$

Maximum Welfare for (1*B*): $W_{1B}^f = \displaystyle\int_{M(\bar{\omega})}^{\bar{F}^1(\bar{\omega})} (CS_1^f + CS_2^f + \Pi_1^f + \Pi_2^f)dF$

$$= \int_{M(\bar{\omega})}^{F^1(\bar{\omega})} [162F2(2\bar{\omega} - 1) - 324F^2 + F(\bar{\omega} - 2)^2(5\bar{\omega}^2 - 14\bar{\omega} + 8) -$$

$$(\bar{\omega} - 2)^2(\bar{\omega}^2 - 4\bar{\omega} + 4)]/324FdF$$

Maximum Welfare under Free Market: $W^f(\bar{\omega}) = W_{1A}^f + W_{1B}^f$

CASE 2: Tight Patent Policy

$$0 < F \le \bar{F}^2(\bar{\omega})$$

$$CS^m = \int_{\bar{\omega}/2}^{\bar{\omega}} 2(\hat{\omega} - \bar{\omega}/2)d\hat{\omega} \qquad \Pi^m = 2\bar{\omega}^2/4 - F$$

Maximum Welfare under Monopoly: $W^m(\bar{\omega}) = \displaystyle\int_0^{\bar{F}^2} (CS^m + \Pi^m)dF$

$$= 9\bar{\omega}^4/32$$

CASE 3: Cooperative Alliance

(3*A*) : $0 < F \le 9M(\bar{\omega})/4$

$$CS_1^c = \int_{\underline{\omega}}^{\bar{\omega}/2} [\hat{\omega} - \underline{\omega}]d\hat{\omega} \quad CS_2^c = \int_{\bar{\omega}/2}^{\bar{\omega}} [2\hat{\omega} - (\underline{\omega} + \bar{\omega}/2)]d\hat{\omega}$$

$$\Pi^c = 2(\bar{\omega} - 1) + (\bar{\omega} - 2)^2/4 - 2F$$

Maximum Welfare for (3*A*): $W_{3A}^c = \displaystyle\int_0^{9M(\bar{\omega})/4} (CS_1^c + CS_2^c + \Pi^c)dF$

$$= \int_0^{9M(\bar{\omega})/4} [42(2\bar{\omega} - 1) - 16F + 3\bar{\omega}^2 - 8\bar{\omega} + 4]/8dF$$

(3*B*): $9M(\bar{\omega})/4 < F \le \bar{F}^3(\bar{\omega})$

$$CS_1^c = \int_{\underline{\omega}}^{\bar{\omega}/2} (\hat{\omega} - \underline{\omega})(2 - 9M(\bar{\omega})/4)d\hat{\omega}$$

$$CS_2^c \int_{\bar{\omega}/2}^{\bar{\omega}} [2\hat{\omega} - \{\underline{\omega}(2 - 9M(\bar{\omega})/4F) + \bar{\omega}9M(\bar{\omega})/8F\}]d\hat{\omega}$$

$$\Pi^c = 2(\bar{\omega} - 1) - F + (\bar{\omega} - 2)^2(\bar{\omega}^2 - 4\bar{\omega} + 4)/64F$$

Maximum Welfare for (3B): $\displaystyle W^c_{3B} = \int\limits_{9M(\bar{\omega})/4}^{\bar{F}^3(\bar{\omega})} (CS^c_1 + CS^c_2 + \Pi^c)dF$

$$= \int\limits_{9M(\bar{\omega})/4}^{\bar{F}^3} \{[32F(2\bar{\omega} - 1) - 32F^2 + \bar{\omega}(\bar{\omega} - 2)]32F\}dF$$

Maximum Welfare under Cooperative Venture: $W^c(\bar{\omega}) = W^c_{3A} + W^c_{3B}$
Making the calculations I find that:

$W^m(\bar{\omega}) > W^f(\bar{\omega})$ for $1.33 < \bar{\omega} < 2$

$W^m(\bar{\omega}) > W^c(\bar{\omega})$ for $1.33 < \bar{\omega} < 1.43$ and $1.71 < \bar{\omega} < 2$

$W^m(\bar{\omega}) < W^c(\bar{\omega})$ for $1.43 < \bar{\omega} < 2$.

Notes

*   This chapter is based on a paper presented at the 21st Annual Conference of EARIE in Crete, Greece, September 1994. I acknowledge the helpful comments and discussion by the participants of the conference.

1.   In an article in *The New York Times*, 20 February 1996, page A1, on copyright piracy in China, the author notes that exports made up most of the 45 million compact disks illegally copied in 1995. Similarly, in an article in *The Economist*, 13 January 1996, p. 65, on intellectual property rights, it is reported that Italy accounts for 44 per cent of the 50 million pirate recordings sold each year in the European Union.

2.   The following representation is taken from Tirole (1988) p. 97.

3.   For an analysis of the finiteness property in models of vertical product differentiation, see Shaked and Sutton (1982, 1983), or Beath and Katsoulacos (1991) pp. 114–32.

4.   This result is shown to hold in Pepall (1996).

References

Beath, J. and Y. Katsoulacos (1991) *The Economic Theory of Product Differentiation* (Cambridge University Press).

Chin, J. and G. Grossman (1990) 'Intellectual Property Rights and North–South Trade', in Jones, R and A. Krueger (eds), *The Political Economy of International Trade: Essays in Honor of Robert E. Baldwin* (Oxford and Cambridge, MA; Blackwell), pp. 90–107.

Deardorff, A. (1992) 'Welfare Effects of Global Patent Protection', *Economica*, 59, pp. 35–51.

Diwan, I. and D. Rodrik (1991) 'Patents, Appropriate Technology and North–South Trade', *Journal of International Economics*, 30, pp. 27–47.

Gabszewicz, J.J. and J. Thisse (1979) 'Price Competition, Quality and Income Disparities', *Journal of Economic Theory*, 20, pp. 340–79.

Gabszewicz, J.J. and J. Thisse (1980) 'Entry (and Exit) in a Differentiated Industry', *Journal of Economic Theory*, 22, pp. 327–38.

Gilbert, R. and C. Shapiro (1990) 'Optimal Patent Length and Breadth', *Rand Journal of Economics*, 21, pp. 106–12.

Helpman, E. (1993) 'Innovation, Imitation and Intellectual Property Rights', *Econometrica*, 61, pp. 1247–80.

Klemperer, P. (1990) 'How Broad Should the Scope of Patent Protection Be?', *Rand Journal of Economics*, 21, pp. 113–30.

Pepall, L. (1997) 'Innovation and Imitation in Duopoly Model of Vertical Product Differentiation', *Economica*, May.

Pepall, L. and D. Richards (1994) 'Innovation, Imitation and Social Welfare', *Southern Economic Journal*, 60, pp. 673–84.

Scotchmer, S. and J. Green (1990) 'Antitrust Policy, The Breadth of Patent Protection and the Incentive to Develop New Products', mimeo, Harvard University.

Shaked, A. and J. Sutton (1982) 'Relaxing Price Competition through Product Differentiation', *Review of Economic Studies*, 49, pp. 1–13.

Shaked, A. and J. Sutton (1983) 'Natural Oligopolies', *Econometrica*, 51, pp. 1469–83.

Tirole, Jean (1988) *The Theory of Industrial Organization* (Cambridge: MIT Press).

5 Market Integration and the Benefits of National versus International R&D Cooperation

Geert Steurs*

5.1 INTRODUCTION

Many countries have set up national cooperative R&D programmes for some well-defined research areas. The same happens at the international level. The EC, for example, subsidizes R&D cooperation between participants located in different EC countries once a proposal is accepted. This happens in an environment of increasing international competition caused by, among other things, the integration of world markets. However, when discussing R&D cooperation, most authors only consider national R&D cooperation in segmented markets, i.e. the firms which cooperate are located in the same country and the market in which they cooperate is perfectly segmented from the markets in which firms located in other countries are operating. This chapter is an attempt to address this double limitation by comparing national with international R&D cooperation both when markets are segmented and when they are integrated.

The framework we use is an extension of the model by D'Aspremont and Jacquemin (1988). We consider the case of two symmetric duopolies each located in a different country. Figure 5.1 represents the four R&D-cooperation scenarios we look at in the subsequent sections. In the first two cases, the cooperating firms are located in the same country (national R&D cooperation). In the third and fourth cooperative settings, the cooperating firms are located in different countries (international R&D cooperation). In all the scenarios in this chapter, only two out of the four firms are involved in an R&D-cooperation agreement. Moreover, we do not consider settings in which there is more than one R&D-cooperation agreement. This is done in order to limit the number of scenarios to be compared.

When comparing and discussing these different settings, we try to answer the following kind of research questions. When discussing national R&D

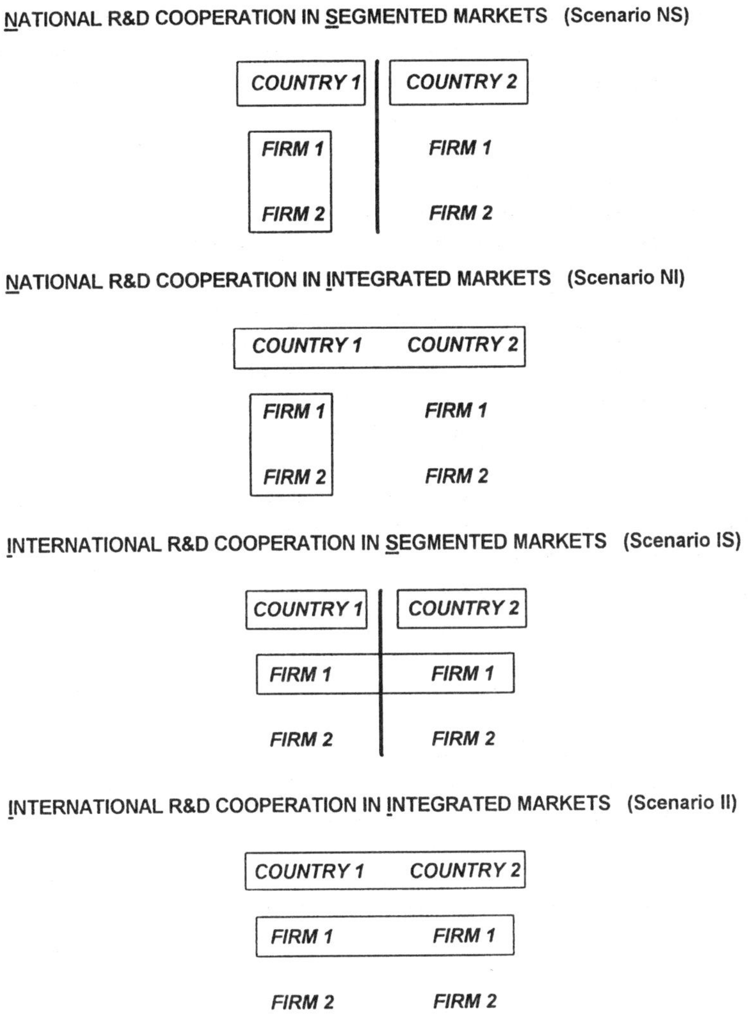

NATIONAL R&D COOPERATION IN SEGMENTED MARKETS (Scenario NS)

```
┌──────────────┐ ┌──────────────┐
│  COUNTRY 1   │ │  COUNTRY 2   │
├──────────────┤ │              │
│   ┌────────┐ │ │   FIRM 1     │
│   │ FIRM 1 │ │ │              │
│   │        │ │ │              │
│   │ FIRM 2 │ │ │   FIRM 2     │
│   └────────┘ │ │              │
└──────────────┘ └──────────────┘
```

NATIONAL R&D COOPERATION IN INTEGRATED MARKETS (Scenario NI)

```
┌──────────────────────────────┐
│  COUNTRY 1      COUNTRY 2     │
│  ┌────────┐                   │
│  │ FIRM 1 │     FIRM 1        │
│  │        │                   │
│  │ FIRM 2 │     FIRM 2        │
│  └────────┘                   │
└──────────────────────────────┘
```

INTERNATIONAL R&D COOPERATION IN SEGMENTED MARKETS (Scenario IS)

```
┌──────────────┐ ┌──────────────┐
│  COUNTRY 1   │ │  COUNTRY 2   │
│  ┌───────────┼─┼───────────┐  │
│  │ FIRM 1    │ │    FIRM 1  │  │
│  └───────────┼─┼───────────┘  │
│    FIRM 2    │ │    FIRM 2    │
└──────────────┘ └──────────────┘
```

INTERNATIONAL R&D COOPERATION IN INTEGRATED MARKETS (Scenario II)

```
┌──────────────────────────────┐
│  COUNTRY 1      COUNTRY 2     │
│ ┌────────────────────────────┐│
│ │ FIRM 1        FIRM 1       ││
│ └────────────────────────────┘│
│   FIRM 2        FIRM 2        │
└──────────────────────────────┘
```

Figure 5.1 National and international R&D-cooperation scenarios

cooperation, we try to determine the impact of market integration on the conditions under which national R&D cooperation has beneficial effects. Equivalently, when discussing international R&D cooperation, we examine under what conditions international R&D cooperation leads to higher R&D investments, output, profits and welfare, both when markets are segmented and when they are integrated.

To lend a real-world interpretation to these research questions, we sometimes consider two EC member states, for example, France (country 1) and the UK (country 2).[1] By simplification, a French firm can choose between national R&D cooperation with another French firm and international R&D cooperation with a firm from the UK. Of course, a third option remains, i.e., not to cooperate at all. In this chapter, we look at the welfare maximizing mode of R&D cooperation to see whether or not this optimal choice is influenced by the integration of the French and British market.

Our results have some interesting analogies with two other branches in the I.O. literature (Motta, 1994). The first is the literature on horizontal mergers and cartels. In particular, dependent on the level of national and international R&D spillovers and on whether markets are segmented or integrated, R&D cooperation may result in higher profits for the non-cooperating firms than for the cooperating firms, the latter always being more profitable than with R&D competition. This result is similar to the one obtained by Salant, Switzer and Reynolds (1983) that a merger may result in higher profits for the fringe firms versus the cartel members. However, in their model, cooperation may reduce the profitability of the cartel members relative to the non-cooperative case which is not true in our model.

Our discussion can also be related to the literature on strategic trade policy, more specifically, the papers by Spencer and Brander (1983), Ruiz-Mier (1989), Papaconstantinou (1992) and Rutsaert (1994). The strategic trade literature emphasizes the possibility for a government to intervene in the process of international competition by helping national firms which, thanks to the commitment of their national authority, are in a more favourable position in an international oligopoly. If one considers national R&D cooperation as a special type of strategic trade policy, we see that, dependent on the level of national and international R&D spillovers and on the level of market integration, national R&D cooperation in one country may raise the welfare level in the cooperating country. But, contrary to most results reported in the strategic trade literature, this may be true for the non-cooperating country.

We know of only one paper which addresses the same kind of research questions within a model similar to ours. Motta (1994) also considers a perfectly symmetric two-country setting with two firms in each country. There are, however, a number of important differences between his work and ours. First, he only considers the case in which markets are integrated. Second, he makes no distinction between national and international R&D spillovers, but assumes that spillovers between cooperating firms are higher than between non-cooperating firms. Finally, there is also a difference in the scenarios. Motta (1994) considers a scenario where two firms cooperate on their research activities while the remaining two firms do not. This setting is equivalent to our scenario of national R&D cooperation in integrated markets. He further considers the case where two cooperative agreements are formed simultaneously, each involving two firms. Both scenarios are compared with the fully non-cooperative equilibrium (cf. our scenario of R&D competition in integrated markets) and the case where all four firms cooperate. However, he does not consider scenarios with cross-border R&D cooperation.

The rest of the chapter is organized as follows. In section 5.2 we present the model. We proceed with a discussion of national R&D cooperation in section 5.3 followed by a discussion of international R&D cooperation in section 5.4. In section 5.5 a comparison is made between the equilibrium outcomes with national and international R&D cooperation, including some policy implications. In a final section we give some concluding remarks.

5.2   THE MODEL

The model we use is an extension of D'Aspremont and Jacquemin (1988). We consider two countries and in each country there are two firms. These firms all produce the same homogeneous output: x_i is produced by firm i in country 1 and y_i by firm i in country 2 ($i = 1,2$). We assume that the markets in which these firms sell their products are either perfectly segmented or perfectly integrated.[2]

When the markets are segmented, the firms in each country sell their product only in their home market. Export is assumed to be impossible.[3] Country and market borders are therefore the same. The firms in country 1 and 2, respectively, face the following linear inverse demand functions which share the same characteristics:

$$P_1 = a - b(x_1 + x_2) \tag{5.1}$$
$$P_2 = a - b(y_1 + y_2) \tag{5.2}$$

When both markets integrate, the 4 firms face a unique world market whose consumers are represented by the citizens of both countries. So if markets are integrated, the (world) market is composed of the two countries.[4] We further assume that the linear inverse-demand of this world market is simply the sum of the original segmented markets:

$$P_w = a - b(x_1 + x_2 + y_1 + y_2)/2 \tag{5.3}$$

All firms initially produce with the same marginal production cost c while there are no fixed costs.[5] Firms can invest in R&D which leads with certainty to a reduction in their marginal production costs. These R&D investments are indicated by u_i (v_i) for the firms in country 1 (2). Moreover, firms benefit from R&D (or 'technological') spillovers. Between firms located in the same country national R&D spillovers exist which equal β. Firms also benefit from spillovers from the firms in the other country through international R&D spillovers which equal Φ.[6] We assume that national R&D spillovers are equal in both countries, that international R&D spillovers are independent of the direction of the spillovers and that market integration doesn't change the level of international R&D spillovers.[7] Finally, we also assume that R&D cooperation, on a national or international scale, does not affect the level of spillovers.

The existence of both national and international R&D spillovers results in the following effective R&D-investment levels[8] U_i and V_i ($i = 1, 2$) for the firms in country 1 and 2, respectively:

$$U_i = u_i + \beta u_j + \Phi(v_1 + v_2) \qquad (i, j = 1, 2; i \neq j) \qquad (5.4)$$

$$V_i = v_i + \beta v_j + \Phi(u_1 + u_2) \qquad (i, j = 1, 2; i \neq j) \qquad (5.5)$$

The cost of R&D is assumed to be quadratic and equal to $(\Gamma/2)u_i^2$ ($i = 1, 2$) for the firms in country 1 and $(\Gamma/2)v_i^2$ ($i = 1, 2$) for the firms in country 2, where Γ is a measure of R&D efficiency. This specification implies that the total costs of a firm are convex with respect to the level of R&D investments.

The firms play a two-stage game. In the first stage they decide simultaneously on their R&D investments while in the second stage they decide on the quantity they will produce and sell on the market. Cooperation is limited to the R&D stage of the game. By backward induction we derive the subgame perfect Nash equilibria. This is done, for all the scenarios which will be compared, in the Appendix.

This model is probably too simple to draw strong policy conclusions. It does not take into account the benefits from R&D cooperation such as synergy-effects or the achievement of a critical mass of R&D investments. The assumptions like, for instance, two perfectly symmetric countries or symmetric international R&D spillovers may be far from realistic. Introducing asymmeties however would divert the analysis from the issue we want to focus on, i.e. a comparison between national and international R&D cooperation and the impact of market integration on this comparison.[9]

5.3 MARKET INTEGRATION AND THE BENEFITS OF NATIONAL R&D COOPERATION

In this section we compare the consequences of national R&D cooperation in segmented versus integrated markets in order to determine whether or not market integration affects the benefits of national R&D cooperation for the cooperating and non-cooperating firms (or country). Essentially we compare the conditions under which national R&D cooperation leads to higher R&D investments, output, profits and welfare both in the cooperating and non-cooperating country when markets are segmented versus when they are integrated. This is different from comparing the actual equilibrium values, i.e., whether, for instance, national R&D cooperation results in higher R&D investments by the cooperating firms when markets are integrated versus when they are segmented. This is a less relevant research question from our point of view since we assume that market integration is exogenous.[10] We also relate some of the results with the literature on horizontal mergers and cartels as well as with the strategic trade literature. Finally note that we were only able to prove the first two results analytically by comparing the relevant expressions in the Appendix. All other results are based on simulations.

A Comparison of the Innovative Investment and Output Levels

First of all, it can easily be verified that when markets are segmented, national R&D cooperation compared with R&D competition leads to higher (lower) R&D investments (and output) by the cooperating firms if $\beta > 1/2$ ($\beta < 1/2$), i.e. just like in D'Aspremont and Jacquemin (1988). When markets are integrated, national R&D cooperation will imply higher (lower) R&D investments (and output) by the cooperating firms if $\beta > (1 + 2\Phi)/4$ ($\beta < (1 + 2\Phi)/4$). This condition becomes more stringent when international R&D spillovers increase because this reduces, for a given level of national R&D spillovers, the strategic complementarity between the R&D investments of firms in the same country.

When comparing these conditions we observe two differences. First, when markets are integrated, a comparison between the R&D investments (and output) by the cooperating firms with national R&D cooperation versus R&D competition is no longer independent of the level of international R&D spillovers because the cooperating firms are now operating in an integrated world market. Second, there is a different stringency imposed on the level of national R&D spillovers for national R&D cooperation to result in higher R&D investments and output by the cooperating firms. This difference can be summarized as follows.

Result 1: *When international R&D spillovers are small ($\Phi < 1/2$), national R&D cooperation in integrated markets is more likely to result in higher R&D investments and output in the cooperating country than when markets are segmented. When international R&D spillovers are large ($\Phi > 1/2$), the reverse is true.*

If, for example, there are no international R&D spillovers between France and the UK, R&D cooperation in France leads to higher R&D investments and output by the French firms as soon as $\beta > 1/4$ if the French and UK markets are integrated, while β must be higher than 1/2 if these markets are segmented. However, if there are perfect international R&D spillovers between France and the UK, R&D cooperation in France leads to higher R&D investments and output by the French firms only if $\beta > 3/4$ when the French and UK markets are integrated, while when these markets are segmented, β must exceed 1/2.

The preceding discussion focused on the cooperating firms (country). The next result deals with the impact of national R&D cooperation on the levels of R&D investment and output of the non-cooperating firms (country). We only consider the cases where national R&D cooperation leads to higher R&D investments and output by the cooperating firms when compared with R&D competition. More precisely, we consider the cases in which $\beta > 1/2$ when markets are segmented and $\beta > (1 + 2\Phi)/4$ when markets are integrated. The question then is whether or not these beneficial effects 'spill over' to the country where the firms do not cooperate. It turns out that this is dependent on the level of market integration:

Result 2: *When markets are segmented and national R&D cooperation leads to higher R&D investments and output in the cooperating country when compared with R&D competition, the same is typically true for the non-cooperating country. When markets are integrated and national R&D cooperation leads to higher R&D investments and output in the cooperating country when compared with R&D competition, the same may or may not be true for the non-cooperating country.*

Referring to our example, when R&D cooperation by the French firms results in higher R&D investments and output in France, the same is true in the UK.[11] The reason is that there is no 'strategic' effect of the higher R&D investments by the cooperating firms on the non-cooperating firms since the two countries are perfectly segmented. The higher R&D investments of the cooperating firms, however, lead to lower marginal costs for the non-cooperating firms thanks to the international R&D spillovers, which implies higher outputs and higher marginal gains from R&D. This induces the non-cooperating firms to increase their R&D investments.

When markets are integrated, however, R&D investments and output in the non-cooperating country may be lower when compared with R&D competition because now the cooperating and non-cooperating firms compete in the same world market, which implies strategic interactions. For instance, R&D cooperation by the firms in France will result in lower R&D investments and output in the UK when compared with R&D competition when international R&D spillovers are 'low', more precisely if $\Phi < (1 + \beta)/3$.[12]

A comparison of the Profit and Welfare Levels

Our comparisons of the profitability and welfare effects of national R&D cooperation, both for the cooperating and non-cooperating firms, are to a large extent based on simulations which show the following.

Result 3: *National R&D cooperation typically results in higher profits for the cooperating firms when compared with R&D competition, irrespective of the level of market integration. The non-cooperating firms, however, may become less profitable when compared with R&D competition, but on the other hand they may also be more profitable than the cooperating firms.*

National R&D cooperation in segmented markets typically leads to higher profits for the cooperating firms. The same is true when markets are integrated. The impact on the profits of the non-cooperating firms is less clear-cut however. When markets are segmented and if there are international R&D spillovers, circumstances exist under which R&D cooperation by the firms in one country means a disadvantage to the non-cooperating firms in the other country. This is true if $\Phi > 0$ and $\beta < 1/2$. On the other hand, simulations also show us that when $\beta > 1/2$ and when the level of international R&D spillovers is not too low, the non-cooperating firms are more profitable than the cooperating firms (see Table 5.1). The intuition is that under these circumstances the non-cooperating firms benefit from the higher R&D investments by the cooperating firms while they incur lower R&D-investment costs. When there is market integration, we get very similar results (see Table 5.1).

These results can be discussed in the context of the literature on horizontal mergers and cartels. Salant, Switzer and Reynolds (1983), for instance, show that when firms produce homogeneous products and compete in terms of quantity, members of a cartel might earn lower profits than with competition

Table 5.1   Profits of the cooperating and non-cooperating firms with national R&D cooperation in segmented and integrated markets (with $a = 100$, $b = 1$, $c = 80$, $\Gamma = 10$, $n = 2$)[a]

		Segmented markets					Integrated markets			
	1	112.03	105.27	100.00	96.02	93.18	(b)	(b)	111.58	100.00	95.12
Φ	$\frac{1}{2}$	107.32	103.00	100.00	98.21	97.57	114.95	103.75	100.00	104.61	121.29
	0	102.49	100.62	100.00	100.62	102.49	92.11	100.00	133.67	284.52	8371.11
		0	$\frac{1}{4}$	$\frac{1}{2}$	$\frac{3}{4}$	1	0	$\frac{1}{4}$	$\frac{1}{2}$	$\frac{3}{4}$	1
				β					β		

[a]A number above 100 implies that the cooperating firms earn higher profits when compared with the non-cooperating firms.
[b]Profit are undefined here (see Appendix).

while the fringe firms become more profitable. The basic intuition for this result is that the cooperating firms act as producers of a public good for which the non-cooperating firms free ride.[13] In our model, however, the cooperating firms are typically more profitable than with R&D competition, which is a first important difference. On the other hand, the non-cooperating firms may be more or less profitable when compared with R&D competition. Therefore, the fringe firms do not always benefit from the existence of an R&D agreement.

When analyzing the impact of market integration on the welfare effects of national R&D cooperation for the cooperating as well as for the non-cooperating country, we get the following result:

Result 4: *When national R&D cooperation results in higher welfare for the cooperating country, the same will typically be true for the non-cooperating country when markets are segmented while the reverse may be true when markets are integrated.*

National R&D cooperation in segmented markets results in higher welfare, defined as the sum of consumer and producer surplus, in the cooperating country if $\beta > 1/2$, i.e. under the same condition as when it results in higher R&D investments and output by the cooperating firms. Similarly, national

R&D cooperation in integrated markets leads to a greater welfare in the cooperating country if $\beta > (1 + 2\Phi)/4$. When national R&D spillovers are below these critical levels, welfare is lower in the cooperating country as a consequence of national R&D cooperation.

But what about the impact on the welfare level of the non-cooperating country? Evidently, if there are no international R&D spillovers when markets are segmented, national R&D cooperation in one country has no impact on the welfare level in the other country. But simulations show that if there are international R&D spillovers, a comparison of the welfare levels typically leads to the same classification as a comparison of the output levels. This implies that if $\beta > 1/2$, national R&D cooperation not only results in a higher welfare level in the cooperating country, but also in the non-cooperating country, and, under certain conditions, to higher welfare in the non-cooperating country than in the cooperating country (see Table 5.2). However, when national R&D cooperation in integrated markets results in greater welfare in the cooperating country, this is only true for the non-cooperating country when international R&D spillovers are sufficiently high. This implies that when markets are integrated, welfare may be lower in the non-cooperating country when compared with R&D competition.

Table 5.2 Welfare in the cooperating and the non-cooperating country with national R&D cooperation in segmented and integrated markets (with $a = 100$, $b = 1$, $c = 80$, $\Gamma = 10$, $n = 2$)[a]

		Segmented markets					*Integrated markets*				
Φ	1	108.04	103.39	100.00	97.76	96.63	(b)	(b)	103.67	100.00	98.39
	$\frac{1}{2}$	103.49	101.16	100.00	100.00	101.18	104.48	101.16	100.00	101.32	105.80
	0	98.84	98.82	100.00	102.45	106.29	97.96	100.00	108.06	127.87	171.62
		0	$\frac{1}{4}$	$\frac{1}{2}$	$\frac{3}{4}$	1	0	$\frac{1}{4}$	$\frac{1}{2}$	$\frac{3}{4}$	1
				β					β		

[a]A number above 100 implies that welfare in the cooperating country is higher when compared with the non-cooperating country.
[b]Welfare levels are undefined here (see Appendix).

If national R&D cooperation is considered as a special form of government intervention, these results can be compared with the strategic trade literature. Spencer and Brander (1983), for example, have shown that an R&D subsidy leads domestic firms to choose a higher level of R&D, thus enabling them to capture a larger share of export markets which is to the detriment of foreign firms and results in higher domestic net welfare. Ruiz-Mier (1989) uses a framework similar to Spencer and Brander. However, he does not consider R&D subsidies, but the promotion of cooperative research as a way in which a government may be able to influence the institutional environment so as to confer a competitive advantage upon its national firms.

In both papers, however, domestic and foreign firms compete in a third 'export' market, which is crucially different from our set-up. Moreover, Spencer and Brander (1983) do not take R&D spillovers into account, while Ruiz-Mier (1989) assumes that R&D spillovers exist but only between the cooperating firms. Nevertheless, a discussion of our results within this framework of international trade theory allows us to draw at least two interesting conclusions.

First, like Motta (1994), we can conclude that if national R&D spillovers are sufficiently high ($\beta > 1/2$ if markets are segmented and $\beta > (1 + 2\Phi)/4$ if markets are integrated), the promotion of national R&D cooperation results in higher domestic welfare. Second, and more important, if markets are segmented, the same is true in the foreign country, which implies that the promotion of cooperative research (unlike subsidies) is not a 'beggar-thy-neighbour' policy. If markets are integrated, R&D cooperation may or may not result in greater welfare in the other country. In any case, when national R&D cooperation results in higher welfare in both countries when compared with R&D competition, chances are smaller that the foreign government will react against such a policy. Other benefits of an R&D cooperative policy are that it does not imply higher costs to the government because the firms turn out to have a private incentive to cooperate, it does not provoke the same distortions as a subsidy and it is politically acceptable (e.g. GATT rules do not exclude R&D-cooperation agreements) (Motta, 1994).

We now continue with a discussion of international R&D cooperation, both in segmented and integrated markets.

5.4 MARKET INTEGRATION AND THE BENEFITS OF INTERNATIONAL R&D COOPERATION

Before we proceed with a comparison between the equilibrium outcomes resulting from international R&D cooperation with those resulting from

R&D competition, we would like to point out that we will not only compare the equilibrium outcomes for the cooperating and non-cooperating firms separately, but also the resulting total R&D-investment, output and profit levels for each country, i.e., by adding these together for the cooperating and non-cooperating firms. These total equilibrium levels are the same in each country since in each country one of the firms is involved in an international R&D agreement while the other is not. This is an important difference with the national R&D-cooperation scenarios.

A Comparison of the Innovative Investment and Output Levels

It can easily be verified that when markets are segmented, international R&D cooperation leads to higher R&D investments and output by the cooperating firms as soon as there are international R&D spillovers ($\Phi > 0$). However, international R&D cooperation in integrated markets only results in higher R&D investments and output for the cooperating firms when international R&D spillovers are sufficiently 'high' ($\Phi > (1 + \beta)/3$). The reason is that only if $\Phi > (1 + \beta)/3$, there exists a positive externality which is internalized by international R&D cooperation, and therefore results in higher R&D investments (and output). So if markets are integrated the level of international R&D spillovers must be sufficiently high in order for international R&D cooperation to result in higher R&D investments and output. Moreover, the restriction on the level of international R&D spillovers becomes more stringent when national R&D spillovers increase.[14] The intuition here is that if both R&D investments and national R&D spillovers increase, domestic competitors benefit, which inhibits firms from investing more in R&D.

What about the impact of international R&D cooperation on the R&D investments and output of the non-cooperating firms? With international R&D cooperation in segmented markets, the non-cooperating firms typically invest less in R&D and produce less output than the cooperating firms, but they invest more in R&D and produce higher output when compared with R&D competition, at least when national R&D spillovers are sufficiently 'high' ($\beta > (1 - \Phi)/2$). However, if national R&D spillovers are 'small', more precisely if $\beta < (1 - \Phi)/2$, the non-cooperating firms invest less in R&D and produce less output when compared with R&D competition. This is important to know in order to get an idea of the impact of international R&D cooperation on the total innovative investments and output of a country. Simulations show that these are higher with international R&D cooperation compared with R&D competition, at least when there are international R&D spillovers.

When markets are integrated, the effects of international R&D cooperation on the non-cooperating firms are difficult to disentangle. The non-cooperating firms invest less in R&D and typically produce less output than the cooperating firms when international R&D spillovers are 'high', since under these circumstances the cooperating firms increase their R&D investments. The reverse is true if international R&D spillovers are 'low'. When compared with R&D competition, the non-cooperating firms invest more in R&D and produce greater output when national and international R&D spillovers are both 'high' or both 'low'. So when international R&D cooperation results in greater R&D investments and output for the cooperating firms, the reverse may be true for the non-cooperating firms. But on the other hand, when international R&D cooperation results in less R&D investments and output for the cooperating firms, this need not be true for the non-cooperating firms.

Again it is important to see what happens with the total level of R&D investments and output. It turns out that, analogous to the case of segmented markets, the total level of R&D investments and output is higher with international R&D cooperation when compared with R&D competition if $\Phi > (1 + \beta)/3$, i.e. under the same condition as when the cooperating firms invest more in R&D and produce greater output. So if the non-cooperating firms invest less in R&D or produce less output when compared with R&D competition, this is more than compensated by the higher R&D investments and output of the cooperating firms.

Summarizing the impact of market integration on the total R&D and output levels with international R&D cooperation results in the following result:

Result 5: *When markets become integrated, international R&D cooperation is less likely to result in higher total R&D investments and output when compared with R&D competition.*

A Comparison of the Profit and Welfare Levels

Similar to the case of national R&D cooperation, we find that also international R&D cooperation typically results in higher profits for the cooperating firms, irrespective of the level of market integration. A comparison between the profits of the non-cooperating and those with R&D competition turns out to be solely dependent on output when markets are segmented as well as when they are integrated. This implies that when markets are segmented, the non-cooperating firms are more profitable when

Table 5.3 Profits of the cooperating and the non-cooperating firms with international R&D cooperation in segmented and integrated markets (with $a = 100$, $b = 1$, $c = 80$, $\Gamma = 10$, $n = 2$)[a]

		Segmented markets					Integrated markets				
Φ	1	103.05	99.92	97.36	95.15	93.18	(b)	(b)	101.32	97.23	95.12
	$\frac{1}{2}$	102.22	100.67	99.36	98.21	97.16	104.65	100.98	100.00	100.79	102.99
	0	100.00	100.00	100.00	100.00	100.00	92.11	96.54	101.73	107.78	114.95
		0	$\frac{1}{4}$	$\frac{1}{2}$	$\frac{3}{4}$	1	0	$\frac{1}{4}$	$\frac{1}{2}$	$\frac{3}{4}$	1
				β					β		

[a]A number above 100 implies that the cooperating firms earn higher profits when compared to the non-cooperating firms.
[b]Profits are undefined here (see Appendix).

compared with R&D competition, unless national R&D spillovers are 'small', i.e., $\beta < (1 - \Phi)/2$. In addition, simulations indicate that when national R&D spillovers are sufficiently high, the non-cooperating firms are more profitable than the cooperating firms (see Table 5.3). The intuition for this is that while the non-cooperating firms incur lower R&D-investment costs, they benefit from the higher R&D investments made by the cooperating firms if national R&D spillovers are 'high'. Overall, when the profits earned by the cooperating and non-cooperating firms are added, we find that only if both national and international R&D spillovers are 'small', total profits may be lower with international R&D cooperation in segmented markets when compared with R&D competition.

When the markets are integrated we get that the non-cooperating firms are more profitable than with R&D competition when national and international R&D spillovers are both 'high' or 'low'. Under these circumstances, they may even be more profitable than the cooperating firms (see Table 5.3).

When the profits earned by the cooperating and non-cooperating firm are added together, we find circumstances under which the higher profits of the cooperating firms do not compensate for the lower profits of the non-cooperating firms, implying that total profits may be lower with international R&D cooperation in integrated markets when compared with R&D

competition. Since this was also true with international R&D cooperation within segmented markets, we conclude that:

Result 6: *Irrespective of the level of market integration, international R&D cooperation may result in lower total profits in each country.*

As indicated before, the reason for this result is that international R&D cooperation may result in lower profits for the non-cooperating firms which are not always compensated for by the higher profits of the cooperating firms. Without formal analysis, Katz and Ordover (1990) warned of the possibility that,

> The technology transfer through the (international) cooperative agreement may substantially strengthen the foreign partner and thereby diminish the rents accruing to domestic firms that were not party to the agreement. (Katz and Ordover, 1990, p. 157)

This is the case in our model, at least for particular combinations of national and international R&D spillovers.

With respect to the impact of international R&D cooperation on welfare, we find that when markets are segmented, total welfare is always higher when there are international R&D spillovers. When markets are integrated this is only true when international R&D spillovers are sufficiently 'high'. This allows us to draw the following conclusion which is very similar to Result 5:

Result 7: *When markets become integrated, international R&D cooperation is less likely to result in higher welfare when compared with R&D competition.*

5.5   NATIONAL VERSUS INTERNATIONAL R&D COOPERATION: A COMPARISON

This section focuses on the impact of market integration on the comparison of the welfare levels which result from national and international R&D cooperation. The most important conclusion is that the conditions under which national R&D cooperation results in higher welfare when compared with international R&D cooperation, change when markets become integrated. We find indeed that:

Result 8: *National R&D cooperation will, compared with international R&D cooperation, more likely result in a higher welfare level in the cooperating country when markets integrate.*

It is the comparison of the R&D investments which drives this intuitively appealing result. Partly based on simulations, it can be shown that when markets are segmented, the R&D investments, and typically also the output of the cooperating and non-cooperating firms, are only higher with national R&D cooperation when compared with international R&D cooperation if international R&D spillovers are 'small', more precisely when $\Phi < 2\beta - 1$.

The intuition for this result is as follows. With national R&D cooperation, the cooperating firms invest more in R&D (and produce a higher output level) when compared with R&D competition if $2\beta - 1 > 0$. The same is true for the cooperating firms involved in an international R&D agreement if $\Phi > 0$. Whether national or international R&D cooperation results in highest R&D investments (and output) depends on which pair of firms' R&D investments have a stronger strategic complementarity. When $\Phi < 2\beta - 1$, the strategic complementarity between the R&D investments of firms located in the same country is stronger than the strategic complementary between the R&D investments of firms located in different countries. Therefore, we get that the firms which cooperate with a firm in the same country will invest more in R&D (and produce more) than the cooperating firms involved in an international R&D agreement. The reverse holds if $\Phi > 2\beta - 1$. A comparison between the R&D investments and output of the non-cooperating firms is in about the same way dependent upon a comparison between Φ and $2\beta - 1$.

Our simulations indicate that not only the level of R&D investments but also welfare in country 1 is higher with national R&D cooperation when $\Phi < 2\beta - 1$ (see Table 5.4). The same conclusion is valid for country 2. So, referring to our example, if international R&D spillovers are 'low', both France and the UK are better off if both firms in France cooperate with each other, while if they are 'high', an international R&D agreement between a French and a UK firm results in higher welfare. There is no conflict between France and the UK with respect to what is optimal from a welfare point of view. However, the optimal state from a welfare point of view does not always correspond with the profit-maximizing choice for the firms. When $\Phi > 2\beta - 1$, i.e., when international R&D cooperation is preferred from a welfare point of view, the French firms may prefer to cooperate on a national basis, implying that there may be room for intervention by the French government which would make the welfare-maximizing choice also the profit-maximizing choice. This could be done for example by subsidizing

Table 5.4 Welfare with international R&D cooperation and welfare in the cooperating country with national R&D cooperation in segmented markets (with $a = 100$, $b = 1$, $c = 80$, $\Gamma = 10$, $n = 2$)[a]

		0	1/4	1/2	3/4	1	0	1/4	1/2	3/4	1
	1	107.37	107.83	107.03	104.99	101.74	(b)	(b)	112.25	107.35	100.82
Φ	1/2	102.57	102.95	102.09	100.00	96.74	103.52	102.76	100.00	95.02	87.52
	0	101.18	101.20	100.00	97.61	94.09	101.18	99.53	94.35	83.82	63.92
				β					β		

[a] A number above 100 implies that welfare with international R&D cooperation is higher when compared with welfare in the cooperating country with national R&D cooperation.
[b] Welfare levels are undefined here (see Appendix).

participation in an EC Research Programme. There is also a third option, i.e., no R&D cooperation, but typically either national or international R&D cooperation results in higher welfare for France when compared with R&D competition.

When markets are integrated, we find, again partly based on simulations, that when national R&D spillovers are higher than international R&D spillovers, the cooperating firms invest more in R&D and produce more with national R&D cooperation when compared with international R&D cooperation. The non-cooperating firms invest more in R&D and produce more with national R&D cooperation when national and international R&D spillovers are both 'high' or both 'low'.

The intuition for these results is the same as in the case of segmented markets. Whether national or international R&D cooperation results in higher R&D investments by the cooperating firms depends on which pair of firms' R&D investments have a stronger strategic complementarity. These are measured by $4\beta - 1 - 2\Phi$ for firms in the same country and by $3\Phi - \beta - 1$ for firms in different countries (see Appendix, equations (5A.7) and (5A.7′)). Therefore, if $4\beta - 1 - 2\Phi > 3\Phi - \beta - 1\Phi$, i.e., if $\beta > \Phi$, the firms which are involved in a national R&D agreement invest more in R&D and produce more than the firms which cooperate on an international basis. The reverse result holds if $\Phi > \beta$.

Our simulation results indicate that also when markets are integrated, a comparison of the welfare levels with national and international R&D

cooperation results in very similar conclusions to those of the R&D-investment levels comparison. We find indeed that welfare in country 1 is higher with national R&D cooperation when $\beta > \Phi$ (see Table 5.4). The same is true for country 2 where national R&D cooperation also results in higher welfare when national R&D spillovers are 'low', but international R&D spillovers are 'high'.

With respect to possible policy implications we find that for specific combinations of national and international R&D spillovers, the firms in France prefer to cooperate with one another, while it would be better, from a welfare point of view, if one of them cooperated with a UK firm. Inversely, it is possible that a French firm prefers to cooperate on an international basis while welfare in France would be higher with national R&D cooperation. Similar to segmented markets, this implies that there may be room for intervention by the French government to make the welfare-maximizing choice also the profit-maximizing choice. But contrary to the case when markets are segmented, the third option, i.e., no R&D cooperation, may result in the greatest welfare in integrated markets when compared with national or international R&D cooperation.

All this allows us to derive the result stated in Result 8. Indeed, when markets are segmented, national R&D cooperation results in higher welfare in the cooperating (but also in the non-cooperating) country when $2\beta - 1 > \Phi$. When markets integrate, this condition becomes $\beta > \Phi$, which is less stringent and therefore national R&D cooperation is more likely to result in higher welfare compared with international R&D cooperation.

The intuition for this result may be as follows. If markets are segmented you care less about one of your domestic firms cooperating with a foreign firm since they do not compete with one another. It may even be true that the higher R&D investments by the domestic firm involved in the cross-border R&D coalition incite the non-participating domestic firm also to invest more in R&D. However, when markets are integrated, domestic and foreign firms compete on the same world market and therefore national R&D cooperation is more often preferred. International R&D cooperation may under these circumstances indeed result in a stronger foreign competitor, which implies a disadvantage for the non-participating domestic firm which must compete on the same world market.

5.6 CONCLUDING REMARKS

Typically, when discussing R&D cooperation, only national R&D cooperation in segmented markets is considered; i.e., the firms which cooperate are located in the same country and the market in which they operate is perfectly segmented from the markets in which firms located in other countries are operating. Since international R&D spillovers have not been taken into account, the impact of R&D cooperation in one country on companies in other countries has never been studied. In addition, international R&D-cooperation scenarios have also never been analyzed before. This chapter was an attempt to fill these gaps in the theoretical literature on R&D cooperation. We were able to derive some interesting and intuitively appealing results which shed some light on the interrelated issues of national and international R&D cooperation, market integration and R&D policy.

However, all the results we discussed were obtained using a model containing many simplifying assumptions. We indicated above that R&D cooperation in our model only implies that potential externalities between the R&D investments of the cooperating firms are internalized. We did not take into account other possible benefits from R&D cooperation, such as, for example, the realization of synergy effects or the achievement of a critical mass of R&D investments.

Another important limitation of our analysis is that we do not consider settings in which there are two national R&D agreements, i.e., in France and in the UK. Evidently, the choice of the French firms or the French government has consequences for the optimal strategy of UK firms and UK government. National R&D cooperation by the firms in France, for example, may result in lower profits for the UK firms which may incite them to also cooperate, and/or in lower welfare for the UK citizens which may incite the UK government to 'retaliate'. Including such 'retaliation' scenarios into our analysis as well as relaxing some of the assumptions would probably allow us to draw stronger (policy) conclusions. But this will not at all be an easy task since even with the present simple model we had to rely to a large extent upon simulations to derive our results.

APPENDIX: DERIVATION OF THE NASH EQUILIBRIA

R&D Competition in Segmented and Integrated Markets

When markets are *segmented* (scenario S), total profits of each firm in country 1 and country 2 are, respectively:

$$\Pi_{i1} = (a - bX - c + U_i)x_i - (\Gamma/2)u_i^2 \qquad (i = 1, 2) \tag{5A.1}$$

$$\Pi_{i2} = (a - bY - c + V_i)y_i - (\Gamma/2)v_i^2 \qquad (i = 1, 2) \tag{5A.1'}$$

where $X = x_1 + x_2$, $Y = y_1 + y_2$, $U_i = u_i + \beta u_j + \Phi (v_1 + v_2)$ and $V_i = v_i + \beta v_i + \Phi(u_1 + u_2)$ with $i, j = 1,2$ and $i \neq j$. In the second stage, each firm maximizes its profits with respect to output conditional on its investments in R&D in the first stage. This results in the following second-stage equilibrium output levels:

$$x_i = Z + Au_i + Bu_j + C(v_1 + v_2) \qquad (i, j = 1, 2; i \neq j) \qquad (5A.2)$$

$$y_i = Z + Av_i + Bv_j + C(u_1 + u_2) \qquad (i, j = 1, 2; i \neq j) \qquad (5A.2')$$

where $Z = (a - c)/3b > 0$, $A = (2 - \beta)/3b > 0$, $B = (2\beta - 1)/3b$ and $C = \Phi/3b$.

In the first stage, firms decide on their level of R&D investments. This results in the following symmetric equilibrium R&D-investment, output and profit levels (the subscripts are deleted):

$$u^s = \frac{AZ}{\Gamma' - AD - 2AC} = v^s \qquad (5A.3)$$

$$x^s = \frac{\Gamma Z}{\Gamma' - AD - 2AC} = y^s \qquad (5A.4)$$

$$\Pi^s = b(x^s)^2(1 - A^2/\Gamma') = b(y^s)^2(1 - A^2/\Gamma') \qquad (5A.5)$$

where $D = A + B = (1 + \beta)/3b$ and $\Gamma' = \Gamma/2b$. The conditions for stability of the R&D-stage outcome will always be assumed to be satisfied, and Γ is assumed to be sufficiently large so as to result in positive R&D investments, output and profits.

When markets are *integrated* (scenario I), the total profits of each firm in country 1 and country 2 are, respectively:

$$\Pi_{i1} = \left(a - b\frac{X + Y}{2} - c + U_i\right)x_i - (\Gamma/2)u_i^2 \qquad (i = 1, 2) \qquad (5A.6)$$

$$\Pi_{i2} = \left(a - b\frac{X + Y}{2} - c + V_i\right)y_i - (\Gamma/2)v_i^2 \qquad (i = 1, 2) \qquad (5A.6')$$

In the second stage, each firm again maximizes its profits with respect to output conditional on its investments in R&D in the first stage. This results in the following second-stage equilibrium output levels:

$$x_i = Z' + A'u_i + B'u_j + C'(v_1 + v_2) \qquad (i, j = 1, 2; i \neq j) \qquad (5A.7)$$

$$y_i = Z' + A'v_i + B'v_j + C'(u_1 + u_2) \qquad (i, j = 1, 2; i \neq j) \qquad (5A.7')$$

where $Z' = 2(a - c)/5b > 0$, $A' = 2(4 - \beta - 2\Phi)/5b > 0$, $B' = 2(4\beta - 1 - 2\Phi)/5b$, and $C' = 2(3\Phi - \beta - 1)/5b$.

In the first stage, firms decide on their level of R&D investments. This results in the following symmetric equilibrium R&D investment, output and profits (the subscripts are deleted):

$$u' = \frac{A'Z'}{2\Gamma' - A'D' - 2A'C'} = v' \qquad (5A.8)$$

$$x' = \frac{2\Gamma'Z'}{2\Gamma' - A'D' - 2A'C'} = y' \qquad (5A.9)$$

$$\Pi' = (b/2)(x')^2(1 - A'^2/2\Gamma') = (b/2)(y')^2(1 - A'^2/2\Gamma') \qquad (5A.10)$$

where $D' = A' + B' = 2(3 + 3\beta - 4\Phi)/5b$ and $\Gamma' = \Gamma/2b$.

National R&D Cooperation in Segmented and Integrated Markets

When there is national R&D cooperation in *segmented* markets (scenario NS), both firms in country 1 cooperate with respect to R&D while the firms in country 2 decide on their R&D investments noncooperatively. In the second stage, all four firms decide noncooperatively on their output. The outcome of the second stage is therefore equivalent to the one we obtained for the case of R&D competition in segmented markets (cf. equations (5A.2) and (5A.2')).

In the first stage, both firms in country 1 decide on their R&D investments by maximizing their combined profits, while each firm in country 2 maximizes its own profits. Because of the difference in the objective functions, the equilibrium R&D investments, output and profits are different between the firms in the cooperating and noncooperating countries (the subscripts are deleted):

$$u^{NS} = \frac{DZ(\Gamma' - AD + 2AC)}{(\Gamma' - D^2)(\Gamma' - AD) - 4AC^2D} \qquad (5A.11)$$

$$v^{NS} = \frac{AZ(\Gamma' - D^2 + 2CD)}{(\Gamma' - D^2)(\Gamma' - AD) - 4AC^2D} \qquad (5A.11')$$

$$x^{NS} = \frac{\Gamma'Z(\Gamma' - AD + 2AC)}{(\Gamma' - D^2)(\Gamma' - AD) - 4AC^2D} \qquad (5A.12)$$

$$y^{NS} = \frac{\Gamma'Z(\Gamma' - D^2 + 2CD)}{(\Gamma' - D^2)(\Gamma' - AD) - 4AC^2D} \qquad (5A.12')$$

$$\Pi_{i1}^{NS} = b(x^{NS})^2(1 - D^2/\Gamma') \qquad (i = 1, 2) \qquad (5A.13)$$

$$\Pi_{i2}^{NS} = b(y^{NS})^2(1 - A^2/\Gamma') \qquad (i = 1, 2) \qquad (5A.13')$$

When markets are *Integrated* (scenario NI), there is one important difference: all four firms compete in the same integrated market. The R&D agreement between the firms in country 1 can therefore be considered as an example of less than industry-wide R&D cooperation. In the second stage, the firms continue to decide noncooperatively on their output which is, therefore, equal to the second-stage equilibrium, output levels we derived for the R&D competition case in integrated markets, i.e., equations (5A.7) and (5A.7').

In the first stage, both firms in country 1 decide on their R&D investments by maximizing their combined profits while each firm in country 2 maximizes its own profits. By focusing on a symmetric equilibrium, we get (the subscripts are deleted):

$$u^{NI} = \frac{D'Z'(2\Gamma' - A'D' + 2A'C')}{(2\Gamma' - D^2)(2\Gamma' - A'D') - 4A'C'^2D'} \qquad (5A.14)$$

$$v^{NI} = \frac{A'Z'(2\Gamma' - D^2 + 2C'D')}{(2\Gamma' - D^2)(2\Gamma' - A'D') - 4A'C'^2D'} \qquad (5A.14')$$

$$x^{NI} = \frac{2\Gamma'Z'(2\Gamma' - A'D' + 2A'C')}{(2\Gamma' - D'^2)(2\Gamma' - A'D') - 4A'C'^2D'} \tag{5A.15}$$

$$y^{NI} = \frac{2\Gamma'Z'(2\Gamma' - D'^2 + 2C'D')}{(2\Gamma' - D'^2)(2\Gamma' - A'D') - 4A'C'^2D'} \tag{5A.15'}$$

$$\Pi_{i1}^{NI} = (b/2)(x^{NI})^2(1 - D'^2/2\Gamma') \qquad (i = 1, 2) \tag{5A.16}$$

$$\Pi_{i2}^{NI} = (b/2)(y^{NI})^2(1 - A'^2/2\Gamma') \qquad (i = 1, 2) \tag{5A.16'}$$

D' must be bigger than zero. Therefore, we must exclude values of Φ bigger than or equal to $(3 + 3\beta)/4$ which corresponds with high international R&D spillovers in combination with low national R&D spillovers.

International R&D Cooperation in Segmented and Integrated Markets

With international R&D cooperation in *segmented* markets (scenario IS), the first firm in country 1 cooperates with the first firm in country 2 while the two other firms decide noncooperatively on their R&D investments. Again, all four firms decide noncooperatively on their output in the second stage, the outcome of which is therefore equivalent to the R&D-competition case in segmented markets (cf. equations (A2) and (A2')).

In the first stage, firm 1 in country 1 and firm 1 in country 2 decide on their R&D investments by maximizing their combined profits. The two other firms each maximize their own profits. The resulting symmetric equilibria are:

$$u_1^{IS} = \frac{EZ(\Gamma' - AE + AF)}{(\Gamma' - E^2)(\Gamma' - AE) - AEF^2} = v_1^{IS} \tag{5A.17}$$

$$u_2^{IS} = \frac{AZ(\Gamma - E^2 + EF)}{(\Gamma - E^2)(\Gamma - AE) - AEF^2} = v_2^{IS} \tag{5A.17'}$$

$$x_1^{IS} = \frac{\Gamma'Z(\Gamma' - AE + AF)}{(\Gamma' - E^2)(\Gamma' - AE) - AEF^2} = y_1^{IS} \tag{5A.18}$$

$$x_2^{IS} = \frac{\Gamma'Z(\Gamma' - E^2 + EF)}{(\Gamma' - E^2)(\Gamma' - AE) - AEF^2} = y_2^{IS} \tag{5A.18'}$$

$$\Pi_{11}^{IS} = b(x_1^{IS})^2(1 - E^2/\Gamma) = b(y_1^{IS})^2(1 - E^2/\Gamma') = \Pi_{12}^{IS} \tag{5A.19}$$

$$\Pi_{21}^{IS} = b(x_2^{IS})^2(1 - A^2/\Gamma') = b(y_2^{IS})^2(1 - A^2/\Gamma') = \Pi_{22}^{IS} \tag{5A.19'}$$

where $E = A + C = (2 - \beta + \Phi)/3b$ and $F = B + C = (2\beta - 1 + \Phi)/3b$.

International R&D cooperation in *Integrated* markets (scenario II) is different from the preceding one only because now both markets are integrated. As in the three other scenarios, all four firms decide R&D-competition case in integrated markets (cf. equations (5A.A7) and 5A7')).

In the first stage, firm 1 in country 1 and firm 1 in country 2 decide on their R&D investments by maximizing their combined profits while the two other firms each maximize their own profit function. Focusing on a symmetric equilibrium, we get:

$$u_1'' = \frac{E'Z'(2\Gamma' - A'E' + A'F')}{(2\Gamma' - E'^2)(2\Gamma' - A'E') - A'E'F'^2} = v_1''$$

(5A.20)

$$u_2'' = \frac{A'Z'(2\Gamma' - E'^2 + E'F')}{(2\Gamma' - E'^2)(2\Gamma' - A'E') - A'E'F'^2} = v_2''$$

$$x_1'' = \frac{2\Gamma'Z'(2\Gamma' - A'E' + A'F')}{(2\Gamma' - E'^2)(2\Gamma' - A'E') - A'E'F'^2} = y_1''$$

$$x_2'' = \frac{2\Gamma'Z'(2\Gamma' - E'^2 + E'F')}{(2\Gamma' - E'^2)(2\Gamma' - A'E') - A'E'F'^2} = y_2''$$

$$\Pi_{11}'' = (b/2)(x_1'')^2(1 - E'^2/2\Gamma') = (b/2)(y_1'')^2(1 - E'^2/2\Gamma') = \Pi_{12}''$$

$$\Pi_{21}'' = (b/2)(x_2'')^2(1 - A'^2/2\Gamma') = (b/2)(y_2'')^2(1 - A'^2/2\Gamma') = \Pi_{22}''$$

where $E' = A' + C' = 2(3 - 2\beta + \Phi)/5b > 0$ and $F' = B' + C' = 2(3\beta - 2 - \Phi)/5b$.

Notes

*.   This chapter is based on chapter 7 of my PhD-thesis 'Spillovers and Cooperation in Research and Development' (Steurs, 1994). Comments and suggestions from R. De Bondt (Promotor), P. Van Cayseele, R. Veugelers, J. Poyago-Theotoky and participants at the 22nd EARIE conference in Juan les Pins are gratefully acknowledged. The usual disclaimer applies.

1.   While any other pair of EC Member States could serve as an example, we prefer to use France and the UK because both their GDP and population are comparable. Moreover, they are separated by the sea which lends more perspective to the notion of segmented versus integrated markets.

2.   Katz and Ordover (1990) distinguish between 'competitive' and 'technological' spillovers. Using their terminology, there are no competitive spillovers when markets are segmented while there are perfect competitive spillovers when markets are integrated.

3.   This assumption is made in order not to complicate the analysis, but it is not that stringent given the symmetric set-up we consider, especially with regard to the initial level of marginal costs (see below).

4.   An alternative interpretation could be to consider integration between industries: for example, between the computer and electronics industries.

5.   The introduction of fixed costs would not alter our analysis and therefore we didn't take them into account.

6.   Coe and Helpman (1995, p. 860), estimating to what extent a country's total factor productivity depends not only on domestic R&D capital but also on foreign R&D capital, distinguish between direct and indirect benefits from foreign R&D: 'Direct benefits consist of learning about new technologies and materials, production processes, or organization methods. Indirect benefits emanate from imports of goods and services that have been developed by trade partners.' Since we assumed export to be impossible, we only consider the direct benefits of foreign R&D.

7. These assumptions, made to keep the problem tractable, imply that we cannot address several interesting situations which could arise. National R&D spillovers may be larger in one of the two countries, for example, because of the creation of a 'national system of innovation' in that country. Or international R&D spillovers may be (mainly) unilateral due to the cultural background of a country or legal restrictions imposed by a government.

8. The effective R&D-investment level is the amount of money a firm alone would have to invest in R&D, if there were to be no national or international R&D spillovers, to achieve the same unit cost reduction (Katz, 1986; Kamien, Muller and Zang, 1992).

9. Even this simple model did not always allow us to prove analytically the results we will discuss. That's why we sometimes refer to simulations which were run with the aid of a Turbo Pascal Program. By changing the values of all exogenous variables, one by one and in combination, we checked whether a systematic pattern arose in the comparison of the equilibrium outcomes. These typical patterns are commented on in the main text.

10. For the effects of market integration on the actual equilibrium levels when firms compete in R&D, see Steurs (1994).

11. Note that while the R&D investments of the non-cooperating (UK) firms will always be lower than those of the cooperating (French) firms, output and therefore also consumer surplus may be higher in the non-cooperating country, i.e. the UK, which is the case if the level of international R&D spillovers is sufficiently 'high', more precisely if $\Phi > (1 + \beta)/2$.

12. On the other hand, if $\Phi > (1 + \beta)/2$, the non-cooperating firms produce more output than the cooperating firms, which is similar to the case of segmented markets.

13. De Bondt and Wu (1997) obtain a similar result when discussing the profitability of an RJV cartel for the case in which cooperation results only in coordinated investments and no better information transfer (as in our model). However, information-sharing between the cooperating partners quickly results in higher profits for the member firms.

14. For example, when $\beta > 0$, Φ must be larger than $1/3$, while if $\beta = 1$, Φ must be larger than $2/3$.

References

Coe, D.T. and E. Helpman (1995) 'International R&D Spillovers'. *European Economic Review*, 39, 5, pp. 859–87.

D'Aspremont, C. and A. Jacquemin (1988) 'Cooperative and Noncooperative R&D in a Duopoly with Spillovers', *The American Economic Review*, pp. 1133–7.

De Bondt, R. and C. Wu (1997) 'Research Joint Venture Cartels and Welfare', ch. 3 in this book.

Kamien, M.I., Muller, E. and I. Zang (1992) 'Research Joint Ventures and R&D Cartels', *American Economic Review*, 82, 5, pp. 1293–306.

Katz, M.L. (1986) 'An Analysis of Cooperative Research and Development', *Rand Journal of Economics*, 17, 4, pp. 527–43.

Katz, M.L. and J.A. Ordover (1990) 'R&D Cooperation and Competition', *Economic Activity: Brooking Papers: Microeconomics*, pp. 137–203.

Motta, M. (1994) 'Research Joint Ventures in an International Economy', Working Paper, Universitat Pompeu Fabra, Barcelona, 25 pp.

Papaconstantinou, G. (1992) 'International R&D Spillovers and Strategic Subsidies', Working Paper, OECD, Paris, 25 pp.

Ruiz-Mier, L.F. (1989) 'Cooperative Research and International Rivalry' in Link, A.N. and G. Tassey (eds), *Cooperative Research and Development: The Industry–University–Government Relationship* (Kluwer Academic Publishers).

Rutsaert, P. (1994) 'To Promote R&D Cooperation: A Strategic Trade Policy?', Working Paper, MERIT, Maastricht. 30 pp.

Salant, S., W. Switzer and R. Reynolds (1983) 'Losses from Horizontal Merger: The Effect of an Exogenous Change in Industry Structure on Cournot–Nash Equilibrium', *Quarterly Journal of Economics*, 98, pp. 185–99.

Spencer, B.J. and J.A. Brander (1983) 'International R&D Rivalry and Industrial Stategy', *Review of Economic Studies*, L, pp. 707–22.

Steurs, G. (1994) 'Spillovers and Cooperation in Research and Development', PhD thesis, Faculty of Economics and Applied Economics, Katholieke Universiteit Leuven, 252 pp.

Steurs, G. (1995) 'Strategic Rivalry with Spillovers within Segmented versus Integrated Markets', forthcoming in *Economics of Innovation and New Technology*, 26 pp.

6 R&D Cooperation between Asymmetric Partners

Katrien Kesteloot and Reinhilde Veugelers

6.1 INTRODUCTION

Confronted with newly opening international markets and intensified competition, firms are readjusting their scope of operations, backed by technological developments that allow for producing and marketing on a global scale. In their quest for efficient global operations, firms increasingly revert to alliances, national or cross-border, involving production, research, distribution and other functional activities.

The advantages of such alliances are compelling (Pfeffer and Nowak, 1976; Mariti and Smiley, 1983; Harrigan, 1985; Porter and Fuller, 1986; Contractor and Lorange, 1988; Hagedoorn and Schakenraad, 1994): alliances are an expedient way to crack new markets, gain skills and technologies, realize economies through reorganization and exploitation of complementarities, share risks, fixed costs and resources as well as to monitor and control competitive forces. Despite these apparent benefits of cooperation, scattered evidence suggests that alliances carry a disturbingly high risk of trouble or failure (see, e.g., Kogut, 1988). Partners may fail to coordinate and jointly manage the dynamics of the alliance (Killing, 1983). In addition, firms expose and develop valuable know-how through the alliance (Thomas and Trevino, 1993). Such information flows, when uncontrolled in a world of opportunism, can undermine the comparative technological advantages of the firms, endangering their long-term viability (Baumol, 1990; Hamel, Doz and Prahalad, 1989).

The selection of partners influences the success of alliances not only by affecting the net gains from cooperation, but also through its impact on the stability of alliances. Alliances are more successful when partners stand to gain from each other, which requires complementarity in technological and managerial know-how. Not only will this create synergy effects, but given that each partner is necessary to exploit these synergy effects, partners will need to stay together, which implies less incentives for opportunism. Symmetric partners may have less synergy effects to exploit than asymmetric partners but coordination may be easier to achieve.

97

In this chapter it will be investigated if and under which circumstances firms should be advised to seek similar, rather than asymmetric partners when setting up cooperative ventures. A first section provides an overview of the empirical evidence, which mainly deals with the frequency of occurrence of various types of asymmetries, pointing out a number of factors affecting the task of investigating the impact of asymmetries on venture performance empirically. Among other things, it is difficult to evaluate the success rate of cooperative alliances, because success can be conceptualized in many different ways, and moreover very few data are available to measure performance accurately. Therefore, the impact of firm asymmetries on the performance of cooperative ventures will be dealt with by summarizing the (few) theoretical models that deal with this topic and by providing some additional analytical insights in the stability of cooperative agreements. A final section concludes with some suggestions for further research.

6.2   EMPIRICAL EVIDENCE

The general findings on the nature of partners' asymmetries and their expected impact on venture performance reported in the literature are briefly summarized and illustrated by means of some data, from the database generated by the research group on managerial economics and industrial organization, Catholic University of Leuven and reported in detail in Veugelers (1993 and 1994). Few empirical research deals exclusively with research alliances, but the arguments that are put forward to explain the advantages and drawbacks of (a)symmetric alliances in other activities will to a large extent carry over to research alliances.

In terms of organizational format, two types of alliances will be distinguished: joint venture and coordination. The joint venture involves a separate entity shared by the partners and usually involves a substantial setup cost, and hence commitment from the partners. 'Coordination' involves the coordination and/or integration of R&D, production, and/or distribution between the partner companies as well as a transfer of know-how among the partners. Such coordination can involve an explicit format, such as cross-participation or cross-licensing, but also more implicit forms, without any extra infrastructure, can be envisaged. Throughout the chapter, the concepts 'alliance' or 'cooperative venture' will be used as generic concepts, whereas 'coordination' and 'joint venture' will be used to identify the above mentioned forms of cooperation, that is without or with setting up a separate entity (see also Harrigan, 1988).

In our database, a majority of alliances engages in production (23 per cent), distribution (26 per cent) or the combination of both activities (14 per cent), whereas only 18 per cent incorporate some research activity, either as exclusive scope (6 per cent) or in combination with other activities (12 per cent).[1] US and Japanese alliances are slightly more research oriented, with, respectively, 28 per cent and 25 per cent research alliances (Veugelers, 1994). The small share of research alliances may reflect the specific problems accompanying these types of agreements.[2] The value of the partner's know-how, as well as the know-how generated by the alliance, may be hard to assess among the partners. In addition, control of the input, transfer and use of know-how may be difficult to realize. The typically uncertain nature of R&D activities makes it more difficult to disentangle non-compliance of partners from exogeneous sources of failure of the alliance. In addition, the implications for the long-run survival chances of such opportunistic behaviour are more critical in research alliances: a company risks exposing valuable know-how to the partner, who may use this know-how to improve its competitive position, while failing to reciprocally expose its own valuable know-how. The specific advantages and problems of research versus non-research alliances are further reflected in the organizational choice of each type of alliance. Although joint ventures remain the most frequent organizational format in any type of alliance, the occurrence of simple coordination is significantly higher for research alliances: coordination is the organizational format in 44 per cent of research alliances whereas only 33 per cent of the non-research alliances are simple forms of coordination. The higher risks involved in R&D alliances may call for less explicit types of cooperation, allowing for more flexibility. In addition, if the research alliance only involves transfer of know-how, a simple coordination format, such as a cross-licensing, may suffice.

Regarding the objectives for strategic partnering, market access and control motives are most eminent in a multitude of international horizontal coordinations involving production and/or distribution, whereas the quest for synergies is more apparent in the asymmetric interregional and vertical relations involving R&D activities that move beyond simple transfers of technology, and where typically partner characteristics such as size and experience and a tighter organizational joint venture structure may limit opportunism and strengthen commitment.

Obviously, the costs and benefits of asymmetric partners in alliances will be specific to the origin of the asymmetry. This section summarizes the evidence on asymmetries from various sources such as national origin, technological origin, size and allying experience of the partners. Hereby, special attention is given to alliances involving R&D activities.

Our database consists of 668 alliances, as they appeared in the financial press between January 1986 and July 1991.[3] Data have been collected and coded on a number of structural characteristics in order to typify the sectors and nations most active in alliances, the organizational format and functional activities organized within the alliance. Unlike most other databases on alliances which focus on technological cooperation (such as Hagedoorn and Schakenraad, 1994; Cainarca *et al.*, 1989), or on international cooperation (Hergert and Morris, 1988; Ghemawat *et al.*, 1986; Bleeke and Ernst, 1992), or on specific technologies (Burgers *et al.*, 1993), no *a priori* restriction on content and/or (inter)national scope of the alliance is withheld in the database, to allow for a fuller set of comparisons.

National versus International Alliances

Although about half of the alliances included in our database tend to be within regions, only 21 per cent remains within the same country (Veugelers, 1994). The high number of cross-national alliances may aim at entering new markets where alliances are an alternative to direct investment, export or licences. Alliances are a quick mode of serving foreign markets, which exploits the local partner's know-how of its home market, provides access to distribution channels or may be driven by government regulation: cf. the Eastern European alliances. In addition skill complementarity is more likely among international partners, given the heterogeneity of environments. But this heterogeneity may at the same time increase the coordination costs.

Research alliances tend to be organized more frequently between partners from different nationalities: 80 per cent of all alliances that involve R&D can be classified as international, versus 78 per cent for non-research alliances, a difference which is, however, not statistically significant.

Inter versus Intra Industry Alliances

The technological relationship between the partners and the venture will influence benefits as well as costs of engaging in alliances. The drive for exploiting complementary capabilities is more apparent when partners operate in vertical and unrelated business, given that it is more likely that firms lack the know-how partners may have. Companies may look for vertical or unrelated partners for alliances, providing access to new products, where these vertical alliances may be a quicker and more efficient mode of vertical integration or diversification. Companies may engage in alliances in their own markets with a vertical or unrelated partner, as a defensive strategy, to control entry into their own line of business. Horizontal alliances among (potential) competitors offer the extra benefits of allowing for (reciprocal) access to (international) markets for the same products, exploiting scale economies and monitoring and controlling the industry supply and intensity of competition.

The stability of vertical and unrelated alliances may be more problematic to the extent that the heterogeneity among partners exacerbates differences in corporate culture and management. Horizontal alliances, on the other hand, may suffer from instability given that partners as direct competitors share less compatible goals.

In our database, a large majority of alliances, 78 per cent, are situated in the same technology (i.e. NACE-3 digit classification) as one of the parents. This higher frequency of horizontal alliances confirms most other studies (Harrigan, 1988; Ghemawat *et al.*, 1986). In addition, most of the alliances, 55 per cent, are among parents that originate from the same technology. Vertical alliances are significantly more engaged in research activities than horizontal alliances, whereas alliances between partners that are technologically not related, involve significantly less research activities. This pattern suggests a more intense search for complementarities within these alliances, a characteristic which may explain the more intense vulnerability of vertical alliances (see also Harrigan, 1988).

Asymmetries in Size

When partners differ in size, asymmetric positions arise in terms of financial and non-financial input to the alliance as well as different benefits that each partner expects out of the alliance. Large firms may seek to team up with smaller firms to acquire access to the innovative potential of smaller companies and to overcome some of their own rigidities. Smaller firms may have an interest in the larger firms' research, production and/or marketing and financial infrastructure in order to reach markets and products quickly. While the complementarity between small and large partners is obvious, so are the higher coordination costs when size asymmetries between partners exist. The obstacles relate to differences in corporate culture, divergence in purpose as well as organizational structure as reflected in different decision-making processes and varying levels of management (e.g. Doz, 1988).

Teaming up with equally sized companies may forgo the benefits from complementarity but may limit these coordination costs. In addition smaller firms may shun larger partners to avoid the risk of larger partners appropriating the technology of the smaller partner to exploit in their own operations. The problematic divergence between ex ante and ex post bargaining power is asymmetric, applying more for the smaller than the

Table 6.1   Size asymmetries in alliances (all alliances versus R&D alliances)

	Both 'large'	Both 'small'	'Large'/'small'
Total	16%	48%	36%
Research alliances	28%	38%	48%

Large = belonging to the Fortune 500.
Source: Veugelers (1993).

larger partner. Larger firms explicitly seek larger partners when the objective of the alliance is strategically controlling and monitoring the competition (Burgers *et al.*, 1993).

In our database, about 36 per cent of the alliances are between partners of unequal size (i.e. only one partner in the Fortune 500 ranking), leaving a majority of alliances between equally sized categories: 16 per cent of the alliances are between partners that are both in the Fortune ranking and 48 per cent of the alliances are between both 'small' operators.[4] Comparing these numbers with the sample composition, suggests that large firms have a somewhat higher preference for entering into an alliance with small firms, as in Burgers *et al.* (1993) for the auto industry. Research alliances are significantly more asymmetric, with 48 per cent of such alliances between partners of unequal size, again pointing out a more intense quest for complementarities. The higher share of both large partners reflects the correlation between size and R&D activities. (See Table 6.1.)

Measurement Problems

Our method of sample composition (i.e. appearance in the financial press), which is used extensively in the literature, obviously has a number of drawbacks, of which the reader should be aware. First of all, in the European financial press, alliances whereby European firms are involved may typically get relatively more attention than ventures without European partners. Furthermore, only the most important alliances (e.g. between large firms, with truly innovative products) are likely to get press attention. Finally, the major source of these newspaper and magazine articles will typically be press releases from the partner firms, who may have very specific motives for (not) revealing their true intentions and hence this information may be slightly biased (Hergert and Morris, 1988). All of this implies that the database need not be representative for the entire population of strategic alliances among firms.

Furthermore, for all of the alliances included in the database, it is not easy to measure the (a)symmetries between partners in a precise way. For instance, even if financial statements of all included firms were available, it would still be difficult to include an accurate, that is, non-biased, size measure. But most often, the researchers only have access to a very limited set of financial statements, and they have to revert to even more crude size measures. In our dataset, size of the partners was measured through a dichotomous variable that takes the value of 1 if the company belongs to the Fortune Global 500 for industry and service sectors (*Fortune* in 1991); otherwise 0. The fact that about 44 per cent of the partners in our dataset have a rank in Fortune may provide an illustration of the bias induced by the data collection process (i.e. press attention is focused on large firms). Obviously, this considerable number may also be related to the larger net benefits these companies can acquire out of alliances as well as their larger attractiveness as partner.[5]

Although the data allow the detailing of the pattern of (a)symmetries in alliances, the link with long-run performance still needs to be assessed. Here, only information on the frequency of occurrence of certain types of strategic alliances is used as a crude proxy for the attractiveness of ventures. Such an analysis may yield more valuable insights into how different types of alliances can be used to (re)build, improve or defend competitive positions. This is an even more difficult problem, since no consensus has yet been reached on how venture performance can be measured most accurately. Performance evaluation is complicated by the fact that strategic alliances can be set up for many different motives, that they often work under uncertain and risky conditions and, by their very nature, they are different from conventional firms. Hence, many different authors all propose divergent performance measures (for different viewpoints, see, for example, Harrigan, 1985; Anderson, 1990; Lorange and Roos, 1990; Geringer and Hebert, 1991; Bleeke and Ernst, 1992; Mohr and Spekman, 1994). Many different performance measures are conceivable, but they all have their advantages and drawbacks. For instance, there is the controversy on the use of subjective (that is, personal evaluation by the managers or partner firms) versus objective performance (that is, evaluation based on facts, published data) measures (Killing, 1983; Anderson, 1990). 'Objective' measures may include financial measures such as profitability, growth rates and other indicators such as duration of the agreement (Chowdury, 1992; Harrigan, 1985), and the stability of share ownership (Killing, 1983). Very often these data are not published separately for the alliance, but they have to be deduced from the consolidated financial statements (Killing, 1983). Subjective measures may include a simple evaluation by the venture managers, or the degree of satisfaction of the partner firms (Killing, 1983). Moreover, it is often very difficult, if not impossible, to obtain precise data on each of these measures. Another interesting way to evaluate performance may be by investigating firms' stock price responses to announcements of strategic alliances (Sleuwaegen *et al.*, 1995; Wu *et al.*, 1994). An extension of the database directly measuring performance in alliances is therefore a much needed addition, but requires innovativeness in the selection of accurate performance measures, disentangling alliance activities from other influences on partner performance. In addition, such performance needs to be traced over a sufficiently large time period. After all, within a fast changing environment, meeting the requirements of change is the ultimate test of success in alliances.

Although the link between partner asymmetries and venture performance cannot yet be assessed empirically, a number of insights have recently emerged from the theoretical literature. While this literature is still in an early developmental stage, it is beginning to improve our understanding of this complex phenomenon. The following section summarizes these analytical insights.

6.3 THEORETICAL MODELS

The analytical papers dealing with the impact of firm asymmetries on successful cooperation among firms are still very scarce. In these models, the success of cooperation is conceptualized in different ways: new product development, expected profits and the stability of cooperative agreements.

These models all assume that horizontal partners cooperate in research and development. In the case of a separate joint venture, most often it only generates know-how, and if it develops a product, it is independent from the parents' products. This line of research is still quite recent and the reader will notice that improved insights on the impact of asymmetries on successful cooperation are only just beginning to emerge.

New Product Development

Chaudhuri (1994) examines the question of whether technologically similar firms are, in a joint venture, more likely to succeed in the development of a new product, than dissimilar firms in a duopoly setting. The probability of successful development depends on the joint, non-verifiable effort stream of both firms. The technological asymmetry is modelled in terms of the marginal costs of effort (more dissimilarity equals larger mean preserving spread of marginal costs).

In this paper, it is found that joint, rather than own, product development will be the preferred alternative, if the technological asymmetry is not too large and if the cost levels are not too high. Further, once a cooperative venture has been set up, an increase in the technological asymmetry augments the probability of successful development.

Expected Profits

Sinha and Cusumano (1991) were the first to focus explicitly on the impact of complementarity in skills and resources on the success of R&D cooperation. They assume that two firms, operating in a homogeneous goods industry, differ in their R&D abilities, thereby generating asymmetries in technology and size. They investigate how this asymmetry may affect the expected profits from setting up a research joint venture, relative to own development. The R&D project is a patent race, with only one winner, able to reduce its production costs after successful completion of the project. The research joint venture has the advantage that (asymmetric) resources can be pooled, thereby creating synergies and the possibility of sharing the costs and returns of R&D.

The asymmetric R&D capabilities may create complementarities, which are simply incorporated through the chance of successful development. In the case of complementaries, the probability of successful development is higher in the joint venture than if firms pursue their own projects. In the absence of complementaries, the probability of succesful own development is higher than for the venture.

In this paper it is found that, obviously, firms are more likely to prefer cooperation to own development, if their resources are more complementary and if the cost of the R&D project is high. Furthermore, if firms have highly complementary skills, they will prefer to cooperate in areas where the technology is highly appropriable. Big firms have a larger incentive to cooperate than small firms, because they are better positioned to capture the venture benefits. However, firms prefer as small a partner as possible to limit the sharing of research results.

Van Long and Soubeyran (1997) show that even symmetric firms may have an incentive to engage in a research joint venture with asymmetric participation rates, since they are hence able to reap larger industry profits, because of the uneven cost structure which allows to create the same aggregate amount of R&D at lower costs. Unfortunately this paper does not deal with cheating and hence neither with stability problems, which are indeed more likely to occur in case of firm asymmetries.

The present chapter examines in detail the incentives to cheat on a loyal partner (unilateral) and on a non-loyal partner (mutual cheating), in terms of these different asymmetries. Taking into account the incentives to form a joint venture, as well as the incentives to cheat, it can be established under which conditions successful, stable joint ventures will emerge.

Given the complexity of the model, these conditions can only be pinpointed by means of numerical simulations. These indicate that in order to establish a successful joint venture, high enough synergies are required to keep especially the advantaged firm (in terms of productive efficiency, R&D efficiency and absorptive capacity) interested, while know-how needs to be kept sufficiently proprietary within the venture to curb cheating, at least with equal sharing among partners. Bargained profit shares leave a larger share for the advantaged firm, for which the own development option is relatively more lucrative, although expected synergies diminish the inequality in shares caused by the asymmetry. By giving more to the big firm according to his advantage, the latter will always have an incentive to join an alliance, even if synergies are low within the venture. In addition, in case of high spillovers, a successful joint venture with bargained shares can be established, since the latter will curb the big firm's incentive to cheat. Only in the case of low synergies combined with high spillovers will bargained shares fail to establish successful joint ventures.

Smaller asymmetries between partners imply that successful joint ventures are less likely with bargained shares if spillovers are high and synergies are not too pervasive. With equal sharing, on the contrary, joint ventures cannot be established when partners are too asymmetric, since in this case the advantaged firm prefers own development.

Expected Profits and Stability of Cooperation in an R&D Coordination Setting

This section summarises ongoing research, focusing on the impact of partner asymmetries on the profitability and stability of R&D cooperation in an analytical framework. Given the empirically observed stronger prevalence of asymmetries in R&D coordination, the problem is modelled in a supergame framework whereby two asymmetric firms repeatedly take sequential R&D and production decisions, with the R&D decisions being coordinated in order to maximize joint profits. In our setting, R&D decisions are coordinated and firms undertake innovative efforts in their own research lab – cf. the empirically observed higher preference for coordination – and R&D coordination is sustained by grim trigger strategies (Friedman, 1971).

Model Structure

An asymmetric duopoly, where firms produce differentiated products, with constant marginal costs c_i is envisaged. Demand for their products is:

$$p_i = a_i - bq_i - dq_j \qquad \forall i \neq j = 1, 2 \tag{6.1}$$

where p_i (q_i) is firm i's price (quantity) and $b > 0$, $b \geq |d|$.

Firms can improve their profitability by undertaking investments in R&D, which lower their production costs and which may entail positive spillovers on the rival's cost.

If no R&D is undertaken, unit production costs are $c_i = A_i$ ($i = 1, 2$ and $A_i < a_i$). Production costs may be reduced through own R&D efforts, as well as through the rival's R&D. Incremental innovations, yielding improvements in the production process, rather than drastic innovations, are envisaged. The importance of the spillover effect is captured through the parameter β_i, which reflects the extent of such technological leakage as well as the capacity to absorb this externally generated know-how:

$$c_i = A_i - \alpha_i(x_i + \beta_i x_j) \qquad 1 \geq \beta_i \geq 0 \tag{6.2}$$

β_i is assumed to be technology-specific and is exogenous. It reflects the level of automatic, uncontrollable know-how spillovers. The parameter α_i reflects the ability to apply and implement know-how, i.e. to transfer know-how into cost savings. x_i and x_j refer refer to R&D efforts.

Innovative efforts involve diminishing returns, specified as increasing marginal costs of R&D. Total R&D costs are $\tau x_i^2/2$, whereby τ is inversely related to the efficiency of the innovation process.

All of this allows us to specify firms' total profits, V_i as follows:

$$V_i = \pi_i(q_i, q_j) - \tau x_i^2/2$$
$$\text{with } \pi_i(q_i, q_j) = (p_i - c_i)q_i = [a_i - A_i + \alpha_i(x_i + \beta_i x_j) - \tag{6.3}$$
$$bq_i - dq_j]q_i$$

Firm Asymmetries

Our model incorporates size and technological asymmetries between partners. Other forms of asymmetries are ignored to keep the model tractable (see below). In order to simplify the notation and to focus on the asymmetries, an s-vector is introduced, whereby the elements of the vector reflect the size of the asymmetries. To fix ideas, the 'advantaged' firm is labelled as the big (B) firm, while its partner is identified as the small (S) firm:

$$s = (s_a, s_\beta, s_\alpha) \qquad\qquad (6.4)$$

$$\text{with } s_a = (a_s - A_s)/(a_B - A_B)$$

$$s_\alpha = \alpha_s/\alpha_B$$

$$s_\beta = \beta_s/\beta_B \qquad \text{with } 1 \geq s_a, s_\beta \text{ and } s_\alpha \geq 0$$

In case all s-parameters are equal to 1, both firms are symmetric.

Size asymmetries in terms of market size (a_s versus a_B) and in terms of production costs (A_s versus A_B) are reflected by the parameter s_a; s_a is smaller than one, reflecting that the small firm faces a smaller net demand intercept than the big firm, which may be due to lower demand for its product and/or higher production costs. Firms may differ in 'size', because of differences in consumer demand for their products, or in initial production costs. The latter may differ because of former production and innovation experience, because of organizational characteristics of the firm or other reasons.

Furthermore, firms may differ in their technological capabilities, which is captured by two different parameters. s_α reflects the difference in *R&D efficiency*; $s_\alpha < 1$ implies that the big firm can better implement all know-how, or, put alternatively, transfer any R&D input into R&D outputs (cost savings) than its small partner, for example because its R&D process is managed more efficiently, because of a closer interaction between its R&D and production departments, because it has accumulated more innovation experience (learning effects) or attracted better researchers, because its production infrastructure allows to fit in process improvements more easily (De Bondt and Henriques, 1995).

Firms can not only differ in their ability to implement any know-how, but also in their ability to assimilate know-how from other firms: s_β represents this asymmetry in spillovers, or *absorption capacity*; $s_\beta > 1$ implies that the large firm is better able to absorb foreign know-how, or alternatively, is better able to keep its own know-how proprietary than the small rival, for example because of the nature of R&D projects or because of the firm's ability or willingness to learn from rivals.

Strategies

Firms play this innovation and production game for an infinite number of periods. While an infinite horizon is not very plausible, this framework applies also if the game is played for a finite number of periods, but with unknown end date. Empirical research reveals that few alliances (only 5 per cent) determine a fixed end date when setting up an agreement (Veugelers, 1993).

During every period, firms decide on R&D and production sequentially. Each stage-game is thus composed of a two-stage game in R&D and output, which is repeated infinitely. In order to focus exclusively on the stability of R&D cooperation, it is assumed that firms want to establish a cooperative equilibrium in R&D only, while they continue to compete in output markets (Cournot–Nash), an assumption which can be supported by antitrust legislation. It is assumed that R&D does not carry over across periods, for example of the speed of technological progress or short product life-cycles, which allows us to apply the supergame framework.

The stability of such cooperative agreements is investigated in a setting where the equilibrium is supported by (non-cooperative) grim trigger strategies (Friedman, 1971). Both firms start out in the cooperative phase. If one firm deviates from the cooperative outcome, both firms revert to the punishment phase from the next period on, for all remaining periods of the game. If this punishment is severe enough, *i.e.* if forgone profits, due to the punishment, offset the initial profit increment from deviating, it will prevent firms from defecting in the first place. Hence, a stable cooperative outcome exists.

By sticking to the cooperative equilibrium, firms realize cooperative profits (V_i^c) for an infinite number of periods. The net present value of this flow of profits is $V_i^c/(1 + 1/r_i)$, with r_i the interest rate for firm i.[6] Given that its rival is loyal, a firm may go for maximal profits by deviating from the cooperative outcome. Defection profits are indicated by $V_i^d (V_i^d > V_i^c)$. Such a defection will be punished, by reverting to the Nash equilibrium, whereby both firms realize punishment profits V_i^n $(V_i^n < V_i^c)$. Given that detection and consequent punishment are assumed to take one period to unfold, the net present value of profits realised with cheating is $V_i^d + V_i^n/r_i$.

A cooperative outcome will be stable, if the following inequality holds for each firm:

$$V_i^c(1 + 1/r_i) \geq V_i^d + V_i^n/r_i \qquad (6.5)$$

$$\text{or } (V_i^c - V_i^n)/(V_i^d - V_i^c) \equiv r_i^* \geq r_i \qquad (6.6)$$

If inequality (6.6) is satisfied for each firm i, i.e. if each firm's interest rate is lower than a certain firm-specific threshold (r_i^*) a stable cooperative equilibrium exists.[7]

Equilibrium

A scenario of R&D cartelization (in the terminology of Kamien *et al.*, 1992) is envisaged. Firms coordinate their R&D investments, but choose their output levels independently.

In the second phase of each stage-game, firms choose their output levels independently, in order to maximize their own profits. From the first-order conditions the equilibrium output levels in terms of firms' R&D efforts can be derived:

$$q_i = Z_i + A_i x_i + B_i x_i \tag{6.7}$$

$$\forall i, j = 1, 2 \quad i \neq j$$

$$\text{with} \quad Z_i = [2b(a_i - A_i) - d(a_j - A_j)]/(4b^2 - d^2)$$
$$A_i = (2b\alpha_i - d\beta_j\alpha_j)/(4b^2 - d^2)$$
$$B_i = (2b\beta_i\alpha_i - d\alpha_j)/(4b^2 - d^2)$$

For the large firm, the usual economic viability, second order and stability restrictions on the parameter values, applying to the symmetric case, are sufficient to guarantee positive cooperative profits ($V_B^c > 0$), independent of the magnitude of each asymmetry considered separately. For the small firm, this also holds in case of R&D efficiency and spillover asymmetries, but this need not be the case with substantial size asymmetries, of which a numerical example is provided in Figure 6.1.

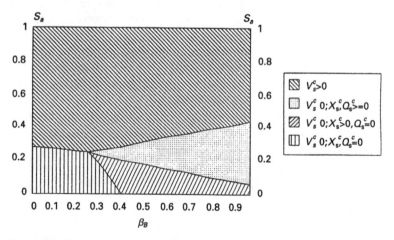

Figure 6.1 Cooperative profits for the small firm, with size asymmetries ($\alpha = 1$, $s_\alpha = 1$, $s_\beta = 1$)

For many parameter values of the size asymmetry, an asymmetric cooperative equilibrium may exist, with both firms innovating and producing.[9] However, with large size asymmetries ($s_a < 0.2$ up to 0.4, depending on the level of the spillovers), the small firm would not be willing to cooperate, because of negative cooperative profits ($V_S^c < 0$). In case of large – symmetric – spillovers, cooperation would imply that both firms innovate ($x_S^c, x_B^c > 0$), but would entail losses for the small firm ($V_S^c + V_B^c$ is maximized, with $V_S^c < 0$ and $V_B^c > 0$). Intuitively, the large market size, together with the large spillovers, implies that joint profit maximization ($V_S^c + V_B^c$) requires performing much R&D (in order to reduce unit production costs, mainly for the large sales market) and performing these R&D efforts in the two laboratories in order to reduce the costs of R&D.[10] Obviously, such high R&D efforts may entail losses for the small firm, which only serves a small market (high R&D costs but low sales profits, and hence $V_S^c < 0$). It may even occur that it is optimal, from this joint profit viewpoint, for the small firm not to produce/sell its product, but only to perform R&D (for the partner market); i.e. joint profits are basically maximized by serving only the largest market (and thus avoiding the detrimental competitive impact of the availability of a substitute) and by spreading the R&D efforts over two laboratories and thus reducing the detrimental impact of diminishing returns in R&D.

With small spillovers, cooperation would imply that the small firm closes down its facilities (joint profit maximization implies $x_S^c = 0$, $q_S^c = 0$) and hence $V_S^c = 0$). In this case the argument of beneficial R&D decentralization (at least for the large firm) does not apply, because of the limited spillovers.

Besides positive cooperative profits, cooperative conduct should additionally yield higher profits than non-cooperative conduct for each firm. This condition is necessary to guarantee that it is worthwhile to join the cooperative agreement in the first place for each firm. Again this condition does not pose particular problems for any asymmetry for the large firm, but it may for the small firm.[11] Figure 6.2 summarizes the possibilities for the above numerical example.

Only with fairly small *market size and/or production costs asymmetries* (s_a above 0.84 to 0.75, depending on the level of spillovers) will the small firm prefer cooperation over independent conduct ($V_S^c > V_S^n$). In the case of more substantial size asymmetries, independent conduct is superior basically since the small firm does not perform so much R&D (which mainly benefits the large firm in a cooperative setup). The case with very large asymmetries (s_a below 0.16 to 0.28 depending on the level of spillovers) will not be further considered here, since the small firm would even in a Nash setting decide to close down in order to avoid losses ($V_S^n < 0$).

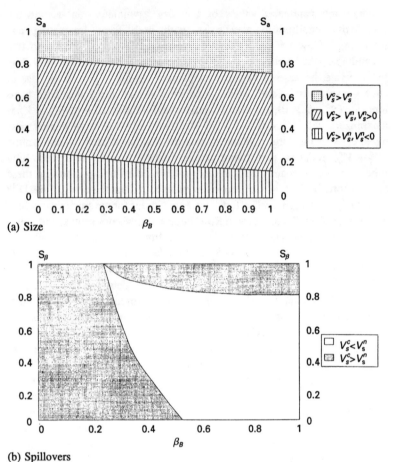

(a) Size

(b) Spillovers

Figure 6.2 Cooperative versus Nash profits for the small firm for different asymmetries ($\alpha = 1$, $s_\alpha = 1$, $s_\beta = 1$)

With *asymmetric spillovers*, the potential profitability of cooperation for the small firm is critically dependent on the level of the large firm's spillover, *vis à vis* the degree of product differentiation and the magnitude of the spillover asymmetry. The critical spillover rate is $\beta_B = d\alpha_s/2b\alpha_B = ds_\alpha/2b$, i.e. where $B_B = 0$, with B_B representing the slope of the big firm's reaction curve, a critical parameter which shows up frequently in these models of strategic R&D investments.[12] Hence, cooperation is potentially beneficial for the small firm (i) in the case of small spillovers for both firms[13] and (ii) in the case of high β_B, only if the spillover asymmetry is not too large (e.g. $s_\beta > 0.8$,

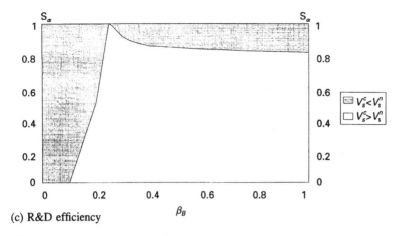

(c) R&D efficiency

Figure 6.2 cont.

or even higher, depending on the level of the spillover, in the numerical example). Intuitively, if β_B is large, cooperation involves a lot of R&D, which mainly benefits the large firm and the small firm will only find cooperation an attractive alternative if it gains quite a lot from coordinating R&D efforts too (i.e. if it absorbs enough know-how from the rival). If not (low β_s), the small firm favours independent conduct, which implies less R&D. If β_B is small, cooperation does not require substantial R&D efforts, and hence the small firm will not be better off by determining its optimal R&D efforts independently.

Similar findings occur with *asymmetries in R&D efficiency.* Cooperative conduct yields higher profits than Nash conduct for the small firm, (i) in any case, if spillovers are very small for both firms, and (ii) only if the asymmetry in R&D efficiency is not too large when spillovers are bigger (e.g. $s_\alpha > 0.8$ if $\beta = 1$ in the numerical example), intuitively, again because the small firm has to benefit enough from cooperation (i.e. sufficiently high α_S compared to α_B). Again, the turning point between both areas lies at $\beta_B = d\alpha_S/2b$.

Hence, according to this model, in the semiconductor industry, where spillovers may be quite large, the small firms would indeed not be interested in joining a cooperative agreement with large firms, such as Sematech, because of too low expected cooperative profits.

Stable R&D Cooperation

For those parameter values for which duopolistic cooperative and non-cooperative equilibria exist, it is now investigated how each type of asymmetry affects the stability of cooperation, taking into account the prevention of deviations by means of a grim trigger strategy. Given that both firms have an incentive to join a cooperative agreement ($V_i^c > V_i^n$), it is analyzed whether they have an incentive to stick to the agreement, i.e. whether the immediate benefits from defection ($V_i^d > V_i^c$, for one period) are outweighed by the disadvantages of the subsequent punishment ($V_i^n < V_i^c$, for all remaining periods of the game), and how this net gain from cheating depends on the type and magnitude of asymmetries. This stability issue can be discussed easily in terms of the maximal interest rate that is required for firms to stick to the cooperative outcome.

Figure 6.3 illustrates the evolution of the critical interest rate (r_i^*) for the big and the small firm, in terms of the different asymmetries and the level of the spillovers.

In the case of *size asymmetries*, the big firm is less inclined to deviate from the cooperative agreement as its rival becomes smaller (smaller S_a) and as symmetric spillovers decrease. The reverse holds for the small firm, which is, even with fairly small size asymmetries (s_a above 0.77) not very likely to stick to the cooperative outcome (i.e. its critical interest rate decreases fast with the asymmetry), intuitively because its own benefits from cooperation are not large enough, which makes cheating more attractive (high one-time gains of $V_s^d - V_s^c$, combined with not so severe punishment – small $V_s^c - V_s^n$, since V_s^c is small).

With *asymmetric spillovers*, similar results hold, at least when the spillovers for the large firm are quite substantial (i.e. if $B_B > 0$, implying $\beta_B > ds_\alpha/2b$, or, put alternatively, if the big firm's and small firm's R&D efforts are strategic complements – cf. Bulow *et al.*, 1985). In this case, cooperation is more and more likely to be supported by the large firm, as the asymmetry becomes larger (i.e. β_s smaller) while the reverse holds for the disadvantaged firm. The small firm experiences quite a strong incentive to perform less R&D than agreed, in order to reduce its R&D costs substantially, without affecting its sales drastically (since it can anyway absorb know-how, from the substantial R&D efforts performed by the large rival). Again, the impact of the asymmetry on the magnitude of the gains from cooperation is the driving force behind this result. Hence, to the extent that a firm can partially control the level of its own know-how that its rival can absorb (i.e. its rival's spillover rate), this suggests that the advantaged firm should be aware of the fact that unilaterally keeping its know-how as proprietary as possible (i.e. enhancing the spillover asymmetry) is likely to result in a breakdown of cooperation, because its small partner is stimulated into cheating. With modest spillovers for the large firm ($B_B < 0$, i.e. if for the big firm R&D efforts are strategic substitutes), the results are reversed. In this

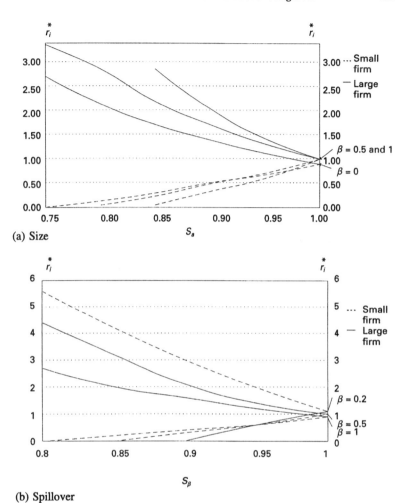

(a) Size

(b) Spillover

Figure 6.3 Stable R&D cooperation with different asymmetries ($\alpha = 1$, $s_\alpha = 1$, $s_\beta = 1$)

situation, the advantaged firm is more likely to defect as the asymmetry grows larger. With low spillovers, cooperative R&D efforts are quite small, and since it does not learn a lot from its small partner, the large firm is tempted to defect by performing more R&D than agreed, in order to enhance its own sales and profits (more R&D, which does not benefit the rival much anyway, because of low β_B and s_β).

With *asymmetries in R&D efficiency*, the stability issue can be described along the same lines, since a similar process is at work and is not further discussed here.

Typically, it is thus the case, at least when spillovers are large enough, that the large firm will be more inclined to stick to the cooperative outcome as any kind of asymmetry grows larger, i.e. as its rival becomes more disadvantaged, while the reverse holds for the small firm, intuitively because the large firm has more to gain from cooperation than the small firm. For the small firm, the immediate gains from cheating $(V_s^d - V_s^c)$ decrease as it becomes more disadvantaged, while the drawbacks from cheating $(V_s^c - V_s^n)$ decrease even faster with the size of the asymmetry for parameter values for which a cooperative equilibrium exists. The reverse holds for the large firm, which experiences less incentive to cheat as the asymmetry grows, because the immediate cheating gains $(V_B^d - V_B^c)$ reduce, while the punishment becomes relatively more severe $(V_B^c - V_B^n$ increases).

Since the disadvantaged firm is not very likely to stick to the cooperative outcome for any kind of substantial asymmetry, it can be concluded that cooperation is not very likely to persist between partners that differ drastically in terms of either (geographical or product) market size, productive efficiency, absorption capacity or R&D efficiency, and this analytical finding is supported by the evidence since ventures between similar partners (in terms of culture, asset size, venturing experience) seem to last longer (Harrigan, 1988).

To the extent that the results from our model can be interpreted from the point of view of selecting an attractive R&D partner, these results imply that R&D cooperation would better be pursued with an advantaged rather than a disadvantaged partner because such cooperation is more likely to persist (i.e. critical interest rate is quite high), while cooperation with a disadvantaged partner would be more likely to break down (or more precisely: not to materialize), because of the attractiveness of cheating for the latter. Hence, if a firm faces a choice of several potential partners, a partner with a more favourable position, in terms of size, R&D efficiency and/or absorption capacity, would be a better choice than a disadvantaged partner, at least from the point of view of stable cooperation. This issue of stability should be weighed against the gains from cooperation however, since typically an individual firm's cooperative profits are higher in case of cooperation with a disadvantaged partner, intuitively, because a more advantaged partner realizes larger cooperative profits!

It can further be analyzed how sensitive the stability of R&D cooperation is to each type of asymmetry. Table 6.2 shows how each firm's critical interest rate responds to a given variation in each asymmetry (each *s*-element

Table 6.2 Sensitivity of stable R&D cooperation to asymmetries ($\alpha_B = \beta_B = 0.8$)

	(maximal interest rate in %)					
	Size asymmetry		*Spillover asymmetry*		*R&D eff. asymmetry*	
s	r_B^*	r_S^*	r_B^*	r_S^*	r_B^*	r_S^*
0.85	213	25	223	19	203	11
0.9	163	47	170	43	163	35
1	96	96	96	96	96	96

varying from 0.85 to 1), in a (numerical) setting where everything else is identical.

For the advantaged firm, the incentive to stick to the cooperative outcome is more or less identical for each kind of asymmetry – in any case its real interest rate will be below its r_B^*, but the disadvantaged firm's optimal strategy is more sensitive to the type of asymmetry. Growing asymmetries in R&D efficiency are most likely to entice the small firm to deviate from the cooperative outcome (largest decrease in r_s^* for a given asymmetry), while augmenting size asymmetries are least likely to stimulate the small firm into cheating. All of this would suggest that asymmetries in size are less harmful for stable cooperation in R&D than asymmetries in R&D efficiency or spillovers. To the extent that 'size' can be interpreted as an industry characteristic, while R&D efficiency and absorption capacity are more firm-specific, the above finding would provide an analytical justification for Harrigan's (1988) observation that industry characteristics are far more important for the stability of cooperation than firm characteristics. This finding should, however, be interpreted with caution and its robustness should be investigated in other settings. For instance, it may be that these results would not hold in the case of cooperation in both R&D and production.

Several Asymmetries

Obviously, if the asymmetries were to occur simultaneously, they would reinforce each other.

Table 6.3   Stability with simultaneous asymmetries

s	*(maximal interest rate in %)*			
	0.85	0.9	0.95	1
$r_B{}^*$	733	400	203	96
$r_s{}^*$	-	-	22	96

No stable outcome.

For a numerical example where the three asymmetries vary simultaneously from 0.85 to 1 (Table 6.3) (i.e. parameter values for which a stable cooperative outcome was possible for each asymmetry considered separately), each firm's critical interest rate was calculated and it is obtained that once the asymmetry is larger than 5 per cent in all areas simultaneously (i.e. $s_a = s_\alpha + s_\beta < 0.95$) the small firm would never stick to the cooperative outcome. Hence R&D cooperation becomes infeasible, even with small asymmetries in different areas. Likewise, the incentive for the large firm to stick to the cooperative outcome is strenghtened as the asymmetries occur simultaneously: r_B^* increases to 733 per cent when $s_a = s_\alpha = s_\beta = 0.85$ whereas it increases to a little over 200 per cent in the case of one asymmetry only – but in each case, the large firm is very likely to stick to the cooperative equilibrium (i.e. $r_B < r_B^*$). Finally, one partner need not be disadvantaged in all areas. A size disadvantage can for example be accompanied by an advantage in R&D efficiency. For instance, a spin-off firm, a small enterprise set up by researchers, may not yet have built a strong market base (size disadvantage), but may enjoy stronger technological expertise both in applying know-how (advantage in R&D efficiency) and in absorbing external know-how (spillover advantage) than the partner firm. In such a situation, the numerical simulations show that the spin-off firm will be more inclined to stick to the cooperative outcomes as all asymmetries increase, while the reverse holds for its partner. The stability advantages associated with higher R&D efficiency and absorption capacity outweigh the disadvantages of smaller size. (see Table 6.4.)

If one partner is able to attract better researchers than its rival, this will lead to higher R&D efficiency and absorption capacity (higher α and β). The advantaged partner, with the better reseachers, will be more inclined to stick

Table 6.4 Critical discount factor with several asymmetries

Scenario	(maximal interest rate in %)		
	r* with symmetry	*r$_i$ with 5% asymmetry*	*r$_i$ with 15% asymmetry*
Spin-off firm	96	150	285
Partner	96	64	16
Best researchers firm	96	186	488
Worse partner	96	43	-
Local partner	96	108	132
Multinational	96	92	89

to the cooperative outcome, while its partner is more tempted to deviate as the asymmetry augments (fast decrease in r_i^*).

A locally operating company may consider R&D cooperation with a large multinational enterprise. The latter may for instance enjoy a size advantage, while the former may be better placed to apply know-how, because of its superior information about the local conditions (no asymmetries in spillovers assumed). In such a scenario the local (multinational) firm will be more (less) inclined to cooperate as both asymmetries grow larger, because R&D efficiency asymmetries are more influential than size asymmetries.

Finally, the analysis also suggests that a scenario whereby one partner is disadvantaged in several areas *vis à vis* its partner is much less likely to result in stable cooperation than a scenario where the asymmetries are distributed across partners, which tends to support the empirical finding that cooperation is much more likely to be stable between partners with complementary skills (Harrigan, 1988).

Conclusions

When the asymmetric scenario is compared with the symmetric case, the following conclusions can be drawn regarding the robustness of the symmetric setup.

The symmetric setup was sufficiently rich to point out the crucial impact of the level of spillovers – *vis-à-vis* the degree of product differentiation – on the gains and stability of R&D cooperation. This characteristic, unsurprisingly, also shows up in the asymmetric setting, and additionally, it was shown that substantial asymmetries in spillovers may render R&D cooperation unprofitable, at least for the disadvantaged firm. Moreover, the numerical examples revealed that the critical level of the other asymmetries for which R&D cooperation turns out to become more or less attractive is very often related to the degree of spillovers.

Contrary to the symmetric case, the asymmetric scenario has pointed out the crucial impact of asymmetries in market size and/or initial production costs (i.e. the net demand intercept) and R&D efficiency on the expected gains from cooperation. Whereas market size, initial production costs and R&D efficiency only affect the level of profits, but not the stability of cooperation in a symmetric setup, they both have a much more substantial impact once asymmetries are incorporated. Large asymmetries (low s_α or s_a) may lead the disadvantaged firm to prefer independent over cooperative R&D conduct, and large size asymmetries could furthermore result in losses for the disadvantaged firm.

All in all, intuitively, this simple analytical scenario suggests that R&D cooperation between asymmetric firms will typically be beneficial for the advantaged firm, and will only be attractive for the disadvantaged firm if the asymmetries are not too substantial, i.e. if its partner does not benefit too much more than itself from cooperation.

6.4   CONCLUSIONS AND SUGGESTIONS FOR FUTURE RESEARCH

Obviously, in order to achieve a fuller understanding of the impact of firm asymmetries on the formation and performance of strategic alliances, much more work still needs to be done.

For instance, in all models it was assumed that both partners are horizontally related (they operate in the same product market), since the empirical research shows that the majority of alliances is established between horizontal partners (e.g. Ghemawat *et al.*, 1986; Harrigan, 1988; Veugelers, 1994). Nevertheless alliances between partners that are vertically related or that produce independent products may pose specific problems (e.g. larger heterogeneity and hence coordination costs) and opportunities (e.g. no product market rivalry and hence less threats to the stability of the cooperative venture) for cooperation, which it would be worthwhile investigating.

Furthermore, most of the analytical papers have modelled incremental innovations, yielding cost reductions, but not drastic innovations, generating for example new products or additional varieties, and this may fundamentally affect the expected profits, but also the persistence of strategic alliances. Chaudhuri (1994) provides such a model, and inspiration for further research on this topic, with asymmetric firms, can be found in the literature that deals with R&D for quality improvements in products that are horizontally or vertically related (see e.g. Poyago-Theotoky, 1997).

Also the incentives for cooperation in other organizational formats, for example in joint ventures, whereby the joint venture's products may likewise be horizontally, vertically or not at all related to the parents' products, should be addressed separately. This was attempted in another paper (Veugelers and Kesteloot, 1995). In this paper, the impact of complementarities between firms, whereby cooperation will yield synergies, is studied in detail. It must also be investigated to what extent the results would be altered if the asymmetric firms cooperate not only in R&D but also in output markets (*i.e.* full cooperation).

Furthermore, it may also be interesting to investigate in more detail the role of the alliance-initiating companies (Hagedoorn, 1995): Which first-mover advantages and disadvantages can be identified? Is their impact affected by for example the nature (size, industry, technology) of the initiating firm and the venture of the cooperative agreement? Which moves and countermoves can be expected from the other firms in the industry? Furthermore, most models start out from duopolistic industries, but, in practice, many industries are oligopolistic and firms may face a choice of several potentially attractive venture partners; moreover several alliances with different numbers of firms being members may emerge. Poyago-Theotoky (1995) provides some insights into the incentives to join an alliance, as against staying out, but her model is restricted to a setting with symmetric firms – hence only the number of firms joining or staying out matters. But with asymmetric firms, not only the number of firms will affect the incentives to join or quit certain alliances, or networks of alliances, but also the nature of each of these firms.

Finally, in practice, the partners may also differ in their venturing experience and hence reputation as an attractive alliance partner, but fully investigating this topic would require a truly dynamic model.

Regarding future empirical work, additional insights on accurate and measurable indicators of firm performance in general, and strategic alliance performance in particular, have a high priority on the research agenda. Also information about accurate measures of firm asymmetries would improve the data used in the empirical work.

APPENDIX: EQUILIBRIUM R&D LEVELS

From the first-order conditions for the different stages of the game:
- during precompetitive R&D coordination:

$$q_i = Z_i + A_i x_i + B_i x_j$$

$$\forall i, j = 1, 2 \quad i \neq j$$

with
$$Z_i = [2b(a_i - A_i) - d(a_j - A_j)]/(4b^2 - d^2)$$
$$A_i = (2b\alpha_i - d\beta_j\alpha_j)/(4b^2 - d^2)$$
$$B_i = (2b\beta_i\alpha_i - d\alpha_j)/(4b^2 - d^2)$$
$$x_i = 2bq_iA_i/\tau + 2bq_jB_j/\tau \qquad \forall i, j = 1, 2 \quad i \neq j$$

- during cheating by firm i:

$$q_i = Z_i + A_i x_i + B_i x_j \qquad \forall i, j = 1, 2 \quad i \neq j$$
$$x_i = 2bq_iA_i/\tau \qquad \forall i = 1, 2$$

- during the Nash punishment:

$$q_i = Z_i + A_i x_i + B_i x_j \qquad \forall i, j = 1, 2 \quad i \neq j$$
$$x_i = 2bq_iA_i/\tau \qquad \forall i = 1, 2$$

the expressions for the equilibrium R&D levels can easily be derived (for $i, j = 1, 2$ and $i \neq j$):

$$x_i^c = \frac{(A_iZ_i + B_jZ_j)(\tau/2b - A_j^2 - B_i^2) + (A_iB_i + A_jB_j)(A_jZ_j + B_iZ_i)}{(\tau/2b - A_i^2 - B_j^2)(\tau/2b - A_j^2 - B_i^2) - (A_iB_i + B_jA_j)^2}$$

$$x_i^d = \frac{A_iZ_i}{(\tau/2b - A_i^2)} + \frac{A_iB_i}{(\tau/2b - A_i^2)} x_j^c$$

$$x_i^n = \frac{A_iZ_i(\tau/2b - A_j^2) + A_iB_iA_jZ_j}{(\tau/2b - A_i^2)(\tau/2b - A_j^2) - A_iA_jB_iB_j}$$

Equilibrium sales and profit levels can be obtained from these optimal R&D levels. They are not reported here, beceause their complex expressions do not provide any additional insights.

The second-order and stability conditions (cf. Henriques, 1990) were checked for all numerical examples.

Notes

1. Nineteen per cent of the alliances remain unspecified on functional activities. Other empirical studies, who focus more on technological cooperation, tend to find higher frequencies of research alliances. For instance, in the Insead database, as reported by Hergert and Morris (1988), 64 per cent involve some research activity. In the LEREA/CEREM database, as reported by Mytelka

(1991), 29 per cent involve knowledge. The MERIT database as reported by Hagedoorn and Schakenraad (1994) focus on technology driven alliances.

2. Also Berg *et al.* (1982) find R&D oriented joint ventures to produce a negative impact on industry average rates of return, whereas non-R&D alliances on average have a positive impact.

3. This procedure, which is common in most other databases of alliances, may cause some misrepresentation, given that the more visible and high impact alliances have a larger probability of being announced in the press. See also Hagedoorn and Schakenraad (1994) for more on this procedure.

4. Note that given the rough measure of size, there may still exist considerable size differences within this category.

5. Previous studies also find a positive correlation between size and cooperative strategies: Berg *et al.* (1982), Schakenraad and Hagedoorn (1994), Ghemawat *et al.* (1986).

6. For simplicity, discounting within each two-stage subgame is ignored.

7. In practice, firms may choose more severe but temporary punishments. Since the length of the punishments is endogeneous in these models, such punishment structures are not pursued here, to keep the results tractable. For other possible strategies and their (dis)advantages, see Abreu (1986) and Tirole (1988).

8. The robustness of the results has been checked for other numerical solutions, which are not reported in the paper.

9. All parameter values imply that x_B^c, q_B^c and $V_B^c > 0$.

10. This is most easily seen when $\beta = 1$, which implies that $x_S^c = x_B^c$, independent of the magnitude of the size asymmetry.

11. In the razor's edge case of $B_i = 0$ for both firms, $V_i^c = V_i^n$, which is an artifact of the model (see also De Bondt and Veugelers, 1991; De Bondt and Henriques, 1995).

12. A similar critical spillover rate was identified in symmetric scenarios in De Bondt and Veugelers (1991) and Kesteloot and Veugelers (1995) and in a setup with asymmetric spillovers (De Bondt and Henriques, 1995).

13. If β_B is low, β_S has to be small too, since $s_\beta < 1$.

References

Abreu, D. (1986) 'Extremal Equilibria of Oligopolistic Supergames', *Journal of Economic Theory*, 39, pp. 191–225.

Anderson, E. (1990) 'Two Firms, One Frontier: On Assessing Joint Venture Performance', *Sloan Management Review*, 31 (2) pp. 19–30.

Baumol, W.J. (1990) 'Technology Cartels, Speed of Technology Transmission and the Market Mechanism', Working paper, New York and Princeton Universities.

Berg, S., J. Duncan and P. Friedman (1992) *Joint Venture Strategies and Corporate Innovation* (Cambridge, MA.: Oelgeschlagel, Gunn & Hain).

Bleeke, J. and W. Ernst (1992) 'The Way to Win in Cross-Border Alliances', *The McKinsey Quarterly*, 1, pp. 113–33.

Bulow, J., J. Geneakoplos and P. Klemperer (1985) 'Multimarket Oligopoly: Strategic Substitutes and Complements', *Journal of Political Economy*, 93, pp. 488–511.

Burgers, W., C. Hill and W. Chan Kim (1993) 'A Theory of Global Strategic Alliances: The Case of the Global Auto Industry', *Strategic Management Journal*, 14, pp. 419–32.

Cainarca, G., M. Colombo, S. Mariotti, C. Ciborra, G. De Michelis and M. Losano (1989) *Tecnologie Dell'Informazione E Accordi Tra Imprese* (Fondazione Olivetti, Edizione di Comunita).

Chaudhuri, P.R. (1994) 'Technological Asymmetry and Joint Product Development', Working Paper, CORE, Louvain-la-Neuve.

Chowdury, J. (1992) 'Performance of International Joint Ventures and Wholly Owned Foreign Subsidiaries: A Comparative Perspective', *Management International Review*, 32(2) pp. 115–33.

Contractor, F. and P. Lorange (eds) (1988) *Cooperative Strategies in International Business* (Lexington: D.C. Heath).

De Bondt, R. and R. Veugelers (1991) 'Strategic Investment with Spillovers', *European Journal of Political Economy*, 7, pp. 345–66.

De Bondt, R. and I. Henriques (1995) 'Strategic Investment with Asymmetric Spillovers', *Canadian Journal of Economics*, 28(3) pp. 656–74.

de Woot, P. (1990) *High Technology Europe: Strategic Issues for Global Competiveness* (Oxford: Basil Blackwell).

Doz, Y. (1988) 'Technology Partnerships between Large and Small Firms: Some Critical Issues', in Contractor and Lorange (1988) pp. 317–38.

Friedman, J. (1971) 'A Noncooperative Equilibrium for Supergames', *Review of Economic Studies*, 28, pp. 1–12.

Geringer, J.M. and L. Hebert (1991) 'Measuring Performance of International Joint Ventures', *Journal of International Business Studies*, 22 (2) pp. 249–64.

Ghemawat, P., M. Porter and R. Rawlinson (1986) 'Patterns of International Coalition Activity', in M. Porter (ed.), *Competition in Global Industries* (Boston: HBS Press) pp. 345–65.

Hagedoorn, J. (1995) 'A Note on International Market Leaders and Networks of Strategic Technology Partnering', *Strategic Management Journal*, 16, pp. 241–50.

Hagedoorn, J. and J. Schakenraad (1994) 'The Effect of Strategic Technology Alliances on Company Performance', *Strategic Management Journal*, 15, pp. 291–309.

Hamel, G., Y. Doz and C. Prahalad (1989) 'Collaborate with Your Competitor and Win', *Harvard Business Review*, 67, pp. 133–9.

Harrigan, K.R. (1985) *Strategies for Joint Ventures* (Lexington: Lexington Books).

Harrigan, K.R. (1988) 'Strategic Alliances and Partner Asymmetries', in Contractor and Lorange (1988) pp. 205–26.

Henriques, I. (1990) 'Cooperative and Noncooperative RandD in Duopoly with Spillovers: Comment', *American Economic Review*, 80, pp. 838–60.

Hergert, M. and D. Morris (1988) 'Trends in International Collaborative Agreements', in Contractor and Lorange (1988).

Kamien, M.I., E. Muller and I. Zang (1992) 'Research Joint Ventures and R&D Cartels', *American Economic Review*, 82(5) pp. 1293–306.

Kesteloot, K. and R. De Bondt (1993) 'Demand-Creating R&D in a Symmetric Oligopoly with Spillovers', *Economics of Innovation and New Technology*, 2, pp. 171–83.

Kesteloot, K. and R. Veugelers (1995) 'Stable R&D Cooperation with Spillovers', *Journal of Economics and Management Strategy*, 4(4) pp. 651–72.

Killing, J.P. (1983) *Strategies for Joint Venture Success* (New York: Praeger).

Kogut, B. (1988) 'A Study of the Life Cycle of Joint Ventures', in Contractor and Lorange (1988) pp. 169–86.

Lorange, P. and J. Roos (1990) *Strategic Alliances* (Oxford: Blackwell Publishers).

Mariti, P. and R. Smiley (1983) 'Cooperative Agreements and the Organisation of Industry', *Journal of Industrial Economics*, 38(2) pp. 183–98.

Mohr, J. and R. Spekman (1994) 'Characteristics of Partnership Success: Partnership Attributes, Communication Behavior and Conflict Resolution Techniques', *Strategic Management Journal*, 15, pp. 135–52.

Mytelka, L. (1991) *Strategic Partnership and the World Economy* (London: Pinter Publishers).

Pfeffer, J. and P. Nowak (1976) 'Joint Ventures and Interorganisational Interdependence', *Administrative Science Quarterly*, 21, pp. 398–418.

Porter, M. and M. Fuller (1986) 'Coalitions and Global Strategy', in M. Porter (ed.), *Competition in Global Industries* (Boston: Harvard Business School Press) pp. 315–43.

Poyago-Theotoky, J. (1995) 'Equilibrium and Optimal Size of a Research Joint Venture in an Oligopoly with Spillovers', *Journal of Industrial Economics*, 43, pp. 209–26.

Poyago-Theotoky, J. (1997) 'Research Joint Ventures and Product Innovations: Some Welfare Aspects', *Economic of Innovation and New Technology*, forthcoming.

Sinha, D.K. and M.A. Cusumano (1991) 'Complementary Resources and Cooperative Research: A Model of Research Joint Ventures Among Competitors', *Management Science*, 37 (9) pp. 1091–106.

Sleuwaegen, L., G. Den Hartog and H. Commandeur (1995) 'International Strategic Alliances of Leading Dutch Firms: Market Responses Following the Type of Alliance and Nationality of the Partner', Working Paper, K.U. Leuven.

Thomas, J. and L. Trevino (1993) 'Information Processing in Strategic Alliance Building: A Multiple-Case Approach', *Journal of Management Studies*, 30, pp. 779–814.

Tirole, J. (1988) *Theory of Industrial Organisation* (Cambridge, MA.: MIT Press).

Van Long, Ngo and A. Soubeyran (1997) 'Greater Cost Dispersion Improves Oligopoly Profit: Asymmetric Contributions to Joint Ventures', ch. 7 in this book.

Veugelers, R. (1993) 'A Profile of Companies in Alliances', Working Paper, K.U. Leuven.

Veugelers, R. (1994) 'An Empirical Analysis of Partner Similarities in Alliances: Mix or Match', Working Paper, K.U. Leuven.

Veugelers, R. and K. Kesteloot (1994) 'The Design of Stable Joint Ventures', *European Economic Review*, 38, pp. 1799–815.

Veugelers, R. and K. Kesteloot (1995) 'Bargained Shares in Joint Ventures Among Asymmetric Partners: Is the Matthew Effect Catalising?', Working Paper, K.U. Leuven.

Wu, C., J.K.C. Wei and Y. Song (1994) 'Cooperative R&D and Stock Market Returns', Working Paper, Hong Kong University of Science and Technology.

7 Greater Cost Dispersion Improves Oligopoly Profit: Asymmetric Contributions to Joint Ventures

Ngo Van Long and Antoine Soubeyran

7.1 INTRODUCTION

The literature on joint ventures has detailed a variety of motives for firms to engage in partnering (see Berg and Friedman, 1980; Connolly, 1984; Harrigan, 1985; Hennart, 1991; Hladik, 1985; Kogut, 1988; Weston and Ornstein, 1984; D'Aspremont and Jacquemin, 1988; Kamien, Muller and Zang, 1992; among others). The motives that are most commonly cited are risk sharing, access to markets and technology, exploitation of economies of scale and scope, and the possibility to control the degree of rivalry. One important motive for joint venture formation seems to have been neglected: the transfer of resources from the participating firms to the joint venture may serve as a coordinating device among these otherwise rival firms, where the coordination takes the form of increasing the asymmetry between firms by asking originally symmetric firms to contribute to the joint venture in a non-uniform way. The present chapter is an attempt to address this issue.

Our basic point is that an increase in the degree of cost asymmetry between firms in a Cournot oligopoly will always increase their combined profit. More precisely, if the mean unit cost is kept constant, an increase in the dispersion of unit costs will leave price and aggregate industry output unchanged, and will raise industry profit.

The result that aggregate output remains unchanged was proved by Bergstrom and Varian (1985); however, they did not ask the question concerning the response of industry profit to an increase in cost dispersion. By deriving a novel formula relating industry profit to the variance of the distribution of the unit costs, we are able to show conclusively that, for any demand function (not necessarily linear), the industry as a whole will gain by raising that variance. Intuitively, this is because of an allocative production efficiency effect. If the variance is increased, firms with relatively low costs will expand and firms with relatively high costs will contract. The result is that the same aggregate output is now produced at lower costs.

An initially symmetric industry (with identical firms) can make itself asymmetric by asking identical firms to transfer non-identical amounts of resources to a joint venture. Apart from the profit earned by the joint venture, the allocative production efficiency effect mentioned above will benefit the oligopoly, even though each firm's unit cost rises because it must transfer resources to the joint venture. In the resulting asymmetric oligopoly, smaller firms will have lower profits than before, but they are compensated by their greater shares of profit in the joint venture. The shares are increasing functions of the amounts of resources contributed by them, and may be determined as an outcome of cooperative Nash bargaining, which itself may be justified by a non-cooperative game of take-it-or-leave-it offers that potentially can repeat over time.

For expositional simplicity, we assume in this chapter that the joint venture gives no direct benefits to the oligopoly. For example, the joint venture may undertake R&D activities on products or processes that are not related to the oligopoly. According to Veugelers and Kesteloot (1994, p. 1802) this assumption corresponds to a substantial part of actual joint ventures: 41 per cent in their reported survey. A more general model would allow the possible feedback effects of the R&D output of the joint venture on the contributing firms. It is clear that our results concerning the profitability of asymmetric contributions would survive such generalizations.

The implications of our results for research joint ventures (RJVs) are as follows. Firstly, oligopolists that are very similar may find it optimal to transfer non-similar amounts of resources to an RJV. Secondly, these oligopolists will initially incur rises in unit costs, but in a non-uniform way. Their combined output will fall, but their aggregate profit (not including RJV profit) may rise, because of the combined effect of a price rise and a non-uniform cost increase across firms, causing a relative improvement in the allocative production efficiency. Thirdly, if the fruit of the RJV is in the form of lower production costs for the participating oligopolists, one would expect that this will not be spread uniformly across firms: the R&D activities may by chosen in a way that favours firms non-uniformly.

The last remark raises an important question: do partners in a RJV have an incentive to cheat? This question is beyond the scope of our chapter. A model that explores this issue (but abstracts from strategic considerations concerning the rivalry within the original oligopoly) has been developed by Veugelers and Kesteloot (1994).

This chapter is organized as follows: In section 7.2 we analyze the effect of an increase in the variance of the distribution of marginal cost on the combined profit of Cournot oligopolists. Section 7.3 presents a model of participation in a joint venture, and proves our results on asymmetric contributions. Section 7.4 offers some concluding remarks.

7.2   THE EFFECT OF AN INCREASE IN COST DISPERSION ON INDUSTRY PROFIT

Consider an industry consisting of n firms producing a homogeneous product under constant returns to scale. Let q_i denote firm i's output. Industry output is

$$Q = \sum q_i \tag{7.1}$$

The market demand function is $P = P(Q)$, with $P' < 0$. Firm i's profit is

$$\pi_i = (P(Q) - c_i)q_i \tag{7.2}$$

where c_i denotes firm i's constant unit cost.

A Cournot equilibrium satisfies the set of first order conditions:

$$P'(Q)q_i + P - c_i = 0, \qquad i = 1, 2, \dots, n \tag{7.3}$$

Summing (7.3) over all firms gives

$$P'(Q)Q + nP(Q) - C = 0 \tag{7.4}$$

where C is the sum of all marginal costs. It follows that Q is a function of C only, and is independent of the distribution of the c_i's, as long as all firms produce a positive output. This result is credited to Bergstrom and Varian (1985).

We wish to determine the effect of an increase in the variance of the distribution of marginal costs on industry profit.[1] Let m_i denote firm i's profit margin in a Cournot equilibrium:

$$m_i = P(Q) - c_i \tag{7.5}$$

From (7.3) and (7.5),

$$m_i = -P'(Q)q_i \tag{7.6}$$

Substitute (7.5) and (7.6) into (7.2) to obtain

$$\pi_i = m_i q_i = -P'(Q)q_i^2 = -(m_i)^2/P' \tag{7.7}$$

Industry profit is

$$\pi^I = \sum \pi_i = (-1/P') \sum m_i^2 \tag{7.8}$$

Let $\bar{c}$ and $\bar{q}$ denote the mean marginal cost and mean output respectively,

$$\bar{c} = C/n, \qquad \bar{q} = Q/n \tag{7.9}$$

From (7.8) and (7.9),

$$
\begin{aligned}
\pi^I &= (-1/P')\Sigma[(P - \bar{c}) + (\bar{c} - c_i)]^2 \\
&= (-1/P')\Sigma[-\bar{q}P' + (\bar{c} - c_i)]^2 \\
&= (-1/P')[n(\bar{q}P')^2 + V(c)]
\end{aligned} \tag{7.10}
$$

where $V(c)$ denotes the variance of the distribution of marginal cost. We have thus proved the following proposition:

Proposition 1: *For any general demand function (not necessarily linear), if the mean marginal cost is fixed, an increase in the variance of the distribution of marginal cost will increase industry profit.*

The intuition behind this result is as follows: in equilibrium, firms with high unit costs have smaller market shares than firms with low unit costs. Consequently, if we can reduce the unit cost of a low cost firm by some small amount, and increase the unit cost of a high cost firm by the same amount, then the cost of producing a given aggregate output is lowered. With the equilibrium industry output and price being unchanged (the result of Bergstrom and Varian that we cited above), there is an increase in allocative production efficiency. This increases industry profit.

By a similar argument, it is easy to show that for any subset consisting of k firms, an increase in the variance of marginal cost within the subset will raise its combined profit. Intuitively, this can be seen by noting that, with the mean marginal cost being kept constant, industry output will remain unchanged, and so will the outputs of firms outside the subset. The increase in industry profit must therefore accrue only to members of the subset. For later reference, we record this result below. Without loss, assume the subset consists of the first k firms. Let

$$\hat{c} = (1/k)\sum_{i=1}^{k} c_i, \qquad \hat{q} = (1/k)\sum_{i=1}^{k} q_i \tag{7.11}$$

$$V^{(k)} = \sum_{i=1}^{k} (\hat{c} - c_i)^2 \tag{7.12}$$

Then it can be shown that

$$\pi^{(k)} = \sum_{i=1}^{k} \pi_i = (-1/P')[k(\hat{q}P')^2 + V^{(k)}] \tag{7.13}$$

From (7.13), an increase in the variance $V^{(k)}$ will increase the combined profit.[2]

It is interesting to note that since Q does not change, consumer surplus remains constant, and an increase in the variance improves welfare, as measured by the sum of industry profit and consumer surplus.

How can an increase in the variance be achieved? One possibility is the transfer of resources (such as the capital stock, or human resources) from one firm to another, while the firms remain Cournot rivals, and their number in the industry is unchanged. In fact, infinitesimal transfers of capital stocks between firms have been an object of study in the horizontal merger literature. Farrell and Shapiro (1990) called such transfers 'infinitesimal mergers', and they assumed that after the transfers the firms retain their independence and remain Cournot rivals. This is in sharp contrast to the model of horizontal mergers by Salant, Switzer and Reynolds (1983) who assumed that the merged firms become a single entity, so that the number of firms in the oligopoly *falls*. Under this assumption, they showed that exogenous mergers are not profitable unless a significant number of firms are involved (at least 80 per cent of all firms, in the case of linear demand).

7.3 THE OPTIMALITY OF ASYMMETRIC CONTRIBUTIONS TO A JOINT VENTURE

We now make use of the results of section 7.2 to show that identical oligopolists that participate in a joint venture (JV) typically find it optimal to do so in an asymmetric way. For simplicity, we assume that the JV in question develops a new technology or a new product that is not related to the business of the participating oligopolists. This is not an extreme assumption. It has been pointed out that 'an average of 41 per cent of all the ventures involving an R&D activity are operating in different sectors than their parent companies' (Veugelers and Kesteloot, 1994, p. 1802).

We now assume that the oligopolists' marginal costs are functions of firm-specific resources (for example, entrepreneurial talent) that are available in limited supply, say K units per firm. Let e_i be the amount of this resource that firm i devotes to the control of its production cost, and $s_i = K - e_i$ be the amount it contributes to the JV. For simplicity, we postulate that

$$c_i = c_0 + s_i, \quad 0 \le s_i \le K \tag{7.14}$$

Consider now a JV formed by firm 1 and firm 2. The reduced form profit function for the JV is

$$J = J(s_1, s_2) \tag{7.15}$$

where J is concave and non-decreasing, with

$$J(0, s_2) = J(s_1, 0) = 0 \tag{7.16}$$

The JV operates in a different industry, or in a different market. This assumption is made in order to focus on the effects of the contributions s_1 and s_2 on the cost structure of the oligopolistic industry. Firm 1 and firm 2 are partners in the JV, but they remain rivals in the oligopolistic market. The structure of the game is as follows. In stage 1, the firms commit the quantities s_1 and s_2 to the JV. This will raise their marginal costs in the oligopoly to $c_i = c_0 + s_i$. In stage 2, they choose their outputs q_1 and q_2 simultaneously and non-cooperatively: they are Cournot oligopolists like the other $n - 2$ firms. Because their Cournot equilibrium profits depend on c_1 and c_2, we denote these by $\pi_i (s_1, s_2)$. Firm i's payoff is $\pi_i(s_1, s_2) + \alpha_i J (s_1, s_2)$ where α_i is its share in the JV's profit. How do they agree on the values of α_1 and α_2? We assume that this is achieved as an outcome of cooperative Nash bargaining. In other words, the shares (α_1, α_2) and the contributions (s_1, s_2) must maximize the Nash product N, where

$$N = [\pi_1(s_1, s_2) + \alpha_1 J(s_1, s_2) - \pi_1(0, 0)][\pi_2(s_1, s_2) + \alpha_2 J(s_1, s_2) - \pi_2(0, 0)] \tag{7.17}$$

subject to $\alpha_1 + \alpha_2 = 1$. Here the disagreement payoffs are $\pi_1 (0, 0)$ and $\pi_2 (0, 0)$.

It is important to note that the cooperative Nash bargaining solution may be justified as an outcome of a non-cooperative game in which players take turn to make take-it-or-leave-it offers. Their relative bargaining powers can be shown to be an increasing function of their relative degree of patience. See Binmore, Rubinstein and Wollinsky (1986). In our model, we assume that all participating firms have equal bargaining powers.

Problem (7.17) can be reformulated as one of finding (R_1, R_2) and (s_1, s_2) that maximizes

$$N = [R_1 - \pi_1(0, 0)][R_2 - \pi_2(0, 0)] \tag{7.18}$$

subject to

$$R_1 + R_2 = \pi_1(s_1, s_2) + \pi_2(s_1, s_2) + J(s_1, s_2) \qquad (7.19)$$

Let $S(s_1, s_2)$ denote the right-hand side of (7.19). It is the total surplus to be shared between the two firms. Clearly the first step in solving problem (7.18) is to find (s_1, s_2) that maximizes the total surplus. Denote this maximum by $S(s^*_1, s^*_2)$. The second step consists of maximizing (7.18) subject to $R_1 + R_2 = S(s^*_1, s^*_2)$. This yields

$$R_i = \frac{1}{2}[S(s^*_1, s^*_2) - \pi_i(0, 0) - \pi_j(0, 0)] \qquad (7.20)$$

This implies that

$$\alpha_i = [R_i - \pi(s^*_1, s^*_2)]/J(s^*_1, s^*_2) \qquad (7.21)$$

The JV agreement therefore specifies s^*_1, s^*_2, α_1 and α_2 that are obtained as described above. Each firm anticipates that in the second stage of the game (competition in the oligopolistic market) it will earn the amount $\pi_i(s^*_1, s^*_2)$.

We are now ready to demonstrate that the optimal choice of s_1 and s_2 is typically characterized by asymmetry. For simplicity, we will assume that the demand function is linear:

$$P = a - Q, \qquad a > c_0 + K \qquad (7.22)$$

The Cournot equilibrium outputs are

$$q_1 = \frac{1}{n+1} \max [0, a - c_0 - ns_1 + s_2] \qquad (7.23)$$

$$q_2 = \frac{1}{n+1} \max[0, a - c_0 - ns_2 + s_1] \qquad (7.24)$$

$$q_h = \frac{1}{n+1}(a - c_0 + s_2 + s_1), h > 2 \qquad (7.25)$$

From (7.13) and (7.22), the combined profit of the first two oligopolists is

$$\pi(s_1, s_2) = \frac{1}{2}[(c_1 - c_2)^2 + (q_1 + q_2)^2]$$

$$= \frac{1}{2}(s_1 - s_2)^2 + \frac{1}{2(n+1)^2}[2(a - c_0) - (n-1)(s_1 + s_2)]^2$$

$$(7.26)$$

provided that both firms produce. In the special case where

$$ns_2 \geq a - c_0 + s_1 \text{ and } ns_1 < a - c_0 + s_2 \tag{7.27}$$

then $q_2 = 0$ and $q_1 > 0$, and, with $n - 1$ active firms,

$$\pi(s_1, s_2) = (1/n^2)[a - c_0 - (n - 1)s_1]^2 \tag{7.28}$$

The case with $q_1 = 0$ and $q_2 > 0$ is obtained by swapping the subscripts in (7.27) and (7.25).

Equation (7.26) clearly indicates that for any given sum of contributions to the JV, $s_1 + s_2 = z$, say, the combined profit $\pi(s_1, s_2)$ attains its maximum if and only if $|| s_1 - s_2 ||$ is maximized, subject to $s_1 + s_2 = z$ and $s_i \geq 0$. We have therefore proved the following proposition:

Proposition 2: *Let the JV's profit function be $J(s_1, s_2) = f(s_1 + s_2)$ if $s_1 \geq \underline{s}$ and $s_2 \geq \underline{s}$ and $J(s_1, s_2) = 0$ otherwise. Then for any given $z = s_1 + s_2 \geq 2\underline{s}$, the optimal contributions that maximize the JVs are asymmetric, with:*

$$s_i = \underline{s}, s_j = z - \underline{s} > \underline{s} \tag{7.29}$$

Proposition 2 shows that if the contributions s_1 and s_2 are perfect substitutes in the JV when they exceed a certain level, then the participation in the JV should be extremely asymmetric, with one firm contributing the barest minimum. This is because, for any given z, the joint profit of the two firms is maximized by making the cost structures as uneven as possible. Intuitively, this is due to the allocative production efficiency effect that we discussed in section 7.2.

Clearly, Proposition 2 can be easily generalized to a JV formed by $k \leq n$ firms. A case of special interest is one where all the n firms participate in the JV. In this case, let z be the sum of all the s_i's. Let $\bar{c}$ denote the mean marginal cost, and $\underline{s}$ the minimum contribution of each firm:

$$\bar{c} = c_0 + (z/n), z \geq n\underline{s}. \tag{7.30}$$

Using (7.10) and (7.30), industry profit in the case of linear demand is

$$\pi^I = V(c) + n\left(\frac{a - \bar{c}}{n + 1}\right)^2 \tag{7.31}$$

Therefore, for a given z, industry profit is maximized by maximizing the variance of the marginal cost, subject to $c_i \geq c_0 + \underline{s}$ and $\Sigma c_i = n\bar{c}, \bar{c}$ given. The solution to this problem is to set all but one c_i at its minimum value $c_0 + \underline{s}$, and the remaining marginal cost, say, c_1, at $c_1 = c_0 + (z - n\underline{s})$, provided that $z - n\underline{s} \leq K$. The maximal variance is

$$V^*(z) = (n-1)[c_0 + \underline{s} - \bar{c}]^2 + [c_0 + z - n\underline{s} - \bar{c}]^2$$
$$= n(n-1)(z/n)^2 - 2\underline{s}(n+1)(z/n) + (n^2+n-1)\underline{s}^2, \qquad (7.32)$$

where $z \geq n\underline{s}$.[3] Let π_0 denote the industry profit when there is no JV and all $c_i = c_0$, and $\pi^I(z)$ the industry profit when all firms participate in the JV and their contribution is $z \geq n\underline{s}$. Then, from (7.31) and (7.32),

$$\pi^I(z) - \pi_0 = V^*(z) + \frac{n}{(n+1)^2}[(z/n)^2 - 2(a - c_0)(z/n)] \qquad (7.33)$$

From (7.33), we obtain the following result:

Proposition 3: *If all firms contribute asymmetrically to a common JV so that the variance of costs is maximized, then the industry profit increases with the average contribution z/n, for z/n greater than some critical level z^*/n. Moreover, there exists a level $z^{**} > z^*$ such that, beyond this level, industry profit (not including the JV's profit) exceeds the pre-joint venture aggregate profit.*

The proof of this proposition is trivial and therefore omitted. The reader can verify that if $n = 2$ and $\underline{s} = 0$, then $z^* = (a - c_0)/5$, and $z^{**} = 2z^*$. The isoprofit curves for $\pi(s_1, s_2)$ are depicted in Figure 7.1 for this case. Note that $\pi^I(z) = \pi(z, 0) = \pi(0, z)$. Both q_1 and q_2 are positive only in the region defined by $2s_2 < a - c_0 + s_1$ and $2s_1 < a - c_0 + s_2$. As can be ascertained from (7.26), the slopes of the isoprofit curves are zero (respectively, infinite) when they cross the line $s_1 = (a - c_0 + 4s_2)/5$ (respectively, $s_2 = (a - c_0 + 4s_1)/5$).

Notice that, starting from a pre-JV symmetric equilibrium, a small transfer of resources to the JV will at first reduce the aggregate profit of the oligopoly. Additional transfers will eventually cause profit to rise, because the price effect will become stronger as the industry's output contracts, provided that the firms become increasingly dissimilar, so that the increases in unit production costs occur only to the smaller firms. In fact, as Figure 7.1 indicates, if $\underline{s} = 0$, then the highest industry profit is achieved in the limiting case where the lowest cost firm becomes a monopoly.

The JV described in Proposition 2 combines resources s_1 and s_2 to make profit, and these resources are perfect substitutes. Therefore, the iso-profit curves for the JV, $J(s_1 + s_2) = $ constant, are straight lines with slope -1. To maximize surplus $S(s_1, s_2)$, it is necessary that $J(s_1 + s_2)$ be maximized subject to $\pi(s_1, s_2) \geq \bar{\pi}$, a constant. But this constraint set is non-convex. It follows that the optimal solution is asymmetric.

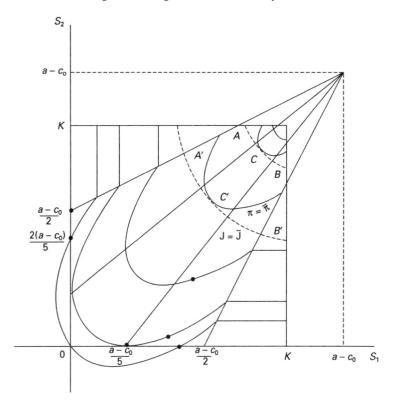

Figure 7.1 Asymmetric contributions to joint ventures

If the resources s_1 and s_2 are not perfect substitutes in the JV, the situation will be slightly different. Specifically, assume that $J(s_1, s_2)$ is strictly quasi-concave, so that the marginal rate of substitution between s_1 and s_2 is diminishing. Then again, a symmetric tangency point such as C or C' is a local minimum. A maximum will occur at a point such as A or A' (or equivalently, B or B'). If $\pi \leq (a - c_0)^2/5$ and $K < (a - c_0)/5$, then it is possible that an optimum is symmetric, but this is not necessarily so.

Our results in this section remain essentially unchanged if the demand curve is not linear. If, on the other hand, the R&D activities of the JV result in the discovery of new processes that lower the production costs of the participating oligopolists, then the model would become much more complicated, because one would have to specify the process of knowledge transmissions and spillover effects between firms. Kamien, Muller and Zang (1992) have developed several models of R&D cooperation. Their results are quite sensitive to the specifications of spillovers and of the nature of the cooperation. They concentrated on symmetric equilibria. However, Salant and Shaffer (1992) have provided counter examples where in one of the models of R&D cooperation of Kamien, Muller and Zang, symmetric solutions are minima, not maxima. Van Long and Soubeyran (1995) have generalized the Salant–Shaffer result by considering any number of firms and any general demand function, and provided necessary and sufficient conditions for R&D cooperation to be asymmetric. They also considered rivalry between two R&D joint ventures.

7.4   CONCLUDING REMARKS

We have shown that, under a wide range of circumstances, contributions to a joint venture by identical oligopolists are typically asymmetric. We explained this in terms of the benefit obtained from having an uneven cost structure in an oligopoly. Our result applies to any general demand function (not necessarily linear) for the oligopoly. The battle of the giants can be avoided by increasing the variance of the distribution of marginal costs. We have restricted attention to the Cournot case. However, in a Bertrand oligopoly with differentiated products, a similar result can be obtained, though the calculations are much more tedious. A detailed treatment of the Bertrand case is the subject of a forthcoming paper.

Notes

1.   It should be stressed that there is no uncertainty in this model.
2.   Note that since Q and all the q_j's ($j > k$) are unchanged, $\hat{q}$ is independent of the variance.
3.   We assume, of course, that costs remain sufficiently low so that all the q_i's are positive.

References

Berg, Sanford V. and Philip Friedman (1980) 'Causes and Effects of Joint Venture Activity: Knowledge Acquisition vs. Parent Horizontality', *The Antitrust Bulletin*, 25(1) (Spring) pp. 142–68.

Bergstrom, Theodore and Hal Varian (1985) 'When are Nash Equilibria Independent of the Distribution of Agents' Characteristics?', *Review of Economic Studies*, pp. 715–18.

Binmore, K., A. Rubinstein and A. Wollinsky (1986) 'The Nash Bargaining Solution in Economic Modelling', *Rand Journal of Economics*, 17, pp. 176–88.

Connolly, Seamus G. (1984) 'Joint Ventures and Third World Multinationals: A New Form of Entry of International Markets', *Columbia Journal of World Business*, Summer, pp. 45–59.

D'Aspremont, Claude and Alexis Jacquemin (1988) 'Cooperative and Non-Cooperative R&D in Duopoly with Spillovers', *American Economic Review*, 78 (December) 1133–7.

Farrell, Joseph and Carl Shapiro (1990) 'Horizontal Mergers: An Equilibrium Analysis', *American Economic Review*, pp. 105–26.

Grossman, Gene and C. Shapiro (1986) 'Research Joint Ventures: An Antitrust Analysis', *Journal of Law, Economics and Organization*, 1986(2), pp. 315–17.

Harrigan, Kathryn (1985) *Strategies for Joint Ventures* (Lexington, MA,: Lexington Books).

Hennart, Jean-François (1987) 'A Transaction Costs Theory of Equity Joint Ventures', *Strategic Management Journal*, 28, pp. 109–21.

Hennart, Jean-François (1991) 'The Transaction Cost Theory of the Multinational Enterprise', in C. Pitelis and R. Sugden (eds), *The Nature of the Transnational Firm*, (London Routhledge,) pp. 81–116.

Hladik, K.J. (1985) *International Joint Ventures: An Economic Analysis of U.S. Foreign Business Partnerships* (Lexington, MA: Lexington Books).

Kamien, Morton, Eitan Muller amd Israel Zang (1992) 'Research Joint Ventures and R&D Cartels', *American Economic Review*, 82(5), pp. 1293–306.

Katz, M. (1986) 'An Analysis of Cooperative Research and Development', *Rand Journal of Economics*, 17, pp. 527–43.

Kogut, Bruce (1988) 'Joint Ventures: Theoretical and Empirical Properties', *Strategic Management Journal*, 9, pp. 319–32.

Ordover, J. and R. Willig (1985) 'Antitrust for High Technology Industries: Assessing Research Joint Ventures and Mergers', *Journal of Law and Economics*, 28, pp. 311–33.

Raubitschek, Ruth and Barbara Spencer (1992) 'High Cost Domestic Joint Ventures and International Competition: Do Domestic Firms Gain?', *International Economic Review*, 37, 2, May, pp. 315–40.

Salant, S., S. Switzer and R.J. Reynolds (1983) 'Losses from Horizontal Mergers. The Effects of An Exogenous Change in Industry Structure on Cournot Nash Equilibrium', *Quarterly Journal of Economics*, 98, pp. 185–99.

Salant, S. and G. Shaffer (1992) 'Optimal Asymmetric Strategies in Research Joint Ventures: A Comment on the Literature', Working Paper No. 93–96, Dept of Economics, University of Michigan.

Shapiro, C. and R.D. Willig (1990) 'On Antitrust Treatment of Production Joint Ventures', *Journal of Economic Perspectives*, 4 (Summer) pp. 113–30.

Van Long, Ngo and Antoine Soubeyran (1995) 'Rivalry between R&D Joint Ventures', unpublished typescript, McGill University.

Veugelers, R. and K. Kesteloot (1994) 'On the Design of Stable Joint Ventures', *European Economic Review*, 38, pp. 1799–815.

Weston, J. Fred and Stanley I. Ornstein (1984) 'Efficiency Considerations in Joint Ventures', *Antitrust Law Journal*, 53(1), pp. 84–95.

8 Commitment and Efficiency in Research Joint Ventures

Rune Stenbacka and Mihkel M. Tombak*

8.1 INTRODUCTION

Competition policy in most industrial countries allows for and even encourages research joint ventures. A research joint venture (RJV) is a contractural arrangement whereby the partners share in the costs and benefits of the research. RJVs are a way in which research funds can be leveraged and a way to mitigate appropriability problems associated with the public goods aspect of the knowledge created through research. The contractual agreements which form the basis of RJVs can take a number of forms. These agreements can irreversibly specify the allocation over time of the outlays of the resources of the partners. Alternatively, RJVs can be based on flexible agreements where the funding is subject to periodic review by the partners. In this chapter we study how the investments of RJVs in cost-reducing R&D are affected by the degrees of commitment implied by the contractual arrangements. We also investigate the main implications for the cost efficiency of the industry as well as the corresponding welfare effect.

Public policy which encourages R&D cooperation has its foundation on the widespread and empirically justified view that private rates of return from R&D investments are generally lower than the social returns. This divergence of private and social returns has a variety of well-known explanations (see Katz and Ordover, 1990, for an execellent overview of this issue). A particularly interesting argument in favour of RJVs is that they encourage investment in R&D and thereby increase dynamic efficiency. In an argument with a long tradition (Schumpeter, 1975, p. 83) it has been suggested that there exists a tradeoff between dynamic and allocative efficiency. RJVs can have an essential impact on this tradeoff. The current literature analyzing RJVs is based on static models (see, for example, Kamien, Muller and Zang, 1992, and the references therein). However, in order to capture dynamic efficiency it is clear that an intertemporal model is required. In addition, the nature of R&D investments suggests that a dynamic framework is necessary. Rosenberg (1982) stresses the relative importance of incremental improvement in processes over discontinuous technological breakthroughs. There is anecdotal evidence for the view that technological progress is more a function of a steady accumulation of many minor improvements than of major innovations: see, for example, Hunter (1949) for evidence from the shipping industry, Fishlow (1966) for the railroad industry, Hollander (1965) for the synthetic material industry, and Enos (1958) for the petroleum industry. Consequently, we diverge from the literature on RJVs by modelling technological development as an on-going process with a lag between the R&D and the realized cost reduction.

The recent contribution of Kamien, Muller and Zang (1992) provides the terminology which is used in this study. They examine various types of industry-wide RJVs and industry-wide R&D cartels and find that the cartelized RJV (in which firms coordinate R&D activities so as to maximize industry profits) makes larger investments in cost reduction, has lower equilibrium prices and higher equilibrium profits than the other forms of organization examined. In another ground–breaking study, d'Aspremont and Jacquemin (1988) find that for sufficiently large spillovers between the firms industry-wide R&D cooperation leads to greater R&D investments than does competitive R&D. Kamien and Zang (1993) compare an industry-wide RJV with two competing RJVs and find conditions under which industry-wide R&D cooperation would be detrimental. We use a differential game approach so as to emphasize the dynamic aspects of investment behaviour. This dynamic formulation allows us to distinguish between contracts which require RJV partners to commit to investment programmes and contracts which are contingent on R&D outcomes over time. Other applications of differential games in economics include Kamien and Schwartz (1991), Fershtman and Kamien (1987) and Reynolds (1987) among others.

The contractual arrangements which form the basis for RJVs can take a variety of forms. Contracts may vary regarding the degree to which partners have to commit to investment levels. For example, members of Sematech (Semiconductor Manufacturing and Technology Institute) were initially required to pay a minimum annual fee of US$ 1 million for at least four years (Erdilek, 1989). We study two important dimensions of these agreements. First, we examine the issue of whether legal institutions should make it sustainable for RJVs to commit to investment programmes at the point in time when the joint venture is formed. We analyze the case in which firms make commitments up front to a time pattern of investments covering the life of the RJV and compare this with the situation where firms make no initial commitment but continually review their investment based on the cost realization. More formally, we compare the open–loop with the feedback equilibrium. Secondly, we explore the issue of whether public policy should encourage cartelized RJVs, where firms collectively decide on investment patterns to maximize the discounted industry payoff. We then contrast this scenario with one in which firms within the RJV decide individually on their investments so as to maximize their own discounted payoffs, given the investment pattern of the other firms. When firms decide on investment levels individually we refer to this situation as the competitive RJV and we compute the Nash equilibrium investment pattern.

We find that shifting from a competitive RJV to a cartelized RJV under the open–loop regime results in increased investments in R&D, decreased costs and an improvement in total welfare. This result can be explained by the free-rider problem inherent in the set-up of the competitive RJV. Because under RJV competition each firm decides on its own contribution to the RJV investment fund and yet all enjoy the same benefit, there is a disincentive to invest. Thus the investment in cost-reducing R&D is less than socially desirable. However, as we move to a more flexible arrangement whereby firms continually review their investment profile and apply the feedback equilibrium decision rule, we find that the 'free rider' problem is to some degree mitigated and investment levels increase. This is an effect which cannot be captured in a static model. As a policy implication we can state that the contracts governing RJVs should not contain commitments to certain investment levels for long periods of time. The practice of reviewing contractual arrangements when RJVs apply for their block exemption from the EC competition law gives the European Commission a way of implementing such a policy.

This chapter is organized in the following manner. Section 8.2 outlines the model, defining the payoff and kinematic functions and describing the parameters. Also, section 8.2 provides the formal definitions of strategy spaces and equilibria. In section 8.3 we compute the open–loop equilibria for the two types of RJVs (cartelized and competitive). The equilibria are compared and comparative statics are performed on two of the parameters (number of firms and the speed with which R&D investments are translated into cost reductions). In section 8.4 the more flexible arrangement is examined with the computation of the feedback equilibrium for the competitive RJV. Section 8.5 contains the welfare comparisons, and finally in section 8.6 we summarize and discuss the results.

8.2 THE MODEL

We examine an industry-wide cost reducing research joint venture consisting of n identical firms. Even though firms cooperate on the research side, in accordance with the legal restrictions in most countries, the firms are assumed to compete in the product markets. Firms are indexed by $i, i = 1, \ldots, n$ and produce a homogeneous good. Let $x_i(t)$ be firm i's investment in R&D, x_{-i} the vector of firm i's rivals' investments, and $c(t)$ be industry's marginal costs at time t. Given the marginal cost, firm i enjoys an instantaneous payoff $\pi_i(c(t, n), n)$ which is based on non-cooperative product market competition.

Firms have the same constant discount rate, r, and choose investment levels $(x_i(t))$ such as to maximize

$$J^i(x_i(t), x_{-i}(t)) = \int_0^\infty \left[\pi_i(c(t, n), n) - \frac{x_i(t)^2}{2} \right] e^{-rt} dt, \quad i = 1, \ldots, n$$

subject to the kinematic equation

$$\dot{c}(t) = \mu[\bar{c} - c(t) - \alpha(x_i(t) + \sum_{j \neq i} x_j(t))]$$

In the above problem $c(t)$ is the state variable and $x_i(t)$ is firm i's control variable chosen from a strategy space S_i. The kinematic expression is a differential equation governing the change in costs as a function of investments in R&D. The parameter μ captures the speed with which R&D results are translated into marginal cost reductions. It is similar to the speed of price adjustment factor in Fershtman and Kamien (1987). The limiting case of $\mu \to \infty$ implies instantaneous adjustment and it is assumed that $\mu \geq 1$. The parameter $\bar{c}$ is the initial marginal cost of the (symmetric) firms, i.e., $\bar{c} = c(0)$. The parameter α measures the productivity of the R&D investments and we assume $0 < \alpha \leq \frac{1}{2}$. Note that we assume, as do Kamien, Muller, and Zang (1992), the spillovers to be at their maximum levels within the RJV. In other words, the marginal cost of production is decreased by the sum of all the R&D efforts of the RJV partners. In principle, the model could be extended to capture incomplete spillovers between the RJV partners. However, on this dimension we wish to retain comparability with the previous work on RJVs and emphasize the effects of dynamics. The kinematic expression yields cost realizations which are a decreasing and convex function of investments. One could interpret this expression as the costs being derived from a knowledge base which depreciates over time. Such a depreciation could, for example, follow from employee turnover.

The current value Hamiltonian for this problem is given by

$$\mathcal{H}^i = \pi(c(t, n)) - \frac{x_i(t)^2}{2} + \lambda_i(t)\mu[\bar{c} - c(t) - \alpha(x_i(t) + \sum_{j \neq i} x_j(t))]$$

$$(8.1)$$

$$i = 1, \ldots, n$$

Definition 1. The investment profile $x_i^*(t)$, $x_{-i}^*(t)$ is a *Nash Equilibrium* if for all $i = 1, \ldots n$,

$$J^i(x_i^*(t), x_{-i}^*(t)) \geq J^i(x_i(t), x_{-i}^*(t)) \quad \forall x_i(t) \in S_i.$$

A Nash equilibrium in such strategies is an n-tuple such that each firm's profile is the best response to its rivals' profiles.

Definition 2. The *open-loop strategy space* for firm i is $S_i^{ol} = \{x_i(t)|x_i$ is piecewise continuous and $x^i(t) \geq 0$ for every $t\}$.

With open-loop strategies each firm chooses an investment profile $x_i(t)$ to which it commits itself at time $t = 0$.

We define the feedback strategy space as follows.

Definition 3. The *feedback strategy space* for firm i is

$$S_i = \{x_i(t, c)|x_i \text{ is continuous in } (t, c) \text{ and}$$

$$|x_i(t, c) - x_i(t, c')| \leq \lambda_i(t) \cdot |c - c'| \text{ for some integrable } \lambda_i(t)\}.$$

The feedback strategies describe decision rules that prescribe an investment rate as a function of time and the realized cost. Thus with the feedback Nash equilibrium the commitment requirements are relaxed. Analogous to the widely used concept of subgame perfection, the feedback Nash equilibrium has a rational expectations character such that empty threats with respect to investment decisions (i.e. threats to withdraw funding) are eliminated.

8.3   IRREVERSIBLE COMMITMENTS

In this section we consider a game in which each firm commits to an irreversible investment profile at the outset. We characterize the open-loop equilibrium under two distinct regimes. The first regime is that which Kamien *et al.* (1992) refer to as RJV competition (NJ). In this situation each firm determines its own R&D investment level given the R&D investments of other firms. The marginal cost of production for all participating firms is decreased by a function of the sum of all R&D efforts in the industry. The second regime is RJV cartelization (CJ) using the terminology of Kamien *et al.* (1992). Under this scenario firms coordinate R&D investments so as to maximize industry profits.

RJV Competition

Here we analyze the situation in which each member of the RJV decides on its level of investment, given the investment levels of the other firms. Those investment funds are then pooled and the results of the R&D effort is disseminated to all RJV members. RJV members, however, are not allowed to cooperate in the product market where they produce homogeneous products at the same marginal cost.

The necessary conditions for open-loop investment plans are

$$\frac{\partial \mathcal{H}^i}{\partial x_i} = -x_i(t) - \lambda_i(t)\mu\alpha = 0 \tag{8.2}$$

$$-\dot{\lambda}_i(t) = -(r + \mu)\lambda_i(t) + \frac{\partial \pi_i(c(t, n), n)}{\partial c} \tag{8.3}$$

and

$$lim_{t \to \infty} \lambda_i(t)e^{-rt} = 0 \tag{8.4}$$

For the case of linear inverse demand ($p(Q) = a - \sum_i^n q_i$) and Cournot competition in the product market it can easily be shown that the instantaneous profit $\pi_i(c(t,n),n) = \frac{(a-c)^2}{(n+1)^2}$. For this case the following proposition holds.

Proposition 1 *For RJV competition the unique steady state open-loop equilibrium is characterized by levels of investment for each firm given by*

$$x_i^{*olNJ} = \frac{2\mu\alpha(a - \bar{c})}{(r + \mu)(n + 1)^2 - 2\mu\alpha^2 n} \quad i = 1, 2, \ldots, n \tag{8.5}$$

and the corresponding steady state cost is

$$c^{*olNJ} = \frac{(r + \mu)(n + 1)^2\bar{c} - 2\mu\alpha^2 na}{(r + \mu)(n + 1)^2 - 2\mu\alpha^2 n} \tag{8.6}$$

Proof

Differentiating equation (8.2) with respect to time and combining with equation (8.3) yields the following first order linear differential equation:

$$\dot{x}_i(t) - (r + \mu)x_i(t) = -\frac{2\mu\alpha}{(n+1)^2}(a - c(t)) \tag{8.7}$$

which describes the open–loop equilibrium investment profile. To show that the open–loop equilibrium strategies are symmetric one can solve the linear differential equation (8.3), apply the transversality condition (8.4) and observe that the resulting expression for $\lambda_i(t)$ is not firm specific.

At steady state $\dot{c}(t) = \dot{x}_i(t) = \dot{x}_j(t) = 0$ which when substituted into equation (8.7) and the kinematic equation yields a system of equations from which the proposition follows. Differentiation of the kinematic equation yields

$$\ddot{c} + \alpha\mu n\dot{x}_i + \mu\dot{c} = 0$$

which when combined with (8.2) and (8.3) gives the following second order linear differential equation:

$$\ddot{c} + A\dot{c} + Bc = D$$

where

$$A = -r$$

$$B = \frac{2n\mu^2\alpha^2}{(n+1)^2} - \mu(r + \mu)$$

$$D = \frac{2n\mu^2\alpha^2 a}{(n+1)^2} + \mu(r + \mu)\bar{c}$$

A particular solution of the above second order differential equation is $c(t) = \frac{D}{B}$ which is exactly the steady state cost (8.6). There are two real roots, one positive and the other negative, associated with the characteristic equation connected to the second order differential equation. Clearly, if we concentrate on the stable solution and use an artitrary initial cost level $\bar{c}$, the trajectory

$$c(t) = c^{*olNJ} + (\bar{c} - c^{*olNJ})e^{z_1 t}$$

with $z_1 = -\frac{1}{2}[A + \sqrt{A^2 - 4B}]$ being the negative root of the characteristic equation, is the open–loop Nash equilibrium trajectory.

Q.E.D.

Straightforward comparative static analysis on the steady state costs shows that

$$\frac{\partial c^{*olNJ}}{\partial n} = \frac{2\alpha^2\mu(a - \bar{c})(n^2 - 1)(\mu + r)}{(\mu + 2\mu n - 2\alpha^2\mu n + \mu n^2 + r + 2nr + n^2 r)^2}$$

which is positive, and

$$\frac{\partial c^{*olNJ}}{\partial \mu} = \frac{2\alpha^2(\bar{c} - a)n(n + 1)^2 r}{(\mu + 2\mu n - 2\alpha^2\mu n + \mu n^2 + r + 2nr + n^2 r)^2}$$

which is negative. It can similarly be shown that $\frac{\partial x^{*olNJ}}{\partial n} < 0$ and that $\frac{\partial x^{*olNJ}}{\partial \mu} < 0$. Thus as the number of firms participating in the RJV increases, the steady state investment per firm decreases and the steady state costs increase. By the above Proposition it holds that $lim_{n\to\infty} x_i^{*olNJ} = 0$ and $lim_{n\to\infty} c^{*olNJ} = \bar{c}$. Together with the comparative statics results, this implies that industry-wide R&D investment shrinks with the number of firms participating in RJV competition. This suggests that the free rider effect is sufficiently strong so that $lim_{n\to\infty} n.x^{*olNJ} = 0$.

This feature of declining industry R&D investment with the number of firms suggests that there is an interesting tradeoff between dynamic and allocative efficiency. For the demand conditions examined in this model, consumer surplus is increasing in n in each particular time period (for the given cost). However, in this model consumer surplus increases with a decrease in cost. Consequently, the effect of the number of firms on the total discounted consumer surplus is ambiguous and a finite number of firms may be optimal.

The comparative statics analysis above also establishes that an increase in the speed with which R&D investments are translated into cost reductions will increase the incentives to invest, which, of course, will imply reductions in costs. We now analyze the 'limit game' in which costs adjust instantaneously to R&D investments, i.e. $\mu \to \infty$. From (8.5) we can see that the steady state investment levels satisfy the following corollary:

Corollary 1

$$lim_{\mu \to \infty} x_i^{*olNJ} = \frac{2\alpha(a - \bar{c})}{(n + 1)^2 - 2\alpha^2 n} \tag{8.8}$$

It is interesting to observe that the steady state investment level with instantaneous adjustment of costs is equivalent to the equilibrium investment level in a static game with

$$c = \bar{c} - \alpha x_i - \alpha \sum_{j \neq i} x_j$$

Thus as $\mu \to \infty$ the stationary open–loop investment level converges to the static investment level. This feature is shared by the models of Fershtman and Kamien (1987) and Reynolds (1987).

RJV Cartelization

In this section we study the case in which firms agree at the outset on a coordinated R&D programme so as to maximize industry profits. Firms agree on a common investment profile and the marginal costs of all firms are decreased by a function of the sum of the R&D efforts.

Formally, this requires the computation of the open–loop equilibrium for the following problem:

$$J(x(t)) = \int_0^\infty \left[n\pi_i(c(t, n), n) - \frac{nx(t)^2}{2} \right] e^{-rt} dt$$

subject to the kinematic equation,

$$\dot{c}(t) = \mu[\bar{c} - c(t) - \alpha n x(t)]$$

An analogous process to that above leads to the following proposition.

Proposition 2 *For a cartelized RJV the unique steady state open–loop equilibrium is characterized by a firm level of investment given by*

$$x^{*olCJ} = \frac{2\mu\alpha n(a - \bar{c})}{(r + \mu)(n + 1)^2 - 2\mu\alpha^2 n^2} \tag{8.9}$$

and the corresponding steady state cost is

$$c^{*olCJ} = \frac{(r + \mu)(n + 1)^2 \bar{c} - 2\mu\alpha^2 n^2 a}{(r + \mu)(n + 1)^2 - 2\mu\alpha^2 n^2} \tag{8.10}$$

Comparing expression (8.9) with (8.5) we can see that $x^{*olCJ} > x^{*olNJ}$. This, in turn, implies that $c^{*olCJ} < c^{*olNJ}$. With RJV competition (the NJ case) the firms are free to choose an investment level given the other partners' contribution. This feature creates a 'free rider' problem as the firms all enjoy the fruits of the R&D investments. This 'free rider' problem provides a natural explanation for the observation that the investment level is lower in the case of RJV competition compared with RJV cartelization. With each RJV partner investing less in the case of RJV competition it is clear that the resulting production costs will be higher than those under RJV cartelization. The comparative statics properties in the CJ case are as follows:

$$\frac{\partial x^{*olCJ}}{\partial n} = \frac{2\alpha\mu(a - \bar{c})(\mu - \mu n^2 + 2\alpha^2\mu n^2 + r - n^2 r)}{(\mu + 2\mu n + \mu n^2 - 2\alpha^2\mu n^2 + r + 2nr + n^2 r)^2} < \frac{\partial x^{*olNJ}}{\partial n} < 0$$

$$\frac{\partial c^{*olCJ}}{\partial n} = \frac{4\alpha^2\mu(\bar{c} - a)n(n + 1)(\mu + r)}{(\mu + 2\mu n + \mu n^2 - 2\alpha^2\mu n^2 + r + 2nr + n^2 r)^2} < 0$$

under the condition given by the upper bound on α, and

$$\frac{\partial c^{*olCJ}}{\partial \mu} = \frac{2\alpha^2(\bar{c} - a)n^2(n + 1)^2 r}{(\mu + 2\mu n + \mu n^2 - 2\alpha^2\mu n^2 + r + 2nr + n^2 r)^2} < 0$$

As in the RJV competition case, $lim_{n\to\infty} x_i^{*olCJ} = 0$. In contrast to RJV competition, however, $lim_{n\to\infty} c^{*olCJ} < \bar{c}$. This, together with the comparative statics results suggests that industry-wide investment increases with n under RJV cartelization. That is, the individual investment levels decrease with the increase of n but at a slower rate than n. In the absense of the free-rider problem each firm can make R&D investments with a higher marginal return. This feature is a result of the quadratic cost function and the implicit diseconomies of scale in R&D investments. Consequently, in our model, with the RJV cartel there is no tradeoff between allocative and dynamic efficiency. Thus, in contrast to the RJV competition case, a larger number of RJV partners increases dynamic efficiency in addition to allocative efficiency.

The intuition for the effect of μ is clear – an increase in the speed with which research results are translated into cost reductions, increases the incentive to invest in that research and thereby decreases the steady state cost.

8.4   RJVs WITHOUT COMMITMENT

In this section we relax the constraint that firms must commit to an irreversible investment profile at the outset and allow firms to revise their plans at any point in time on the basis of the realized cost. To capture this idea we make use of the concept of feedback equilibrium. We analyze only the NJ case, because the case of the cartelized RJV can be shown to have identical results in the feedback and open–loop games. The reason for this is that in the cartel case each firm knows what the other firm invests and consequently the value of the state variable (cost) can be predicted. Hence, in case CJ, the investment levels are solely a function of time.

In order to characterize the feedback Nash equilibrium we follow the value functions approach based on the Hamilton–Jacobi–Bellman equation (see Kamien and Schwartz, 1991, p. 274). This equation is given by

$$rV^i(c) = MAX_{x_i}\left\{\pi_i(c, n) - \frac{x_i^2}{2} + \frac{\partial V^i(c)}{\partial c}\mu\left[\bar{c} - c - \alpha\left(x_i + \sum_{j\neq i}x_j^{*NJ}\right)\right]\right\}$$

(8.11)

where $V^i(c)$ is the value to firm i of the game starting at state c and x_j^{*NJ} is the feedback equilibrium strategy for firm j.

From the FOC of the r.h.s. of (8.11) we can derive

$$x_i^{*NJ} = -\mu\alpha\frac{\partial V^i(c)}{\partial c}$$

(since the r.h.s. of (8.11) is concave with respect to x_i), which when substituted into (8.11) yields

$$rV^i(c) = \pi_i(c, n) - \frac{\left(-\mu\alpha\frac{\partial V^i(c)}{\partial c}\right)^2}{2} + \frac{\partial V^i(c)}{\partial c}\mu\left[\bar{c} - c - \alpha\left(-\mu\alpha\frac{\partial V^i(c)}{\partial c} - \sum_{j\neq i}\mu\alpha\frac{\partial V^j(c)}{\partial c}\right)\right]$$

(8.12)

(8.12) defines a system of partial differential equations. With linear demand and Cournot competition the following proposition holds.[1]

Proposition 3 *The steady state feedback equilibrium is characterized by levels of investment for each firm given by*

$$x_i^{*NJ} = -\mu\alpha(w_2 + 2w_3c^{*NJ}) \quad i = 1, 2, \ldots, n$$

(8.13)

and the corresponding steady state cost is

$$c^{*NJ} = \frac{\bar{c} + \mu\alpha^2 nw_2}{1 - 2n\alpha^2\mu w_3}$$

(8.14)

where[2]

$$w_3 = \frac{1}{4\mu^2(2n-1)\alpha^2}\left\{2\mu + r - \sqrt{(2\mu + r)^2 - \frac{8\mu^2(2n-1)\alpha^2}{(n+1)^2}}\right\}$$

and

$$w_2 = \frac{\frac{2a}{(n+1)^2} - 2\mu\bar{c}w_3}{2(2n-1)\mu^2\alpha^2 w_3 - \mu - r}$$

Proof

See Appendix A.

Whereas w_3 is clearly positive, w_2 would be negative for $a < \mu(n+1)^2\bar{c}w_3$. This implies a convex value function. This is plausible since a higher cost state would lead to lower Cournot profits and higher investment levels in order to bring the costs down. Thus higher starting costs imply a lower value of the game to the firm. Since w_3 is positive, however, the range for the value function should be restricted to the non-increasing portion, i.e. where $\frac{\partial V(c)}{\partial c} \leq 0$. This restriction, in turn, implies positive investment levels x_i^{*NJ}. Consequently, w_2 is restricted to being negative.

The comparative static analysis of the feedback equilibrium is not as straightforward as in section 8.3 and we perform a numerical analysis to illustrate the effect of n. Figure 8.1 illustrates that the steady state cost levels increase with n in the feedback equilibrium case for reasonable parameter values. This means that the total investment level of the RJV decreases with the number of partners. Similarly, Figure 8.2 illustrates the impact of speed of adjustment on the steady state cost levels for both the open-loop and the feedback equilibria. This figure illustrates that the investment levels in a

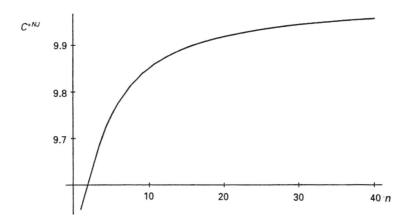

Figure 8.1 Steady state costs vs. number of RJV partners under feedback ($a = 100$, $\bar{c} = 10$, $\alpha = 0.1$, $r = 0.05$, $\mu = 40$)

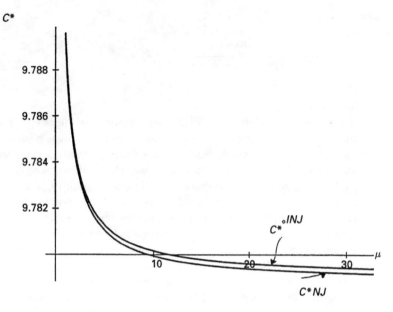

Figure 8.2 Steady state costs vs. speed of cost adjustment ($a = 100$, $\bar{c} = 10$, $\alpha = 0.1$, $r = 0.05$, $n = 6$)

feedback equilibrium exceed those of an open-loop equilibrium and that those investment levels increase as the speed of adjustment increases.

The steady state cost and investment levels are simplified in the 'limit game' in which costs instantaneously adjust as shown in the following corollary.

Corollary 2 *With instantaneous adjustment of costs the steady state investment levels approach*

$$\tilde{x}_i^{*NJ} = \frac{2a\alpha}{g(n+1)^2} - \frac{(\tilde{c}^{*NJ} + \frac{\bar{c}}{g\alpha})(1-g)}{\alpha(2n-1)}$$

and the corresponding steady state cost level approaches

$$\tilde{c}^{*NJ} = \frac{1}{1-\gamma}\left[\bar{c}\left(1+\frac{\gamma}{g}\right) - \frac{2an\alpha^2}{g(n+1)^2}\right]$$

where $g = \sqrt{1 - \frac{2(2n-1)\alpha^2}{(n+1)^2}}$ *and* $\gamma = \frac{n(1-g)}{2n-1}$

Proof

In the limiting case μw_3 approaches,

$$\frac{1-g}{2(2n-1)\alpha^2}$$

Also, μw_2 approaches,

$$\frac{1}{g}\left[\frac{\bar{c}(1-g)}{\alpha^2(2n-1)} - \frac{2a}{(n+1)^2}\right]$$

Substituting these expressions into those of Proposition 3 and taking the limit yields the expressions in the Corollary.

Q.E.D.

The following proposition compares the steady state cost level under the feedback regime to that of the open-loop case in the 'limit' game.

Proposition 4 *Given instantaneous adjustment of costs the steady state cost level is lower in the feedback equilibrium than in the open–loop equilibrium for the competitive RJV, i.e.,*

$$\tilde{c}^{*NJ} < \tilde{c}^{*olNJ}$$

Proof
See Appendix B.

As a consequence of the above proposition, the steady state investment level must be higher in the feedback equilibrium. The reason for the difference between the open-loop and feedback equilibrium investment levels lies in the formulation of the feedback strategy. Under the feedback regime firms take into consideration the optimal reaction to a change in the state variable (c) while in the open-loop regime firms do not. Since w_3 is positive, one can see from (8.13) that the steady state feedback level of investment, x^{*NJ}, is a decreasing function of c. Consequently, each firm will increase its investment when costs decrease. If a firm ignores this reaction by its rivals and simply makes the Nash assumption that its rivals' investments will remain at their present levels, then it will make its investment decision based solely on the effect on c of its own investment. If, however, it takes the competitors' reactions into account, it knows that as it increases investment and causes the cost to fall, its rivals will increase their investments. In this manner, the feedback mechanism creates an incentive to invest as a firm's increase in investment induces its RJV partners to increase their investments. As all members of the RJV take the others' optimal reaction to a cost change into account in the formulation of feedback strategies, the investment will be greater than in the equilibrium of the open-loop strategies where competitors' reactions to cost changes are ignored. This result, *vis-à-vis* the open-loop case, can be explained since with reversible commitments the potential of the rival firm(s) free riding is somewhat mitigated, hence the greater incentive to invest. The free-rider problem still exists, however, since no one firm internalizes the direct increase in other firms' profits on account of the lowering of costs. It should be noted that this effect is absent in static models – which is the setting for most existing analyses.

By conducting additional R&D independently of the RJV a firm may obtain a competitive advantage in marginal costs. Because of the positive feedback effect described above there would be less incentives for the RJV partners to conduct R&D outside of the RJV. In the feedback case, increased investment by a firm increases the investment by its RJV partners, thereby leveraging the initial investment. As a result, the investment in R&D within the RJV is more effective without commitment and the incentives to invest in additional R&D outside of the RJV are reduced.

8.5 WELFARE IMPLICATIONS

In the previous sections we have identified a possible tradeoff between dynamic and allocative efficiency. Kamien, Muller and Zang (1992) provide a welfare comparison between RJV competition and cartelized RJVs for a static model. They find that cartelized RJVs dominate RJV competition in terms of both producer and consumer surplus. The purpose of this section is to analyze the total welfare implications of RJV commitment, which can only be examined in a dynamic context. We define total welfare as the unweighted sum of producer and consumer surplus. We restrict ourselves to the analysis of equilibria in steady state for linear demand and Cournot competition.

With steady state cost levels the total welfare function is defined as

$$W^k(n) = n\left(1 + \frac{n}{2}\right)\left(\frac{a - c^k}{n + 1}\right)^2 - \frac{n}{2}[x_i^k]^2$$

where $k = {}^*olNJ$ refers to the open–loop competitive RJV, $k = {}^*olCJ$ the open–loop cartelized RJV, and $k = {}^*$ the feedback equilibrium.

With instantaneous cost adjustment these total welfare functions are compared in the following proposition.

Proposition 5 *Competitive RJVs under irreversible investment commitments yield lower welfare levels than do cartelized RJVs and competitive*

RJVs with feedback. That is,

$$\tilde{W}^{*olNJ} < \tilde{W}^{*CJ}, \quad and \quad \tilde{W}^{*olNJ} < \tilde{W}^{*NJ}$$

Proof

We first show that total welfare is greater in the regime with lower steady-state costs. In steady-state the change in costs are zero and hence the investment levels computed from the kinematic expression are given by

$$\tilde{x}^{*k} = \frac{(\bar{c} - \tilde{c}^{*k})}{\alpha n}$$

Substituting this steady state investment level into the total welfare function yields

$$\tilde{W}^{*k}(n) = n\left(1 + \frac{n}{2}\right)\left(\frac{a - \tilde{c}^{*k}}{n+1}\right)^2 - \frac{n}{2}\left[\frac{(\bar{c} - \tilde{c}^{*k})}{\alpha n}\right]^2$$

The difference in total welfare under two regimes is then

$$\tilde{W}^{*k}(n) - \tilde{W}^{*-k}(n) =$$

$$(\tilde{c}^{*-k} - \tilde{c}^{*k})\left\{n\frac{(1 + \frac{n}{2})}{(n+1)^2}[2a - (\tilde{c}^{*-k} + \tilde{c}^{*k})] + \frac{1}{2\alpha^2 n}[2\bar{c} - (\tilde{c}^{*-k} + \tilde{c}^{*k})]\right\}$$

Since $\bar{c} > \tilde{c}^{*k}$ $\forall k$ and $a > \bar{c}$ then $sign\ [\tilde{W}^{*k}(n) - \tilde{W}^{*-k}(n)] = sign$ $[\tilde{c}^{*-k} - \tilde{c}^{*k}]$. Therefore the regime with lower steady state costs results in a higher steady state total welfare. Since the open-loop competitive RJV realizes the highest cost level (by comparing (8.5) with (8.9) and by Proposition 4) the proposition follows.

Q.E.D.

The intuition for this result is that under the open–loop competitive RJV regime the free-rider problem and its associated disincentives to invest are severe enough to impair both the welfare of producers and consumers.

8.6 DISCUSSION OF RESULTS

In this chapter we consider research joint ventures which invest in cost-reducing R&D. The salient feature of our model is that these investments and cost reductions take place over time. We consider three different forms of RJV organization. First we examine the case in which each firm commits at the outset to a time pattern of R&D investment given the other firms' patterns of investment. Secondly, we analyze the case of all firms committing to identical patterns of R&D investment at the outset. Thirdly, we study the situation in which firms do not commit to investments at time zero but rather form decision rules which base the investment on the cost realization. In all cases the results of the cost-reducing R&D are disseminated to all RJV partners and the RJV members then compete in the product market with homogeneous products and identical marginal costs.

We find that shifting from a competitive RJV to a cooperative RJV under the open-loop regime results in increased investment in R&D, decreased costs and an improvement in total welfare. This result can be explained by the free-rider problem inherent in the set-up of the competitive RJV. Under RJV competition each firm decides on its own contribution to the RJV investment fund, yet all enjoy the same benefit, so there is a disincentive to invest. Thus the investment in cost-reducing R&D is less than socially desirable. As we move to a more flexible arrangement whereby firms periodically review their investment profile we find that the 'free rider' problem is somewhat mitigated and investment levels increase *vis-à-vis* the competitive open-loop case. This effect is absent in static models – which is the setting of most existing analyses.

This chapter provides comparisons of a number of contractual arrangements to support research joint ventures in the context of a dynamic model. There are many implications for public policy, and for the design of institutions to support the contractual arrangements forming the basis for RJVs in particular. First, we have found in a dynamic context that there is an economic rationale for policy-makers to support and encourage cartelized RJVs. With cartelization firms are free from the disincentives for investment originating in free-rider problems, thus costs are reduced and welfare is enhanced in the long run. Further, without the possibility of cartelized RJVs, we have found that society would gain from flexible contractual arrangements in which the R&D investments would be a function of the state of nature at each point in time. Consequently, society would not benefit from institutions making it possible to make credible commitments to investment programmes at the point in time when the RJV is formed, unless such commitments would also imply cartelized investments.

This analysis can be extended in a number of ways which could potentially change the policy implications. One interesting extension would be the inclusion of less than perfect spillovers between RJV partners. Another interesting possibility would be to allow the RJV partners to continue their R&D efforts outside the RJV. Also, our model includes no uncertainty concerning the future. This feature may enlarge the gain from commitments as firms do not benefit from delaying in order to make their decisions based on information with a higher degree of precision. Further, our model might overstate the gain from cartelization since we have complete information. Clearly, with incomplete information there might be incentive compatibility constraints which would reduce the possibilities of exploiting the gains from cartelization. Both of the qualifications mentioned here represent examples of promising directions for future research efforts.

APPENDIX A

Proof of Proposition 3

Given a linear demand function and Cournot competition the structure of the problem is Linear–Quadratic (LQ) which justifies the quadratic form of the value function given by

$$V^i(c) = w_1^i + w_2^i c + w_3^i c^2 \tag{8A.1}$$

which implies

$$\frac{\partial V^i(c)}{\partial c} = w_2^i + 2w_3^i c \tag{8A.2}$$

Substituting (8A.1) and (8A.2) into (8.12) bringing $rV^i(c)$ to the r.h.s. and thus setting the equation equal to zero implies that the constant term and all of the coefficients of the c-terms must be zero. This yields the system of equations

$$\left(n - \frac{1}{2}\right)\mu^2\alpha^2 w_2^{i2} + w_2^i\mu\bar{c} - rw_1^i + \frac{a^2}{(n+1)^2} = 0$$

$$2(2n-3)\mu^2\alpha^2 w_2^i w_3^i +$$

$$2\mu^2\alpha^2(w_2^j w_3^i + w_2^i w_3^j) - (\mu + r)w_2^i + 2\mu\bar{c}w_3^i - \frac{2a}{(n+1)^2} = 0 \tag{8A.3}$$

$$2(2n-3)\mu^2\alpha^2 w_3^{i2} + 4\mu^2\alpha^2 w_3^i w_3^j - (2\mu + r)w_3^i + \frac{1}{(n+1)^2} = 0 \tag{8A.4}$$

Subtracting the jth firm's counterpart of (8A.4) from (8A.4) yields

$$-(2\mu + r)(w_3^i - w_3^j) + 2\alpha^2\mu^2(w_3^{i2} - (2n-3)w_3^{j2}) + 4\alpha^2\mu^2(n-2)w_3^i w_3^j = 0$$

from which one can see that the intuitive solution for symmetric firms, $w_3^i = w_3^j$ satisfies the above condition. Similarly, subtracting the jth firm's counterpart to (8A.3) from equation (8A.3) yields the following condition

$$-(r + \mu)(w_2^i - w_2^j) +$$

$$2\alpha^2\mu^2(n-2)(w_2^j w_3^i + w_2^i w_3^j) + 2\mu\bar{c}(w_3^i - w_3^j) +$$

$$2\alpha^2\mu^2(w_2^i w_3^i - (2n-3)w_2^j w_3^j) = 0$$

Given $w_3^i = w_3^j$ one can again see that the intuitive solution, $w_2^i = w_2^j$, satisfies the above condition.

The solution to this differential equation has the following form

$$c(t) = c^{*NJ} + Ke^{-(1-2n\alpha^2 w_3)\mu^2 t}$$

where the initial condition $c(0) = \bar{c}$ implies that the constant of integration

$$K = \frac{\bar{c} + n\mu\alpha^2 w_2}{\mu(1 - 2n\alpha^2 w_3)}$$

Convergence requires that

$$w_3 < \frac{1}{2n\alpha^2}$$

which implies that μ is sufficiently large which motivates our assumption $\mu > 1$.

Q.E.D.

APPENDIX B

Proof of Proposition 4

The costs, $\tilde{c}*^{NJ}$, and $\tilde{c}*^{olNJ}$ can be written as

$$\tilde{c}^{*NJ} = \frac{(n+1)^2(g+\gamma)\bar{c} - 2an\alpha^2}{g(1-\gamma)(n+1)^2}$$

and

$$\tilde{c}^{*olNJ} = \frac{(n+1)^2\bar{c} - 2an\alpha^2}{(n+1)^2 - 2\alpha^2 n}$$

Since $g + \gamma \le 1$, the numerator of $\tilde{c}^{*NJ}$ is less than or equal to the numerator of $\tilde{c}^{*olNJ}$. When $\alpha = 0$, it follows that $g = 1$, $\gamma = 0$, and that the denominators of $\tilde{c}^{*NJ}$ and $\tilde{c}^{*olNJ}$ are equal. Since both denominators are decreasing functions of the parameter α we compare the rates of decrease. For the open–loop case this rate is given by

$$\frac{\partial \, Denominator \, [\tilde{c}^{*olNJ}]}{\partial \alpha} = -4\alpha n.$$

In the feedback case this rate is computed by

$$\frac{\partial \, Denominator \, [\tilde{c}^{*NJ}]}{\partial \alpha} = (n+1)^2 \left[\frac{\partial g}{\partial \alpha} - \frac{\partial (g\gamma)}{\partial \alpha} \right]$$

which, given that

$$\frac{\partial g}{\partial \alpha} = \frac{-1}{2g} \frac{4(2n-1)\alpha}{(n+1)^2}, \qquad \frac{\partial g\gamma}{\partial \alpha} = \frac{n}{2n-1} \left[\frac{\partial g}{\partial \alpha} - \frac{\partial g^2}{\partial \alpha} \right]$$

and

$$\frac{\partial g^2}{\partial \alpha} = \frac{-4(2n-1)\alpha}{(n+1)^2}$$

yields

$$\frac{\partial \, Denominator[\tilde{c}^{*NJ}]}{\partial \alpha} = \frac{-4\alpha(2gn-1)}{2g}$$

Since $\frac{2gn-1}{2g} < n$ the denominator of $\tilde{c}^{*NJ}$ decreases at a slower rate than the denominator of $\tilde{c}^{*olNJ}$ as α increases. Therefore, $Denominator[\tilde{c}^{*NJ}] > Denominator[\tilde{c}^{*olNJ}]$ and this combined with the relation between numerators implies the proposition.

Q.E.D.

Notes

*   R. Stenbacka gratefully acknowledges financial support from the Yrjö Jahnsson Foundation and the Academy of Finland. M. Tombak acknowledges support from NSERC grant number OGPO121438. We would like to thank Jim Brander, Barbara Spencer, Morten Hviid, Joanna Poyago-Theotoky and seminar participants at the University of Warwick, INSEAD University of Helsinki, ESEM in Uppsala, EEA in Helsinki and EARIE in Tel-Aviv for helpful comments.

1.   In order to find the feedback equilibrium we make use of the standard method described in Kamien and Schwartz (1991) and applied by Fershtman and Kamien (1987) and Reynolds (1987). This method however, does not solve for asymmetric steady-state equilibria. Obtaining such solutions may be possible by making use of the method developed by Tsutsui and Mino (1990). The method of Kamien and Schwartz suits our purposes as we focus on symmetric equilibria.

2.   Formally, we have two roots for w_3; however, as we shall see in the limiting case as $\mu \to \infty$ only the root reported here implies non-negative investment.

References

D'Aspremont, C. and A. Jacquemin (1988) 'Cooperative and Noncooperative R&D in Duopoly with Spillovers', *American Economic Review*, 78 (December) pp. 1133–7.

Enos, J. (1958) 'A Measure of the Rate of Technological Progress in the Petroleum Refining Industry', *Journal of Industrial Economics*, V (June).

Erdilek, A. (1989) 'Coalitions, Cooperative Research, and Technology Development in the Globalizations of the Semiconductor Industry', in *Cooperative R&D: The Industry–University–Government Relationship*, A. Link and G. Tassey (eds) (London: Kluwer Academic).

Fershtman, C. and M. Kamien (1987) 'Dynamic Duopolistic Competition with Sticky Prices', *Econometrica*, 55 (5) (September) pp. 1151–64.

Fishlow, A. (1966) 'Productivity and Technological Change in the Railroad Sector, 1840–1910', in *Output, Employment and Productivity in the U.S. after 1800*,

Studies in Income and Wealth No. 30 (New York: National Bureau of Economic Research)

Hollander, S. (1965) *The Sources of Increased Efficiency: The Study of Du Pont Rayon Plants* (Cambridge, MA.: MIT Press).

Hunter, L. (1949) *Steamboats on the Western Rivers* (Cambridge, MA.: Harvard University Press).

Kamien, M., E. Muller and I. Zang (1992) 'Research Joint Ventures and R&D Cartels', *American Economic Review*, vol. 82, no. 5 (December) pp. 1293–306.

Kamien, M. and N. Schwartz (1991) *Dynamic Optimization*, 2nd edn (Amsterdam, NL.: North-Holland).

Kamien, M. and I. Zang (1993) 'Competing Research Joint Ventures', *Journal of Economics and Management Strategy*, vol. 2, no. 1 (Spring) pp. 23–40.

Katz, M. and J. Ordover (1990) 'R&D Cooperation and Competition', *Brookings Papers on Economic Activity, Microeconomics*, pp. 137–191.

Reynolds, S. (1987) 'Capacity Investment, Preemption and Commitment in an Infinite Horizon Model', *International Economic Review*, 28 (1) (February) pp. 69–88.

Rosenberg, N. (1982) *Inside the Black Box: Technology and Economics* (Cambridge, UK: Cambridge University Press).

Schumpeter, J. (1975) *Capitalism, Socialism and Democracy* (New York: Harper & Row).

Tsutsui, S. and K. Mino (1990) 'Nonlinear Strategies in Dynamic Duopolistic Competition with Sticky Prices', *Journal of Economic Theory*, 52, pp. 136–61.

9 Dynamic Cooperation in R&D

Sumit Joshi and Nicholas S. Vonortas

9.1 INTRODUCTION

It has long been recognized that dynamic processes underlie technical advance.[1] Moreover, common economic parlance has it that firms in industries considered 'strategic' by developed countries engage in technology-based competition. What we have additionally come to realize, however, is that the structure of the 'technical enterprise' as a whole may be both more complex than earlier economic accounts led us believe and changing fast (e.g., Fusfeld, 1986, 1994). Gone is the conceptualization of the individual firm marshalling its own technological capabilities in order to gain over its rivals. The spread of technological capabilities around the world and the intensifying competition have obliged even the largest firms to look further and beyond their internal research and development (R&D) laboratories in order to keep up with the latest developments of rapidly evolving technologies as well as ease the excessive burden of exploding R&D expenditures on their budgets. Thus, in addition to direct competition, firms have increasingly utilized various forms of vertical and horizontal cooperative agreements (strategic alliances) to pursue their competitive objectives. Inter-firm strategic alliances are generally intended to achieve the following benefits (e.g., Gugler and Dunning, 1993; Vonortas and Safioleas, 1995):

1. Cost sharing for large investments and specific activities, such as R&D.
2. Access to complementary resources, such as synergistic technologies.
3. Acceleration of return on investments through a more rapid diffusion of assets.
4. Spreading of risks.
5. Efficiency creation through economies of scale, specialization and/or rationalization.

6. Creation of otherwise unattainable investment options.
7. Co-opting competition.

Since the beginning of the 1980s, there has been a flurry of interest among business analysts and economists in inter-firm cooperative agreements to create and diffuse technological knowledge.[2] This interest influenced policy promptly. It is no coincidence that the importance of inter-firm cooperative agreements in research and development (R&D) was formally acknowledged in the policies of major industrial forces on both sides of the Atlantic in the same year (1984). The National Cooperative Research Act, sanctioning research joint ventures (RJVs), was passed in the United States; and the first Framework Programme, setting the stage for government support of cooperative R&D, was established in the European Union. Individual country members of the European Union and Japan set in place similar policies even earlier (e.g., Vonortas, 1991).

This chapter is concerned with a subset of inter-firm cooperative agreements. It is concerned with research joint ventures (RJVs) defined as the formation of a new organization jointly controlled by member firms whose only purpose is to engage in research activities. The bulk of the chapter deals with the theory of horizontal RJVs. Its primary objective is to examine the effects of different organizational structures – for conducting R&D and exploiting the returns thereof – on firm incentives to invest in imperfectly appropriable and cumulative R&D. In a general dynamic framework, we attempt to generalize the results obtained in a relevant branch of the industrial organization literature where R&D and production have tended to be analyzed as atemporal multi-stage games often on the basis of parametric functional forms.

The recent theoretical literature in industrial organization dealing with technological competition can perhaps be divided into two major branches. One deals with the 'timing of innovation' where the winner of a technology (patent) race earns the right to some predetermined monopolistic return. Analysis in this tradition has focused on determining the number of firms that enter the race, the aggregate R&D investment and its distribution across firms and time as well as the effects of market power, technological advantage and technological uncertainty (Reinganum, 1989).

By nature, this approach relates more to discrete technological innovations and may not accommodate the technological competition we have in mind here. We envisage a framework where technologies are continuously upgraded but are not radically different from their predecessors, technological knowledge accumulates over time, and there is usually more than one winner in the sense that at least part of the outcome of R&D is communicated among the different players.

Such an approach links better to the other major branch of the literature which concentrates on the 'extent of innovation', usually approximated by the degree of cost reduction (e.g., Dasgupta and Stiglitz, 1980; Brander and Spencer, 1983; Spence, 1984) and, occasionally, product differentiation (e.g., Spence, 1976; Dixit and Stiglitz, 1977). Firms are assumed to invest in R&D in order to, for example, decrease costs and then compete in terms of prices or outputs in the product market.

One must mention here a large number of atemporal analyses (using multi-stage models) of both cooperative and non-cooperative industrial setups with imperfectly appropriable, cost-reducing R&D. They include, for example, Spence (1984), Katz (1986), d'Aspremont and Jacquemin (1988), de Bondt and Veugelers (1991), de Bondt, Slaets and Cassiman (1992), Kamien, Muller and Zang (1992), Suzumura (1992), de Bondt and Wu (1997), Simpson and Vonortas (1994), and Vonortas (1994).[3] These papers generally investigate the relative efficiencies of competition and cooperation in R&D in raising final output production and enhancing social welfare. A consistent finding has been that, by internalizing spillovers, RJVs tend to break the trade-off between externalities and R&D investment.[4] Thus, cooperation may improve firm incentives to undertake highly inappropriable R&D, especially when the product market is relatively not concentrated and/or independent and competing R&D is undertaken.

Unfortunately, the bulk of this literature has essentially been confined to static models of strategic competition – including multi-stage games – and 'naive' dynamic games, namely supergames (Shapiro, 1989). While multiple-stage models constitute a useful first approximation, they cannot substitute for explicitly dynamic treatments. Supergames, where a one-stage game is repeated either eternally or for a fixed period of times while nothing is getting carried from one period over to the next, have also been proven less than entirely satisfactory. For one, the basic assumption of repetition of an identical game disregards the fact that firms can learn from previous actions and that the value of variables such as technical knowledge accumulate over time. For another, supergame solutions have been very sensitive to the number of time periods assumed (finite versus infinite).

Interestingly, the relative paucity in terms of truly dynamic analyses of the effects of R&D investment in the 'extent of innovation' analytical tradition contrasts with the multiple attempts to construct explicitly dynamic models to investigate the strategic effects of production-cost-decreasing capital investment on market structure, entry, exit, production, prices and the like (e.g., Spence, 1979; Fudenberg and Tirole, 1983; and Gilbert and Harris,

1984).[5] Unfortunately, exact translation from one type of investment to the other is prevented by the fact that the output of R&D may not be entirely appropriable by the investor. That is, there is always the potential for positive externalities in technological knowledge which may clearly affect the incentives to engage in R&D in the first place. There is no such potential in the case of investment in physical capital. Other differences may include the way technological knowledge accumulates and depreciates over time.

The lack of formal dynamic economic analysis is particularly apparent when the subject of investigation involves organizational structures other than the stand-alone firm. In light of the proliferating inter-firm technology linkages and extensive joint venturing focusing on technology, this seems to be a rather serious omission. This void provided the incentive for our work.

This chapter takes a more theoretical view of inter-firm cooperation. It lays out and characterizes an explicitly dynamic framework that accommodates imperfectly appropriable and cumulative R&D to study the extent of innovation in technology-intensive industries – i.e., industries where firms engage in R&D in every time period. In every time period, a firm is assumed to take two decisions. First, it decides how much to invest in R&D. This is not a straightforward decision given that the research output is imperfectly appropriable allowing both firms in a duopoly to benefit in each time period from the current effort of one. The research output adds to the firm's intertemporal stock of technical knowledge. This knowledge determines the level of production costs. Second, the firm decides how much to produce on the basis of the achieved cost reduction.

Cooperation is studied under three different cooperative setups, translated here into assumptions concerning the objective function of the cooperative inter-firm arrangement. In the first arrangement (secretariat RJV), firms cooperate by jointly deciding the level of their R&D investments. They undertake, however, the research independently which means that they cannot internalize spillovers completely. Firms compete in the market for final goods. In the second arrangement (operating entity RJV), firms cooperate by both jointly deciding on the level of R&D investment and jointly performing the research. Still, they compete in the market for final goods. In the third arrangement (monopolistic RJV), not only do firms perform the research together but they also choose their outputs jointly.

We find that the R&D policy function (R&D expenses) is increasing in the stock of knowledge. Since the stock of knowledge is a non-decreasing sequence (no abrupt depreciation), aggregate R&D investment is increasing over time. In addition, the rate of spillovers is positively correlated to the aggregate investment in R&D. Note, for example, that an increase in the rate of spillovers, *ceteris paribus*, increases the stock of knowledge for both firms and, hence, the aggregate investment in R&D in each time period. Since an operating entity RJV can be construed in this framework as the limit of a secretariat RJV as the spillover parameter converges to unity, it is shown that the former type of RJV will maintain a higher level of aggregate investment in R&D than the latter in each time period. Moreover, for any initial stock of technical knowledge, the aggregate R&D investment under a monopolistic RJV is greater than the aggregate investment by an operating entity RJV. The rest of the chapter is divided into five sections. Section 9.2 introduces the basic model which underlines the three dynamic cooperative models of investment in R&D. Sections 9.3, 9.4 and 9.5 examine the secretariat RJV, the operating entity RJV and the monopolistic RJV respectively. Finally, section 9.6 discusses the policy implications (and limitations) of this work.

The proofs of all propositions, theorems, and corollaries are relegated to an Appendix.

9.2   THE MODEL

This section outlines the basic model which underlies the various dynamic cooperative models of investment in R&D. It is assumed that there are 2 firms, i and j. The competition between them takes place in discrete time, indexed by $t = 1, 2, \ldots$ There are two stages in each period $t \geq 1$. The following subsections elaborate on the two stages.

The Second Stage Game in Outputs

In Stage 1, the tuple (x_t^i, x_t^j) of R&D levels of the two firms is determined cooperatively. This tuple (x_t^i, x_t^j), via some technical production function, increases the stock of technological knowledge available in period t, (K_t^i, K_t^j). The stocks (K_t^i, K_t^j), in turn, determine the unit cost of production for each firm in period t. The description of the model and the assumptions are presented only for Firm i and are identical for Firm j. The cost function for Firm i in any period $t \geq 1$ is given by:

$$C^i \langle K_t^i, q_t^i \rangle \tag{9.1}$$

where q_t^i denotes the period-t output of Firm i. The cost of production of Firm i is a function of the accumulated stock of technical knowledge of Firm i up to time period t, K_t^i (in addition to being a function of output). Note that the cost function is *time-invariant* in the sense that it does not vary with t. The restrictions on the cost function are given by:

Assumption C:

(C.1) C_i is twice continuously differentiable on R_+^2.
(C.2) $C_K^i \equiv \partial C^i / \partial K^i < 0$: Total cost is strictly decreasing in K^i for any $q^i > 0$. Marginal cost, $C_q^i \equiv \partial C^i / \partial q^i$, is strictly decreasing in K^i for any $q^i > 0$.
(C.3) C_i is convex on R_+^2.

Given the cost of production, in Stage 2 the two firms play a Cournot quantity game in the product market where they face the time-invariant continuous inverse demands:

$$P^i \langle q_t^i, q_t^j \rangle, P^j \langle q_t^i, q_t^j \rangle, \quad P_i^i < 0, P_j^j < 0 \tag{9.2}$$

with $P_i^i \equiv \partial P^i / \partial q^i$. Taking as given the output of Firm j, the objective of Firm i is to maximize its second-stage profits by choosing its output q_t^i from some compact interval $[0, \eta_t]$ where $\eta_t < \infty$ and is allowed to depend on the tuple (K_t^i, K_t^j):

$$\pi_t^i = P^i \langle q_t^i, q_t^j \rangle q_t^i - C^i \langle K_t^i, q_t^i \rangle \tag{9.3}$$

Letting $R^i(q^i, q^j) \equiv P^i(q^i, q^j)q^i$ denote total revenue. It is assumed that:

Assumption R:

(R.1) R^i is twice continuously differentiable on R_+^2.
(R.2) $R_i^i > 0$ and $R_j^i < 0$. Own output has a positive effect and rival's output a negative impact on R^i.
(R.3) $R_{ij}^i < 0$: Output of the two firms are strategic substitutes.[6]
(R.4) R^i is strictly concave on R_+^2.

Assuming that Firm i's second stage maximization problem has an interior solution, the first order condition for this maximization is:

$$R_i^i \langle q_t^i, q_t^j \rangle - C_q^i \langle K_t^i, q_t^i \rangle = 0 \tag{9.4}$$

while the second order conditions require:

$$R_{ii}^i \langle q_t^i, q_t^j \rangle - C_{qq}^i \langle K_t^i, q_t^i \rangle < 0 \tag{9.5}$$

The above is satisfied as a consequence of (C.3) and (R.4).

The quantity game determines the Cournot–Nash equilibrium quantities produced by the two firms in period t as a function of the tuple (K_t^i, K_t^j):

$$q_t^i = Q^i \langle K_t^i, K_t^j \rangle, q_t^j = Q^j \langle K_t^i, K_t^j \rangle \tag{9.6}$$

The functions Q^i and Q^j are referred to as the *output reaction functions* for Firm i and Firm j respectively. Note that the functions Q^i and Q^j are time-stationary because the demand and cost functions do not vary with t. Total differentiation of the first order conditions given by (9.4) for Firm i and j and some manipulation yields:

$$\frac{dq_t^i}{dK_t^i} = \frac{1}{\Lambda^i}\left[R_{jj}^j - C_{qq}^j\right]C_{qK}^i, \quad \frac{dq_t^i}{dK_t^j} = -\frac{1}{\Lambda^i}R_{ij}^i C_{qk}^j \tag{9.7}$$

where we have defined:

$$C_{qk}^i \equiv \partial^2 C^i / \partial q^i \partial K^i, \quad \Lambda^i \equiv \langle R_{ii}^i - C_{qq}^i \rangle \langle R_{jj}^j - C_{qq}^j \rangle - R_{ij}^i R_{ij}^j$$

The Routh–Hurwicz stability condition dictates that $\Lambda^i > 0$ while $C_{qK}^i < 0$ from Assumption (**C.2**). It now follows from (9.5) and Assumption (**R.3**) that Q^i is strictly increasing in K_t^i and strictly decreasing in K_t^j.

The First Stage Profit Function

The analytical simplification afforded by the output reaction functions is that revenues and cost (and profits) in each period can be expressed solely in terms of accumulated technical knowledge (and hence R&D levels), the variables of strategic importance here. In particular, substituting the output reaction functions in (9.3) yields the time-invariant *net revenue function* $\mathfrak{R}^i : R_+^2 \to R_+$ which is defined as:

$$\mathfrak{R}^i \langle K_t^i, K_t^j \rangle = R^i \langle Q^i(K_t^i, K_t^j), Q^j(K_t^i, K_t^j) \rangle - C^i \langle K_t^i, Q^i(K_t^i, K_t^j) \rangle \tag{9.8}$$

From the Berge Maximum theorem (Debreu, 1959, ch. 1), the net revenue function is continuous on R_+^2. The first order properties of $\mathfrak{R}^i$ can be determined from the first order properties of the output reaction functions. Utilizing (9.4) and (9.7) along with Assumptions (**R.2**) and (**C.2**) yields:

$$\mathfrak{R}_i^i = R_j^i Q_i^j - C_K^i > 0 \tag{9.9}$$

$$\mathfrak{R}_j^i = R_j^i Q_j^j < 0 \tag{9.10}$$

The net revenue function is increasing in own stock of knowledge and decreasing in the rival firm's stock of knowledge. The second order property of the net revenue function, however, requires an additional second order restriction on the static output reaction function of the rival firm:

Assumption Q:
Q^j is convex in the tuple (K^i, K^j).

We are now in a position to prove:

Proposition 1 *Under Assumptions (C.3), (R.4) and (Q), the net revenue function is concave in (K^i, K^j).*

The derived (or induced) *first stage profit function* $\Pi^i : R_+^3 \to R_+$ is defined as follows:

$$\Pi^i\langle K_t^i, K_t^j, x_t^i \rangle = \Re^i\langle K_t^i, K_t^j \rangle - x_t^i \tag{9.11}$$

It is an immediate corollary of Proposition 1 that the profit function is concave in the 3-tuple (K^i, K^j, x^i). Further, it is continuous on R_+^3. The intertemporal profit of Firm i evaluated from time period $t = 1$ is:

$$\sum_{t=1}^{\infty} \delta^{t-1} \Pi^i \langle K_t^i, K_t^j, x_t^i \rangle \tag{9.12}$$

where δ is the discount rate. Similarly for Firm j. Since (9.11) is an identity in the 3-tuple (K^i, K^j, x^i), direct differentiation yields the first order properties of the profit function. In particular:

$$\Pi_i^i = \Re_i^i, \ \Pi_j^i = \Re_j^i, \ \Pi_x^i = \left(\Re_i^i \frac{\partial K^i}{\partial x^i} - 1 \right) + \Re_j^i \frac{\partial K^j}{\partial x^i}$$

From (9.9) and (9.10), Firm i's profit function is increasing in own stock of knowledge and decreasing in that of the rival firm. The effect on profits of an increase in R&D expenditure is, however, ambiguous. This is because such investment increases not only the stock of knowledge of Firm i but also, through the ensuing spillovers, the technical knowledge of Firm j. We will assume that the direct effect (given by the parenthetical term in the expression for Π_x^i) dominates the cross effect (given by the second term). It then follows that the last expression above is also non-negative ($\Pi_x^i \geq 0$).

The First Stage R&D Game

Given an initial stock of knowledge $K_0^i \in [0, \infty)$ in period 0, technical knowledge is assumed to evolve according to the law:

$$K_t^i = K_{t-1}^i + k_t^i, \ t \geq 1 \tag{9.13}$$

That is, the technical knowledge in period t, K_t^i, is composed of the technical knowledge accumulated in the previous $(t\text{-}1)$ periods, K_{t-1}^i, and the increment to this stock of technical knowledge in period t, K_t^i, through the R&D expenditures of *both* firms. The reason why k_t^i may depend on the R&D expenditure of Firm j is that the gains to technical knowledge to Firm j from its R&D activity may not be fully appropriable; hence some fraction of the technical knowledge created by Firm j's R&D expenditures may spill over to Firm i. Thus, in each period $t \geq 1$, the addition to Firm i's stock of knowledge is a function of its expenditure on R&D, x_t^i, the expenditure of Firm j on R&D, x_t^j, and the degree of spillover from Firm j, $\theta \in [0, 1]$. It is given by the time-stationary Spence (1984) production function:

$$k_t^i = x_t^i + \theta x_{t}^j, \ t = 1, 2, \ldots \tag{9.14}$$

According to this specification, Firm i's own R&D and the appropriated proportion of the rival firm's R&D are perfect substitutes. Identical considerations apply for Firm j.

Assume now that the two firms cooperate in an RJV. Given the tuple $(K_0{}^i, K_0{}^j)$ of initial stocks of knowledge and the tuple (h_0^i, h_0^j) of initial funds for R&D investment, the two firms maximize *joint* profits given by:

$$\sum\nolimits_{t=1}^{\infty} \delta^{t-1} \left[\Pi^i \langle K_t^i, K_t^j, x_t^i \rangle + \Pi^j \langle K_t^i, K_t^j, x_t^j \rangle \right] \tag{9.15}$$

over the set of all tuples $\{(x_t^i, x_t^j)\}$ satisfying the constraints:

$$x_1^m \leq h_0^m, \ x_t^m \leq \Pi^m \langle K_{t-1}^i, K_{t-1}^j, x_{t-1}^m \rangle, \ t \geq 2 \quad m = i, j \tag{9.16}$$

The jointly determined sequence of R&D expenditures for the two firms for which (9.15) achieves its supremum is called the *optimal* R&D sequence.[7] There are two possible types of RJVs depending on whether cooperation in R&D investment fully internalizes the spillover or not (secretariats and operating entities).[8] A third type, the monopolistic RJV, is basically an operating entity with the additional feature that firms also cooperate in production. These are now treated in the following sections.

9.3 THE SECRETARIAT RJV

In this case, while the two firms jointly determine their R&D expenditures, research takes place separately at the firms' own laboratories. Therefore, the spillovers are *not* internalized. This section first defines the value function and utilizes it to characterize the optimal R&D policy functions in terms of the Optimality, or Bellman, Equation of dynamic programming. The first and second order properties of the value function are then discussed. A new technique exploiting the Optimality Equation is developed to obtain results on the comparative dynamic properties of the optimal R&D policy functions. This method significantly generalizes the classical technique of totally differentiating first order conditions and combining them with stability conditions to conduct comparative dynamic analysis.

Value Function and the Optimal R&D Policy Functions

Consider the *value function* which is defined as:

$$\tilde{J}(K_0^i, K_0^j, h_0^i, h_0^j) = \underset{\{(x_t^i, x_t^j)\}}{Supr} \sum_{t=1}^{\infty} \delta^{t-1}\big[\Pi^i\langle K_t^i, K_t^j, x_t^i\rangle + \Pi^j\langle K_t^i, K_t^j, x_t^j\rangle\big] \tag{9.17}$$

where the supremum is over the set of all feasible R&D sequences satisfying (9.16). From standard dynamic programming arguments, the *Optimality Equation* can be written as:

$$\tilde{J}(K_0^i, K_0^j, h_0^i, h_0^j) = \underset{x^i \le h_0^i, x^j \le h_0^j}{Supr} \big[\{\Pi^i\langle K_1^i, K_1^j, x^i\rangle + \Pi^j\langle K_1^i, K_1^j, x^j\rangle\}\big]$$

$$+\big[\delta\tilde{J}\langle K_1^i, K_1^j, \Pi^i(K_1^i, K_1^j, x^i), \Pi^j(K_1^i, K_1^j, x^j)\rangle\big] \tag{9.18}$$

where $K_1^i = K_0^i + x^i + \theta x^j$ and $K_1^j = K_0^j + x^j + \theta x^i$. The argument in the first term of (9.18) describes the contribution of R&D to profits in the first period. The second term describes the contribution to profits in all subsequent periods. The profit function Π^m, $m = i, j$, is continuous from the continuity of the net revenue function, and the value function is continuous from the Berge Maximum theorem. Further, the interval $[0, h_0^m]$, $m = i, j$, is compact in R_+. Therefore, from a theorem of Weierstrass (Debreu, 1959, ch. 1), there exist values:

$$\tilde{x}^i\langle K_0^i, K_0^j, h_0^i, h_0^j, \theta\rangle, \quad \tilde{x}^j\langle K_0^i, K_0^j, h_0^i, h_0^j, \theta\rangle$$

which achieve the supremum in (9.18). These values are referred to as the *R&D policy functions*. They indicate the joint levels of R&D required for any initial 4-tuple of technological stocks and investment funds to maximize intertemporal profits. Substituting the R&D policy functions in (9.18) yields (suppressing the arguments of the policy functions for notational ease):

$$\tilde{J}\langle K_0^i, K_0^j, h_0^i, h_0^j \rangle = \Pi^i \langle K_0^i + \tilde{x}^i + \theta\tilde{x}^j, K_0^j + \tilde{x}^j + \theta\tilde{x}^i, \tilde{x}^i \rangle$$
$$+ \Pi^j \langle K_0^i + \tilde{x}^i + \theta\tilde{x}^j, K_0^j + \tilde{x}^j + \theta\tilde{x}^i, \tilde{x}^j \rangle$$
$$+ \delta\tilde{J}\langle K_0^i + \tilde{x}^i + \theta\tilde{x}^j, K_0^j + \tilde{x}^j + \theta\tilde{x}^i, \tilde{\Pi}_1^i, \tilde{\Pi}_1^j \rangle \qquad (9.19)$$

where the following notational shorthand has been used:

$$\tilde{\Pi}_1^i \equiv \Pi^i \langle K_0^i + \tilde{x}^i + \theta\tilde{x}^j, K_0^j + \tilde{x}^j + \theta\tilde{x}^i, \tilde{x}^i \rangle,$$
$$\tilde{\Pi}_1^j \equiv \Pi^j \langle K_0^i + \tilde{x}^i + \theta\tilde{x}^j, K_0^j + \tilde{x}^j + \theta\tilde{x}^i, \tilde{x}^j \rangle$$

Proposition 2 *The value function is increasing in K_0^i and h_0^i if $\Re_i^i + \Re_i^j \geq 0$. Further, under Assumptions C,R and Q, the value function is concave on* R_+^4.

Proposition 2 describes the first and second order properties of the value function. Regarding the former, the proof is provided for K_0^i and h_0^i and can similarly be transcribed for K_0^j and h_0^j. The proof shows that the value function is increasing with respect to these parameters if own-effects dominate cross-effects in the sense that an increase in a firm's stock of knowledge enhances its net revenue by a larger amount than the decrease in the net revenue of the rival. Clearly such a condition is required to provide an incentive to firms to form joint ventures for investment in R&D. The second order properties, on the other hand, rely crucially on the concavity properties of the net revenue function.

Characterization of the Optimal R&D Policy

The Optimality Equation is now used to analyze the comparative dynamic properties of the R&D policy functions. The method developed will require two assumptions. The first is the requirement that the profit function, Π^i, is *strictly concave* in x^i, its third argument, given (K^i, K^j). The second requirement is that if the technical knowledge of both firms increase by the same amount due to an increase in both firm's investment in R&D, then the increase in a firm's profit due to the increase in own technical knowledge outweights the decrease in profits due to the increase in the rival firm's technical knowledge. Once again, this assumption is in the spirit of requiring that direct effects are greater than cross effects. Formally:

Assumption P:

(**P.1**) *Given* (K^i, K^j), *the profit function* $\Pi^i(K^i, K^j, x^i)$ *is strictly concave in* x^i.

(**P.2**) *If* $(\overline{K}^i, \overline{K}^j, \overline{x}^i) \geq (\underline{K}^i, \underline{K}^j, \underline{x}^i)$, *with at least one of the coordinates satisfying the inequality strictly, then* $\Pi^i(\overline{K}^i, \overline{K}^j, \overline{x}^i) > \Pi^i(\underline{K}^i, \underline{K}^j, \underline{x}^i)$.

The notation and the methodology in this subsection is immensely simplified by considering the case of *symmetric* firms. Consequently, to present the proof as transparently as possible, the assumption of symmetry is maintained by assuming that both firms face the same demand and cost functions. Such symmetry implies that both firms have the same R&D policy function. We continue, however, to notationally distinguish between the two firms for clarity.

We consider first the monotonicity of the R&D policy function with respect to the initial stock of knowledge. It is assumed that both firms start with the same initial stock of technical knowledge, $\underline{K}_0 = K^i_0 = K^j_0$. We show that an increase in the initial stock of technical knowledge increases *aggregate* investment in R&D.

Theorem 1 *Under Assumptions C, R, Q and P, if* $\overline{K}_0 > \underline{K}_0$, *then:*

$$\tilde{x}^i(\overline{K}_0) + \tilde{x}^j(\overline{K}_0) \geq \tilde{x}^i(\underline{K}_0) + \tilde{x}^j(\underline{K}_0) \tag{9.20}$$

The monotonicity of the time-stationary R&D policy functions with respect to the initial stock of knowledge enables us to characterize the dynamic behavior of the entire *time path* of aggregate investment in R&D. That is, monotonicity of R&D with respect to stock of knowledge, coupled with the fact that the stock of knowledge is non-decreasing over time, allows us to derive monotonicity of R&D along the dimension of time. Given the initial stock of knowledge K_0, the time path of aggregate investment in R&D is given by:

$$y_t = \tilde{x}^i\langle K^i_{t-1}\rangle + \tilde{x}^j\langle K^j_{t-1}\rangle, \ t = 1, 2, \ldots \tag{9.21}$$

That is, aggregate R&D investment is a monotonically increasing function of time for a secretariat RJV.

The following two corollaries of Theorem 1 deal with the monotonicity properties of the R&D policy functions with respect to time and the spillover parameter respectively.

Corollary 1 *Under Assumptions C, R, Q and P,* $y_t \leq y_{t+1}$ *for all* $t \geq 1$.

Corollary 2 *Under Assumptions* **C, R, Q** *and* **P,** *if* $\bar{\theta} > \underline{\theta}$, *then:*

$$\tilde{x}^i(\bar{\theta}) + \tilde{x}^j(\bar{\theta}) \geq \tilde{x}^i(\underline{\theta}) + \tilde{x}^j(\underline{\theta}) \tag{9.22}$$

Note that an increase in the spillover rate, *ceteris paribus*, has the effect of increasing the stock of knowledge for both firms as in the case of an autonomous increase in initial stock of knowledge. Therefore, its impact can be studied as a corollary of Theorem 1. In particular, it is demonstrated that an increase in the rate of spillovers increases *aggregate* investment in R&D.

As a byproduct of Corollary 2, we get an interesting temporal *non-crossing* property of the time path of aggregate investment in R&D with respect to the spillover parameter. Letting $\{y_t(\theta)\}$ denote the time path of aggregate investment when the spillover parameter is θ, it follows from Corollary 2 that for all $t \geq 1$:

$$y_t(\bar{\theta}) \equiv \tilde{x}^i(\bar{\theta}) + \tilde{x}^j(\bar{\theta}) \geq \tilde{x}^i(\underline{\theta}) + \tilde{x}^j(\underline{\theta}) \equiv y_t(\underline{\theta})$$

Therefore, an increase in the rate of spillover ceteris paribus increases the stock of knowledge for both firms, and hence the aggregate investment in R&D, *in each time period.*

9.4 THE OPERATING ENTITY RJV

In this case, the two firms jointly determine their R&D expenditures and conduct the research together. The resulting information is fully and instantaneously disseminated to member firms. Therefore, the spillovers are *fully* internalized (i.e. $\theta = 1$). The value function for this case is given by:

$$\hat{J}\langle K_0^i, K_0^j, h_0^i, h_0^j \rangle = \underset{\{(x_t^i, x_t^j)\}}{Supr} \sum_{t=1}^{\infty} \delta^{t-1} \big[\Pi^i \langle K_t^i, K_t^j, x_t^i \rangle + \Pi^j \langle K_t^i, K_t^j, x_t^j \rangle \big] \tag{9.23}$$

where the supremum is over the set of all feasible R&D sequences satisfying (9.16), $K_t^i = K_{t-1}^i + x_t^i + x_t^j$ and $K_t^j = K_{t-1}^j + x_t^j + x_t^i$, $t \geq 1$. The *Optimality Equation* is:

$$\hat{J}(K_0^i, K_0^j, h_0^i, h_0^j) = \underset{x^i \leq h_0^i, x^j \leq h_0^j}{Supr} \big[\{ \Pi^i \langle K_1^i, K_1^j, x^i \rangle + \Pi^j \langle K_1^i, K_1^j, x^i \rangle \} \big]$$

$$+ \big[\delta \hat{J}\langle K_1^i, K_1^j, \Pi^i(K_1^i, K_1^j, x^i), \Pi^j(K_1^i, K_1^j, x^j) \rangle \big] \tag{9.24}$$

where $K_1^i = K_0^i + x^i + x^j$ and $K_1^j = K_0^j + x^j + x^i$. The supremum is achieved by the R&D policy functions:

$$\hat{x}^i\langle K_0^i, K_0^j, h_0^i, h_0^j\rangle, \quad \hat{x}^j\langle K_0^i, K_0^j, h_0^i, h_0^j\rangle$$

Substituting the R&D policy functions in the Optimality Equation yields:

$$\hat{J}\langle K_0^i, K_0^j, h_0^i, h_0^j\rangle = \Pi^i\langle K_0^i + \hat{x}^i + \hat{x}^j, K_0^j + \hat{x}^j + \hat{x}^i, \hat{x}^i\rangle$$
$$+ \Pi^j\langle K_0^i + \hat{x}^i + \hat{x}^j, K_0^j + \hat{x}^j + \hat{x}^i, \hat{x}^j\rangle$$
$$+ \delta\hat{J}\langle K_0^i + \hat{x}^i + \hat{x}^j, K_0^j + \hat{x}^j + \hat{x}^i, \hat{\Pi}_1^i, \hat{\Pi}_1^j\rangle$$

(9.25)

where the following notational shorthand has been used:

$$\hat{\Pi}_1^i \equiv \Pi^i\langle K_0^i + \hat{x}^i + \hat{x}^j, K_0^j + \hat{x}^j + \hat{x}^i, \hat{x}^i\rangle,$$
$$\hat{\Pi}_1^j \equiv \Pi^j\langle K_0^i + \hat{x}^i + \hat{x}^j, K_0^j + \hat{x}^j + \hat{x}^i, \hat{x}^j\rangle$$

Following the methods developed in section 9.3, it can be shown that the value function is increasing and concave in its arguments. Further, under the symmetry assumption, it can be shown that aggregate investment is increasing in the initial stocks of technical knowledge.

Comparison of Secretariat and Operating Entity RJV

An interesting issue, both from a theoretical as well as a policy point of view, is how complete internalization of the externality created by R&D affects aggregate investment in R&D. The following theorem is important in this regard. It shows how the operating entity RJV can be construed as the limit of secretariat RJVs as the spillover parameter θ converges to unity. Once again, the assumption of symmetric firms is made to facilitate the proof. Further, only the pertinent argument of each function is indicated.

Theorem 2 *Let $\langle \tilde{x}^i(\theta), \tilde{x}^j(\theta)\rangle$ be the R&D policy functions for a secretariat RJV with rate of spillover θ and let $\langle \hat{x}^i, \hat{x}^j\rangle$ be the R&D policy functions for the operating entity RJV. Then, under Assumptions C,R,Q and P*

$$\underset{\theta \to 1}{Lim}\, \langle \tilde{x}^i(\theta), \tilde{x}^j(\theta)\rangle = \langle \hat{x}^i, \hat{x}^j\rangle$$

With the above result, it is now possible to compare aggregate investment in R&D for secretariat and operating entity RJVs. In particular, the operating entity RJV maintains a higher level of aggregate investment in R&D in *each time period.* To see this, consider a secretariat RJV with rate of spillover $\underline{\theta}$. Note from Corollary 2 that if $\bar{\theta} > \underline{\theta}$, then:

$$\tilde{y}_t(\bar{\theta}) \equiv \tilde{x}^i(\bar{\theta}) + \tilde{x}^j(\bar{\theta}) \geq \tilde{x}^i(\underline{\theta}) + \tilde{x}^j(\underline{\theta}) \equiv \tilde{y}_t(\underline{\theta})$$

Therefore, letting $\bar{\theta} \to 1$ and using Theorem 2 it follows that for all $t \geq 1$:

$$\hat{y}_t \equiv \hat{x}^i + \hat{x}^j = \underset{\bar{\theta} \to 1}{Lim} \langle \tilde{x}^i(\bar{\theta}) + \tilde{x}^j(\bar{\theta}) \rangle \geq \tilde{x}^i(\underline{\theta}) + \tilde{x}^j(\underline{\theta}) \equiv \tilde{y}_t(\underline{\theta})$$

The internalization of the spillover reinforces investment in R&D.

9.5 THE MONOPOLISTIC RJV

In this case, not only do the firms choose their R&D levels together, internalizing all externalities, but also cooperate in the product market, choosing their outputs jointly. In contrast to the secretariat and operating entity RJV, the structure of the second stage game is different and, therefore, the profit function will be different. Recalling (9.3), the firms' problem is now given by:

$$\underset{q^i, \, q^j}{Supr}\left[\pi_t^i + \pi_t^j\right]$$

The solution to the firms' problem is given by the output functions:

$$q^i = \overset{\leftrightarrow}{Q}^i\langle K^i, K^j \rangle, q^j = \overset{\leftrightarrow}{Q}^j\langle K^i, K^j \rangle \tag{9.26}$$

Therefore, the profit function of a firm in the monopolistic RJV case is given by:

$$\overset{\leftrightarrow}{\Pi}^i \langle K^i, K^j, x^i \rangle \equiv R^i \langle \overset{\leftrightarrow}{Q}^i(K^i, K^j), \overset{\leftrightarrow}{Q}^j(K^i, K^j) \rangle - C^i(\overset{\leftrightarrow}{Q}^i, K^i) - x^i \tag{9.27}$$

The following proposition highlights the differences between the profit functions of the monopoly and operating entity RJV cases:

Proposition 3 *Under the same initial conditions given by* (K^i, K^j, x^i, x^j):

$$\overset{\leftrightarrow}{\Pi}\langle K^i, K^j, x^i, x^j \rangle \equiv \overset{\leftrightarrow}{\Pi}^i\langle K^i, K^j, x^i \rangle + \overset{\leftrightarrow}{\Pi}^j\langle K^i, K^j, x^j \rangle$$

$$\geq \Pi^i\langle K^i, K^j, x^i \rangle + \Pi^j\langle K^i, K^j, x^j \rangle$$

Consider once again for simplicity the symmetric case where the initial tuple is (K_0, h_0) and note that only the arguments of interest are indicated in the following. The value function for the monopolistic RJV is given by:

$$\overset{\leftrightarrow}{J}\langle K_0^i, K_0^j, h_0^i, h_0^j \rangle = \underset{\{(x_t^i, x_t^j)\}}{Supr} \sum_{t=1}^{\infty} \delta^{t-1} \Pi^m \langle K_t^i, K_t^j, x_t^i, x_t^j \rangle$$

(9.28)

where the supremum is over the set of R&D sequences satisfying (9.16). Once again, the Optimality Equation can be written as:

$$\overset{\leftrightarrow}{J}\langle K_0 \rangle = \underset{x^i \le h_0^i, x^j \le h_0^j}{Supr} \left[\Pi^m \langle K_1^i, K_1^j, x^i, x^j \rangle + \overset{\leftrightarrow}{J}\langle K_1^i, K_1^j \rangle \right]$$

(9.29)

where $K_1^i = K_0^i + x^i + x^j$ and $K_1^j = K_0^j + x^j + x^i$. The supremum is achieved by the R&D policy functions:

$$\overset{\leftrightarrow}{x}^i \langle K_0, h_0 \rangle, \overset{\leftrightarrow}{x}^j \langle K_0, h_0 \rangle$$

which, under the symmetry assumption are identical. Substituting the R&D policy functions in the Optimality Equation yields:

$$\overset{\leftrightarrow}{J}\langle K_0 \rangle = \overset{\leftrightarrow}{\Pi}\langle K_0 + \overset{\leftrightarrow}{x}^i + \overset{\leftrightarrow}{x}^j, K_0 + \overset{\leftrightarrow}{x}^j + \overset{\leftrightarrow}{x}^i, \overset{\leftrightarrow}{x}^i, \overset{\leftrightarrow}{x}^j \rangle$$
$$+ \delta \overset{\leftrightarrow}{J}\langle K_0 + \overset{\leftrightarrow}{x}^i + \overset{\leftrightarrow}{x}^j, K_0 + \overset{\leftrightarrow}{x}^j + \overset{\leftrightarrow}{x}^i \rangle$$

(9.30)

If the profit function satisfies Assumption **P**, then following the methods of Theorem 1 it can be demonstrated that the R&D policy function is increasing in the stock of knowledge. Combined with the fact that the stock of knowledge is a non-decreasing sequence, this implies that aggregate investment is increasing over time.

From Proposition 3, for any sequence $\{(x_t^i, x_t^j)\}$ from the given initial conditions:

$$\sum_{t=1}^{\infty} \delta^{t-1} \overset{\leftrightarrow}{\Pi}\langle K_t^i, K_t^j, x_t^i, x_t^j \rangle \ge \sum_{t=1}^{\infty} \delta^{t-1} \left[\Pi^i \langle K_t^i, K_t^j, x_t^i \rangle + \Pi^j \langle K_t^i, K_t^j, x_t^j \rangle \right]$$

Taking the supremum over the set of all R&D sequences then yields:

$$\overset{\leftrightarrow}{J}\langle K_0, h_0 \rangle \ge \hat{J}\langle K_0, h_0 \rangle$$

(9.31)

Since the two firms operate as a single entity, the notation can be simplified by dropping the distinction between the two firms. Now, combining with

Proposition 3, we have that for any initial stock of knowledge K_0 (and investment funds, h_0):

$$\overset{\leftrightarrow}{\Pi}\langle K_0 + 2\overset{\leftrightarrow}{x}\rangle + \overset{\leftrightarrow}{J}\langle K_0 + 2\overset{\leftrightarrow}{x}\rangle$$
$$-\left[\Pi^i\langle K_0 + \hat{x}^i + \hat{x}^j\rangle + \Pi^j\langle K_0 + \hat{x}^i + \hat{x}^j\rangle + \hat{J}\langle K_0 + \hat{x}^i + \hat{x}^j\rangle\right] \geq 0$$

(9.32)

where the superfluous arguments of the profit and value functions have been omitted.

Comparison of Monopolistic RJV and Operating Entity RJV

This section attempts to compare aggregate investment under a monopolistic RJV with that under the operating entity RJV. Unlike the comparison between secretariat and operating entity RJVs, the analysis here is complicated by the fact that the profit function and the value function for the two cases are different. However, an assumption which strengthens inequality (9.32) allows us to compare the time path of aggregate investment for the two cases. Let:

$$g\langle K_0\rangle \equiv \overset{\leftrightarrow}{J}\langle K_0\rangle - \hat{J}\langle K_0\rangle$$
$$= \overset{\leftrightarrow}{\Pi}\langle K_0 + 2\overset{\leftrightarrow}{x}\rangle + \overset{\leftrightarrow}{J}\langle K_0 + 2\overset{\leftrightarrow}{x}\rangle - \left[\Pi^i\langle K_0 + \hat{x}^i + \hat{x}^j\rangle + \right.$$
$$\left. \Pi^j\langle K_0 + \hat{x}^i + \hat{x}^j\rangle + \hat{J}\langle K_0 + \hat{x}^i + \hat{x}^j\rangle\right]$$

It is assumed that:

Assumption G:
$g:R_+ \to R_+$ *is a strictly increasing function on* R_+.

From inequality (9.32), we know that intertemporal profits are higher for a monopolistic RJV than an operating entity RJV for the same initial stock of knowledge. This is simply a consequence of joint optimization in both stages against non-cooperation in one of the stages. Assumption **G**, in addition, requires that the same increment in the initial stock of knowledge should increase the intertemporal profits of the monopolistic RJV by a strictly greater amount than for the operating entity RJV. With this assumption we can now prove:

Theorem 3   *Under Assumptions **C,R,Q** and Assumption **P** for the profit function* $\overset{\leftrightarrow}{\Pi}$, *for any initial stock of knowledge* K_0:

$$2\overset{\leftrightarrow}{x}\langle K_0\rangle \geq \hat{x}^i\langle K_0\rangle + \hat{x}^j\langle K_0\rangle$$

(9.33)

That is, for the same initial stock, the monopolistic RJV maintains a higher level of investment than the operating entity RJV.

It now follows as a corollary that the time path of aggregate investment for a monopolistic RJV dominates that for the operating entity RJV in each time period. To see this, note that:

$$\overset{\leftrightarrow}{y}_1 = 2\overset{\leftrightarrow}{x}\langle K_0 \rangle \geq \hat{x}^i\langle K_0 \rangle + \hat{x}^j\langle K_0 \rangle = \hat{y}_1$$

Therefore, recalling from Theorem 3 that the R&D policy function for the operating entity RJV is increasing in the stock of knowledge:

$$\overset{\leftrightarrow}{y}_2 = 2\overset{\leftrightarrow}{x}\langle \overset{\leftrightarrow}{K}_1 \rangle = 2\overset{\leftrightarrow}{x}\langle K_0 + 2\overset{\leftrightarrow}{x}(K_0) \rangle$$

$$\geq \hat{x}^i(\overset{\leftrightarrow}{K}_1) + \hat{x}^j(\overset{\leftrightarrow}{K}_1) \geq \hat{x}^i(\overset{\leftrightarrow}{K}_1^i) + \hat{x}^j(\overset{\leftrightarrow}{K}_1^j) = \hat{y}_2$$

where $\hat{K}_1^i = K_0 + \hat{x}^i(K_0) + \hat{x}^j(K_0)$. It follows by induction that $\overset{\leftrightarrow}{y}_t \geq \hat{y}_t$ for all $t \geq 1$.

9.6 REMARKS ON POLICY

The preceding analysis indicates that: (1) industries with high stocks of technological knowledge benefit from cooperative R&D; (2) the more leaky technical knowledge is in an industry, the better positioned an RJV is to undertake the relevant research; (3) closer cooperation leads to higher levels of aggregate R&D. In addition, however, one may wonder how the results of this analysis contribute to the more general policy debate concerning RJVs. Our reading of the relevant policy literature suggests that the main concerns with respect to inter-firm cooperation in R&D have essentially been the following three:

1. How do competition and cooperation in R&D compare in terms of technological progress?
2. Do RJVs help getting us closer to the socially optimal level of R&D expenditure?
3. Should we worry about the extent of permissible collaboration?

The first question has been the main focus of the static multi-stage model appraisals in the 'extent of innovation' approach. We cannot answer this question directly on the basis of the results in this chapter alone, given that we have examined only cooperative setups. It should be noted that the analytical framework used in this chapter may not automatically support analysis of non-cooperative strategic interaction given that its simultaneous-move nature misses the significant action/reaction aspect of independent decisions concerning their R&D investments. However, in a related paper, Joshi and Vonortas (1995) have set up an alternate-move non-cooperative game where firms can condition their R&D investment in any time period t on the observed R&D level of the rival firm from period $t - 1$. Both firms can adjust their output levels in every time period. The rest of the model characteristics are basically the same to those here.

Comparing the results of a dynamic alternative-move game (resulting in Markov dynamic reaction functions for non-cooperative R&D expenditures) and a dynamic simultaneous-move game is anything but simple. Joshi and Vonortas (1995), however, develop a sufficient condition allowing a comparison of the infinite horizon non-cooperative model with the dynamic model of a secretariat RJV. Essentially, this condition requires that an increment in the stock of knowledge of any firm increases the maximal intertemporal profits of the RJV by a greater amount than that of the individual firm. Under this condition, the basic result of the atemporal multistage literature is partially recovered: for the same initial conditions, and by fixing the R&D of the rival firm at the cooperative level dictated by the infinite-horizon RJV, the non-cooperative dynamic reaction function calls for a smaller level of investment in highly inappropriable R&D than that in the cooperative case.

The combination of the above with the analysis in this chapter suggests that the basic result in the static multi-stage model literature carries over to a general dynamic appraisal. The answer to the first question, thus, seems to be that cooperation leads to higher levels of cost-saving R&D expenditure under certain assumptions. As indicated here, these assumptions include fairly standard requirements on the functional forms of the cost, revenue and profit functions. Important were the assumptions that the R&D efforts of the two firms are substitutes, firms compete in outputs, there is no market and technological uncertainty, and there is no abrupt depreciation of the stock of technological knowledge. Finally, the results depend on the assumption that there is no competition outside the joint venture.[9]

We can also say something indirectly with respect to the second question raised at the beginning of this section. In particular, the proposition that oligopolistic firms acting independently would produce suboptimal levels of imperfectly appropriable R&D hardly needs a formal proof at this point (see, e.g., Simpson and Vonortas, 1994).[10] If suboptimality in non-cooperative R&D expenditures carries over to dynamic environments – as we suspect it does – then our analysis suggests a positive answer, given that RJVs have been found to create incentives for raising R&D expenditures over those that would have materialized in a non-cooperative regime.[11]

Our chapter definitely contributes to the third question raised above. Indeed, more extensive cooperation results in higher levels of R&D expenditures and lower production costs. While this outcome depends on our assumptions, we believe that it is a fairly general one given that this has tended to be the case in most of the related theoretical literature. This is an important point, as can be attested from the recent successful bid in the US to extend the provisions of the NCRA to cooperation in downstream activities such as final product prototyping and production as long as the research leading to this product was undertaken collectively.[12]

There were essentially two arguments in favour of the extension. The first (traditional IO) argument was that firm incentives to collaborate in 'pre-competitive' research were being hampered ex ante by restricting the collective exploitation of the research outcome downstream. It has been shown, for example, that head-on competition in development and production between potential co-venturers lowers their ex ante incentive to cooperate in research because they expect the benefits to flow to consumers (e.g., Katz and Ordover, 1990; Simpson and Vonortas, 1994). It was thus argued that 'to the extent that unbridled downstream competition dissipates rents from successful R&D efforts, it may be necessary to allow RJV participants some restraints on ex post competition' (Ordover and Baumol, 1988, p. 30).

The second (non-traditional) argument in favour of NCRA's extension was based on the lack of any detail concerning the process of technological innovation in different industrial sectors in the original version of the NCRA. Being a product of a basically 'linear model of innovation', it was argued, the NCRA was an inappropriate tool for effective policy. By differentiating between different kinds of research and between R&D and production, the legislation implicity contended that there is a clear demarcation between pre-competitive research and development research, on the one hand, and R&D and production, on the other, and that pre-competitive research precedes development and development precedes production. Instead, it was argued, there is often no clear division between pre-competitive research, development and production activities in terms of when each activity occurs and how information flows (e.g., Jorde and Teece, 1990, 1992). In sectors where tight feedback mechanisms operate quickly and efficiently and information flows back and forth, different stages of research, product prototyping and production, vertical as well as horizontal inter-firm linkages often assume important roles in leveraging the in-house technical capabilities of a firm. Thus, policies that do not recognize the nature of innovation in contemporary industrial environments were doomed to fail. The original NCRA was said to be one such policy.

The combination of the traditional and non-traditional arguments made a strong case. The bid was successful, and amendments, extending the NCRA to cover R&D and production, were turned into public law in 1993. Our analysis would seem to support these views. However, the issue should definitely be relegated to empirical verification (which is sorely lacking).

Let us close by saying that the debate over the proper regulation of RJVs could benefit considerably by the introduction of explicit considerations of the actual invention/innovation process in industry. In the presence of significant variations between different industrial sectors, one would expect to go about arguing sector by sector. Why should the repercussions of more extensive collaboration in continuous process industries (say pharmaceuticals or chemicals) be expected to be similar to those in batch processing and assembly industries (say automobiles and computers)? We suspect that often economists have over-reached by attempting to generalize the policy implications of inherently limited theoretical models. Taking this work of ours as an example, one could see useful offshoots utilizing different functional forms for the production function of knowledge, the cost function, the revenue function, and the assumed form of downstream competition to accommodate the operating needs of various industrial settings. Then, one may be more confident to talk about the policy implications of theory.

APPENDIX

Proof of Proposition 1

Consider tuples $(K^i(n), K^j(n))$, $n = 1,2$, and note that:

$$Q^i\langle K^i(n), K^j(n)\rangle \in argmax \{R^i\langle q^i, Q^j(K^i(n), K^j(n))\rangle - C^i\langle K^i(n), q^i\rangle\}, n = 1, 2$$

For any $\epsilon > 0$, there exists output levels, $q^i(n)$, $n = 1,2$, such that:

$$\mathfrak{R}^i\langle K^i(n), K^j(n)\rangle \leq R^i\langle q^i(n), Q^j(K^i(n), K^j(n))\rangle - C^i\langle K^i(n), q^i(n)\rangle + \epsilon$$

(9A.1)

Let $0 < \lambda < 1$. Given any $z(1), z(2)$, we shall use $z(\lambda)$ to denote the following:

$$z(\lambda) \equiv \lambda z(1) + (1 - \lambda)z(2)$$ (9A.2)

and we shall let $Q^j(\lambda) \equiv \lambda Q^j\langle K^i(1), K^j(1)\rangle + (1 - \lambda)Q^j\langle K^i(2), K^j(2)\rangle$. It now follows that

$$\mathfrak{R}^i\langle K^i(\lambda), K^j(\lambda)\rangle \geq R^i\langle q^i(\lambda), Q^j(K^i(\lambda), K^j(\lambda))\rangle - C^i\langle K^i(\lambda), q^i(\lambda)\rangle$$
$$\geq R^i\langle q^i(\lambda), Q^j(\lambda)\rangle - C^i\langle K^i(\lambda), q^i(\lambda)\rangle$$
$$> \lambda[R^i\langle q^i(1), q^j(1)\rangle - C^i\langle K^i(1), q^i(1)\rangle]$$

$$+ (1 - \lambda)\left[R^i\langle q^i(2), q^j(2)\rangle - C^i\langle K^i(2), q^i(2)\rangle\right]$$

$$\geq \lambda\Re^i\langle K^i(1), K^j(1)\rangle + (1 - \lambda)\Re^i\langle K^i(2), K^j(2)\rangle - \epsilon \quad (9A.3)$$

The first inequality follows from the definition of $\Re^i$; the second inequality is a result of Assumption **Q** and (9.9); the third inequality follows from Assumption (**R.**4); the last inequality follows from (9A.1). Since (9A.3) holds for all ϵ, letting $\epsilon \to 0$ yields the concavity of $\Re^i$. ∎

Proof of Proposition 2

First of all note that under the stated assumptions, $\Pi_i^i + \Pi_i^j \geq 0$. Recall that $\overline{K}_0^i \geq K_0^i$ and $\tilde{x}^i, \tilde{x}^j$ are the optimal R&D policy functions. For $n = i, j$, let:

$$\tilde{x}_1^n = \tilde{x}^n\langle K_0^i, K_0^j, h_0^i, h_0^j\rangle, \quad \tilde{x}_t^n = \tilde{x}^n\langle K_{t-1}^i, K_{t-1}^j, \tilde{\Pi}_{t-1}^i, \tilde{\Pi}_{t-1}^j\rangle, \quad t \geq 2$$

Assume $\overline{K}_0^i \geq \overline{K}_0^i$ and let:

$$\overline{K}_t^i = \overline{K}_{t-1}^i + \tilde{x}_t^i + \theta^i \tilde{x}_t^j, \quad t \geq 1$$

Indicating only the argument of the value function which is relevant:

$$\tilde{J}\langle\overline{K}_0^i\rangle \geq \sum_{t=1}^{\infty} \delta^{t-1}\left[\Pi^i\langle\overline{K}_t^i, K_t^j, \tilde{x}_t^i\rangle + \Pi^j\langle\overline{K}_t^i, K_t^j, \tilde{x}_t^j\rangle\right] \quad \text{from definition of } \tilde{J}$$

$$\geq \sum_{t=1}^{\infty} \delta^{t-1}\left[\Pi^i\langle K_t^i, K_t^j, \tilde{x}_t^i\rangle + \Pi^j\langle K_t^i, K_t^j, \tilde{x}_t^j\rangle\right] \quad \text{since } \Pi_i^i + \Pi_i^j \geq 0$$

$$= \tilde{J}\langle K_0^i\rangle \quad \text{from (9.19)}$$

The proof for h_0^i is identical.

Consider any $\epsilon > 0$. Given any initial 4-tuple $(K_0^i(n), K_0^j(n), h_0^i(n), h_0^j(n))$, there exists a sequence $\{x_t^i(n), x_t^j(n)\}$ of R&D investments, $\{K_t^i(n), K_t^j(n)\}$ of stocks of technological knowledge, $n = 1,2$, such that:

$$\tilde{J}\langle K_0^i(n), K_0^j(n), h_0^i(n), h_0^j(n)\rangle \leq \sum_{t=1}^{\infty} \delta^{t-1}\left[\Pi^i\langle K_t^i(n), K_t^j(n), x_t^i(n)\rangle + \right.$$
$$\left. \Pi^j\langle K_t^i(n), K_t^j(n), x_t^j(n)\rangle\right] + \epsilon$$

For any $0 < \lambda < 1$, consider the sequence $\{x_t^i(\lambda), x_t^j(\lambda)\}$ where $x_t^m(\lambda) = \lambda x_t^m(1) + (1 - \lambda)x_t^m(2)$, $m = i, j$, and the initial state $(K_0^i(\lambda), K_0^j(\lambda), h_0^i(\lambda), h_0^j(\lambda))$ where $K_0^i(\lambda) = \lambda K_0^i(1) + (1 - \lambda)K_0^i(2)$ etc. Let $\{\overline{K}_t^i, \overline{K}_t^j\}$ be the sequence of stocks of technological knowledge generated by $\{x_t^i(\lambda), x_t^j(\lambda)\}$ from the initial 4-tuple $(K^i_0(\lambda), K^j_0(\lambda), h^i_0(\lambda), h^j_0(\lambda))$. Given the linearity of the Spence production function, it follows that:

$$\overline{K}_1^i = K_0^i(\lambda) + \langle x_1^i(\lambda) + \theta^i x_1^j(\lambda)\rangle$$
$$= \lambda\left[K_0^i(1) + x_1^i(1) + \theta^i x_1^j(1)\right] + (1 - \lambda)\left[K_0^i(2) + x_1^i(2) + \theta^i x_1^j(2)\right]$$
$$= K_1^i(\lambda)$$

It now follows by induction that for all $t > 1$:

$$\overline{K}_t^i = K_{t-1}^i(\lambda) + x_t^i(\lambda) + \theta^i x_t^j(\lambda) \equiv K_t^i(\lambda)$$

Similarly, $\overline{K}^j_t = K^j_t(\lambda)$ for all $t \geq 1$. Then, using the definition of the value function:

$$\tilde{J}\langle K^i_0(\lambda), K^j_0(\lambda), h^i_0(\lambda), h^j_0(\lambda)\rangle \geq \sum_{t=1}^{\infty} \delta^{t-1}\big[\Pi^i\langle \overline{K}^i_t, \overline{K}^j_t, x^i_t(\lambda)\rangle +$$

$$\Pi^j\langle \overline{K}^i_t, \overline{K}^j_t, x^j_t(\lambda)\rangle\big]$$

$$= \sum_{t=1}^{\infty} \delta^{t-1}\big[\Pi^i\langle K^i_t(\lambda), K^j_t(\lambda), x^i_t(\lambda)\rangle + \Pi^j\langle K^i_t(\lambda), K^j_t(\lambda), x^j_t(\lambda)\rangle\big]$$

$$\geq \lambda \sum_{t=1}^{\infty} \delta^{t-1}\big[\Pi^i\langle K^i_t(1), K^j_t(1), x^i_t(1)\rangle + \Pi^j\langle K^i_t(1), K^j_t(1), x^j_t(1)\rangle\big]$$

$$+ (1-\lambda)\sum_{t=1}^{\infty} \delta^{t-1}\big[\Pi^i\langle K^i_t(2), K^j_t(2), x^i_t(2)\rangle + \Pi^j\langle K^i_t(2), K^j_t(2), x^j_t(2)\rangle\big]$$

$$\geq \lambda \tilde{J}\langle K^i_0(1), K^j_0(1), h^i_0(1), h^j_0(1)\rangle$$

$$+ (1-\lambda)\tilde{J}\langle K^i_0(2), K^j_0(2), h^i_0(2), h^j_0(2)\rangle - \epsilon$$

Since ϵ was chosen arbitrarily, the concavity of the value function follows. ∎

Proof of Theorem 1

To ease the notation, we only indicate those arguments of a function which are relevant to the proof. Suppose to the contrary that:

$$\bar{x}^i + \bar{x}^j \equiv \tilde{x}^i(\overline{K}_0) + \tilde{x}^j(\overline{K}_0) < \tilde{x}^i(\underline{K}_0) + \tilde{x}^j(\underline{K}_0) \equiv \underline{x}^i + \underline{x}^j$$

Appealing to symmetry, let:

$$\overline{K}^i_1 = \overline{K}_0 + \bar{x}^i_1 + \theta\bar{x}^j_1 = \overline{K}_0 + \bar{x}^j_1 + \theta\bar{x}^i_1 = \overline{K}^j_1$$

$$\underline{K}^i_1 = \underline{K}_0 + \underline{x}^i_1 + \theta\underline{x}^j_1 = \underline{K}_0 + \underline{x}^j_1 + \theta\underline{x}^i_1 = \underline{K}^j_1$$

The proof is now divided into the following two cases:

Case 1: $\underline{K}^i_1 = \underline{K}_0 + \underline{x}^i + \theta\underline{x}^j > \overline{K}_0 + \bar{x}^i + \theta\bar{x}^j = \overline{K}^i_1$

Define the tuples $(\check{x}^i, \check{x}^j)$ and $(\mathring{x}^i, \mathring{x}^j)$ such that:

$$\underline{K}_0 + \check{x}^i + \theta\check{x}^j = \overline{K}^i_1 \tag{9A.4}$$

$$\overline{K}_0 + \mathring{x}^i + \theta\mathring{x}^j = \underline{K}^i_j \tag{9A.5}$$

Adding (9A.4) and (9A.5) it follows that:

$$\langle \check{x}^i + \theta\check{x}^j\rangle + \langle \mathring{x}^i + \theta\mathring{x}^j\rangle = \langle \overline{K}^i_1 - \overline{K}_0\rangle + \langle \underline{K}^i_1 - \underline{K}_0\rangle$$
$$= \langle \bar{x}^i + \theta\bar{x}^j\rangle + \langle \underline{x}^i + \theta\underline{x}^j\rangle \tag{9A.6}$$

There exists a $0 < \lambda < 1$ such that:

$$\check{x}^m = \lambda\bar{x}^m + (1-\lambda)\underline{x}^m, \quad m = 1, j \tag{9A.7}$$

Combining (9A.6) and (9A.7) then yields:

$$\mathring{x}^m = (1-\lambda)\bar{x}^m + \lambda\underline{x}^m, \quad m = i, j \tag{9A.8}$$

From the Principle of Optimality:

$$\Pi^i\langle \overline{K}{}^i_1, \overline{K}{}^j_1, \bar{x}^i\rangle + \Pi^j\langle \overline{K}{}^i_1, \overline{K}{}^j_1, \bar{x}^j\rangle + \tilde{J}\langle \overline{K}{}^i_1, \overline{K}{}^j_1\rangle$$

$$\geq \Pi^i\langle \underline{K}{}^i_1, \underline{K}{}^j_1, \hat{x}^i\rangle + \Pi^j\langle \underline{K}{}^i_1, \underline{K}{}^j_1, \hat{x}^j\rangle + \tilde{J}\langle \underline{K}{}^i_1, \underline{K}{}^j_1\rangle \qquad (9A.9)$$

The inequality in (9A.9) is a consequence of the fact that the R&D investment levels $(\hat{x}^i, \hat{x}^j)$ is not optimal from the initial stock $\overline{K}_0$. On the other hand:

$$\Pi^i\langle \underline{K}{}^i_1, \underline{K}{}^j_1, \underline{x}^i\rangle + \Pi^j\langle \underline{K}{}^i_1, K^j_1, \underline{x}^j\rangle + \tilde{J}\langle \underline{K}{}^i_1, \underline{K}{}^j_1\rangle$$

$$> \Pi^i\langle \underline{K}{}^i_1, \underline{K}{}^j_1, \check{x}^i\rangle + \Pi^j\langle \underline{K}{}^i_1, \underline{K}{}^j_1, \check{x}^j\rangle + \tilde{J}\langle \underline{K}{}^i_1, \underline{K}{}^j_1\rangle$$

$$\geq \Pi^i\langle \underline{K}{}^i_1, \underline{K}{}^j_1, \check{x}^i\rangle + \Pi^j\langle \underline{K}{}^i_1, \underline{K}{}^j_1, \check{x}^j\rangle + \tilde{J}\langle \overline{K}{}^i_1, \overline{K}{}^j_1\rangle \qquad (9A.10)$$

where the first inequality is a consequence of Assumption **P** and the second follows from Proposition 2 that the value function is increasing. Adding (9A.9) and (9A.10) yields:

$$\Pi^i\langle \overline{K}{}^i_1, \overline{K}{}^j_1, \bar{x}^i\rangle + \Pi^j\langle \overline{K}{}^i_1, \overline{K}{}^j_1, \bar{x}^j\rangle + \Pi^i\langle \underline{K}{}^i_1, \underline{K}{}^j_1, \underline{x}^i\rangle + \Pi^j\langle \underline{K}{}^i_1, \underline{K}{}^j_1, \underline{x}^j\rangle$$

$$> \Pi^i\langle \underline{K}{}^i_1, K^j_1, \hat{x}^i\rangle + \Pi^j\langle \underline{K}{}^i_1, \underline{K}{}^j_1, \hat{x}^j\rangle + \Pi^i\langle \underline{K}{}^i_1, \underline{K}{}^j_1, \check{x}^i\rangle + \Pi^j\langle \underline{K}{}^i_1, \underline{K}{}^j_1, \check{x}^j\rangle \qquad (9A.11)$$

From the strict concavity of the profit function in its third argument (Assumption **P**):

$$\Pi^i\langle K^i_1, K^j_1, \hat{x}^i\rangle + \Pi^j\langle K^i_1, K^j_1, \hat{x}^j\rangle > (1-\lambda)[\Pi^i\langle \underline{K}{}^i_1, \underline{K}{}^j_1, \bar{x}^i\rangle + \\ \Pi^j\langle \underline{K}{}^i_1, \underline{K}{}^j_1, \bar{x}^j\rangle]\lambda + [\Pi^i\langle \underline{K}{}^i_1, \underline{K}{}^j_1, \underline{x}^i\rangle + \Pi^j\langle \underline{K}{}^i_1, \underline{K}{}^j_1, \underline{x}^j\rangle] \qquad (9A.12)$$

Recall (9A.5). Using the fact that $\hat{x}^m > \bar{x}^m$, $m = i,j$, and Assumption **P** yields:

$$\Pi^i\langle \underline{K}{}^i_1, \underline{K}{}^j_1, \bar{x}^i\rangle = \Pi^i\langle \overline{K}_0 + \hat{x}^i + \theta\hat{x}^j, \overline{K}_0 + \hat{x}^j + \theta\hat{x}^i, \bar{x}^i\rangle$$

$$\geq \Pi^i\langle \overline{K}{}^i_1, \overline{K}{}^j_1, \bar{x}^i\rangle$$

and similarly for Π^j. Inequality (9A.12) now becomes:

$$\Pi^i\langle \underline{K}{}^i_1, \underline{K}{}^j_1, \hat{x}^i\rangle + \Pi^j\langle \underline{K}{}^i_1, \underline{K}{}^j_1, \hat{x}^j\rangle > (1-\lambda)[\Pi^i\langle \overline{K}{}^i_1, \overline{K}{}^j_1, \bar{x}^i\rangle + \Pi^j\langle \overline{K}{}^i_1, \overline{K}{}^j_1, \bar{x}^j\rangle]$$

$$+ \lambda[\Pi^i\langle \underline{K}{}^i_1, \underline{K}{}^j_1, \underline{x}^i\rangle + \Pi^j\langle \underline{K}{}^i_1, \underline{K}{}^j_1, \underline{x}^j\rangle] \qquad (9A.13)$$

An identical argument yields:

$$\Pi^i\langle \underline{K}{}^i_1, \underline{K}{}^j_1, \check{x}^i\rangle + \Pi^j\langle \underline{K}{}^i_1, \underline{K}{}^j_1, \check{x}^j\rangle > \lambda[\Pi^i\langle \overline{K}{}^i_1, \overline{K}{}^j_1, \bar{x}^i\rangle + \Pi^j\langle \overline{K}{}^i_1, \overline{K}{}^j_1, \bar{x}^j\rangle]$$

$$+ (1-\lambda)[\Pi^i\langle \underline{K}{}^i_1, \underline{K}{}^j_1, \underline{x}^i\rangle + \Pi^j\langle \underline{K}{}^i_1, \underline{K}{}^j_1, \underline{x}^j\rangle] \qquad (9A.14)$$

Adding (9A.13) and (9A.14) yields:

$$\Pi^i\langle \underline{K}^i_1, \underline{K}^j_1, \check{x}^i\rangle + \Pi^j\langle \underline{K}^i_1, \underline{K}^j_1, \check{x}^j\rangle + \Pi^i\langle \underline{K}^i_1, \underline{K}^j_1, \check{x}^i\rangle + \Pi^j\langle \underline{K}^i_1, \underline{K}^j_1, \check{x}^j\rangle$$
$$> \Pi^i\langle \overline{K}^i_1, \overline{K}^j_1, \bar{x}^i\rangle + \Pi^j\langle \overline{K}^i_1, \overline{K}^j_1, \bar{x}^j\rangle + \Pi^i\langle \underline{K}^i_1, \underline{K}^j_1, \underline{x}^i\rangle + \Pi^j\langle \underline{K}^i_1, \underline{K}^j_1, \underline{x}^j\rangle$$

$$(9A.15)$$

However, (9A.15) is a contradiction of (9A.11).

Case II: $\underline{K}^i_1 = \underline{K}_0 + \underline{x}^i + \theta\underline{x}^j \le \overline{K}_0 + \bar{x}^i + \theta\bar{x}^j = \overline{K}^i_1$

In this case, choose the tuple $(\ddot{x}^i, \ddot{x}^j)$ such that:

$$\ddot{K}^i_1 \equiv \underline{K}_0 + \ddot{x}^i + \theta\ddot{x}^j > \overline{K}^i_1$$

It now follows using the Principle of Optimality and Proposition 2 respectively that:

$$\Pi^i\langle \underline{K}^i_1, \underline{K}^j_1, \underline{x}^i\rangle + \Pi^j\langle \underline{K}^i_1, \underline{K}^j_1, \underline{x}^j\rangle + \tilde{J}\langle \underline{K}^i_1, \underline{K}^j_1\rangle$$
$$\ge \Pi^i\langle \ddot{K}^i_1, \ddot{K}^j_1, \ddot{x}^i\rangle + \Pi^j\langle \ddot{K}^i_1, \ddot{K}^j_1, \ddot{x}^j\rangle + \tilde{J}\langle \ddot{K}^i_1, \ddot{K}^j_1\rangle$$
$$\ge \Pi^i\langle \ddot{K}^i_1, \ddot{K}^j_1, \ddot{x}^i\rangle + \Pi^j\langle \ddot{K}^i_1, \ddot{K}^j_1, \ddot{x}^j\rangle + \tilde{J}\langle \underline{K}^i_1, \underline{K}^j_1\rangle \qquad (9A.16)$$

However, from Assumption **P**:

$$\Pi^i\langle \ddot{K}^i_1, \ddot{K}^j_1, \ddot{x}^i\rangle + \Pi^j\langle \ddot{K}^i_1, \ddot{K}^j_1, \ddot{x}^j\rangle > \Pi^i\langle \underline{K}^i_1, \underline{K}^j_1, \underline{x}^i\rangle + \Pi^j\langle \underline{K}^i_1, \underline{K}^j_1, \underline{x}^j\rangle$$

which contradicts (9A.16). ∎

Proof of Corollary 1

For any $t \ge 1$, $K^m_t \ge K^m_{t-1}$, $m = i, j$. It then follows from Theorem 1 that:

$$y_{t+1} = \tilde{x}^i\langle K^i_t\rangle + \tilde{x}^j\langle K^j_t\rangle \ge \tilde{x}^i\langle K^i_{t-1}\rangle + \tilde{x}^j\langle K^j_{t-1}\rangle = y_t$$

yielding the desired monotonicity. ∎

Proof of Corollary 2

Assume to the contrary that:

$$\bar{x}^i + \bar{x}^j \equiv \tilde{x}^i(\bar{\theta}) + \tilde{x}^j(\bar{\theta}) < \tilde{x}^i(\underline{\theta}) + x^j(\underline{\theta}) \equiv \underline{x}^i + \underline{x}^j$$

Appealing to symmetry, define:

$$\overline{K}^i_1 = K_0 + \bar{x}^i_1 + \bar{\theta}\bar{x}^j_1 = K_0 + \bar{x}^j_1 + \bar{\theta}\bar{x}^i_1 = \overline{K}^j_1$$
$$\underline{K}^i_1 = K_0 + \underline{x}^i_1 + \underline{\theta}\underline{x}^j_1 = K_0 + \underline{x}^j_1 + \underline{\theta}\underline{x}^i_1 = \underline{K}^j_1$$

Further, define the tuples $(\check{x}^i, \check{x}^j)$ and $(\hat{x}^i, \hat{x}^j)$ such that:

$$K_0 + \check{x}^i + \underline{\theta}\check{x}^j = \overline{K}^i_1$$
$$K_0 + \hat{x}^i + \bar{\theta}\hat{x}^j = \underline{K}^i_1$$

The argument of Theorem 1 can now be mimicked to yield the desired monotonicity.

■

Proof of Theorem 2

Under *strict* concavity of the profit functions, and concavity of the value function, the R&D policy for both types of RJVs is unique. Given any initial tuple (K_0, h_0), the time path of R&D expenditures for the secretariat RJV is given by:

$$\tilde{x}^m_t(\theta) = \tilde{x}^m(\tilde{K}^i_{t-1}(\theta), \tilde{K}^j_{t-1}(\theta), \theta), \tilde{K}^i_t(\theta) = \tilde{K}^i_{t-1}(\theta) + \tilde{x}^i_t(\theta) + \tilde{x}^j_t(\theta), \ t \geq 1$$

Similarly, let $\{(\hat{x}^i_t, \hat{x}^j_t)\}$ be the time path of R&D expenditures associated with the operating entity RJV.

Since $\{(\hat{x}^i_t, \hat{x}^j_t)\}$ may not be optimal for the secretariat RJV, there exists a $T' < \infty$ such that for all $T \geq T'$:

$$\sum_{t=1}^{T} \delta^{t-1} \big[\Pi^i \langle \tilde{K}^i_t(\theta), \tilde{K}^j_t(\theta), \tilde{x}^i_t(\theta) \rangle + \Pi^j \langle \tilde{K}^i_t(\theta), \tilde{K}^j_t(\theta), \tilde{x}^j_t(\theta) \rangle \big]$$

$$\geq \sum_{t=1}^{T} \delta^{t-1} \big[\Pi^i \langle \hat{K}^i_t(\theta), \hat{K}^j_t(\theta), \hat{x}^i_t \rangle + \Pi^j \langle \hat{K}^i_t(\theta), \hat{K}^j_t(\theta), \hat{x}^j_t \rangle \big] \qquad (9A.17)$$

where we have defined:

$$\hat{K}^i_1(\theta) = K_0 + \hat{x}^i_1 + \theta \hat{x}^j_1, \quad \hat{K}^i_t(\theta) = \hat{K}^i_{t-1}(\theta) + \hat{x}^i_t + \theta \hat{x}^j_t, \ t \geq 1$$

Recall from Corollary 2 that:

$$\bar{\theta} > \underline{\theta} \Rightarrow \tilde{x}^i(\bar{\theta}) + \tilde{x}^j(\bar{\theta}) \geq \tilde{x}^i(\underline{\theta}) + \tilde{x}^j(\underline{\theta})$$

Under symmetry of firms (so that the R&D policy functions are the same), we have:

$$\tilde{K}^i_1(\bar{\theta}) = K_0 + \tilde{x}^i_1(\bar{\theta}) + \bar{\theta}\tilde{x}^j_1(\bar{\theta}) \geq \tilde{K}^i_1(\underline{\theta}) = K_0 + \tilde{x}^i_1(\underline{\theta}) + \underline{\theta}\tilde{x}^j_1(\underline{\theta})$$

Therefore, by induction, $\tilde{K}^i_t(\bar{\theta}) \geq \tilde{K}^i_t(\underline{\theta})$ for all $t \geq 1$. It follows from Assumption **P** that the left hand side of (9A.17) is increasing in θ. Now let, passing to some subsequence if necessary:

$$\langle \acute{x}^i, \acute{x}^j \rangle = \underset{\theta \to 1}{Lim} \langle \tilde{x}^i(\theta), \tilde{x}^j(\theta) \rangle$$

Since (9A.17) is valid for all θ, a passage to limits yields from the continuity of the profit function and the Monotone Convergence theorem that:

$$\sum_{t=1}^{\infty} \delta^{t-1} \big[\Pi^i \langle \acute{K}^i_t, \acute{K}^j_t, \acute{x}^i_t \rangle + \Pi^j \langle \acute{K}^i_t, \acute{K}^j_t, \acute{x}^j_t \rangle \big] \geq \sum_{t=1}^{\infty} \delta^{t-1} \big[\Pi^i \langle \hat{K}^i_t, \hat{K}^j_t, \hat{x}^i_t \rangle +$$
$$\Pi^j \langle \hat{K}^i_t, \hat{K}^j_t, \hat{x}^j_t \rangle \big]$$

where:

$$\hat{K}^i_1 = K_0 + \hat{x}^i_1 + \hat{x}^j_1, \ \hat{K}^i_t = \hat{K}^i_{t-1} + \hat{x}^i_t + \hat{x}^j_t, \ t \geq 1$$
$$\acute{K}^i_1 = K_0 + \acute{x}^i_1 + \acute{x}^j_1, \ \acute{K}^i_t = \acute{K}^i_{t-1} + \acute{x}^i_t + \acute{x}^j_t, \ t \geq 1$$

The result now follows from the uniqueness of the R&D policy functions. ∎

Proof of Proposition 3

For any $\epsilon > 0$ there exists $(\bar{q}^i, \bar{q}^j)$ such that:

$$\pi^i\langle \bar{q}^i, q_2 \rangle \geq \underset{q^i}{Max}\, \pi^i\langle q^i, q^j \rangle - \frac{\epsilon}{2}$$

$$\pi^i\langle q^i, \bar{q}_2 \rangle \geq \underset{q^j}{Max}\, \pi^j\langle q^i, q^j \rangle - \frac{\epsilon}{2}$$

It then follows that:

$$\underset{q^i, q^j}{Max}\, [\pi^i(q^i, q^j) + \pi^j(q^i, q^j)] \geq \underset{\bar{q}^i, q^j}{Max}\, [\pi^i(q^i, q^j) + \pi^j(q^i, \bar{q}^j)]$$

$$\geq \underset{q^i}{Max}\, \pi^i(q^i, q^j) + \underset{q^j}{Max}\, \pi^j(q^i, q^j) - \epsilon$$

In particular, evaluating the right hand side at the product market Cournot equilibrium and letting $\epsilon \to 0$ yields the result. ∎

Proof of Theorem 3

Assume to the contrary that:

$$2\overset{\leftrightarrow}{x}\langle K_0 \rangle < \hat{x}^i\langle K_0 \rangle + \hat{x}^j\langle K_0 \rangle \tag{9A.18}$$

Since the value function is increasing (Proposition 2), it follows that:

$$\delta \hat{J}\langle K_0 + \hat{x}^i + \hat{x}^j \rangle \geq \delta \hat{J}\langle K_0 + 2\overset{\leftrightarrow}{x} \rangle \tag{9A.19}$$

On the other hand, from the Principle of Optimality:

$$\overset{\leftrightarrow}{\Pi}\langle K_0 + 2\overset{\leftrightarrow}{x} \rangle + \delta \overset{\leftrightarrow}{J}\langle K_0 + 2\overset{\leftrightarrow}{x} \rangle \geq \overset{\leftrightarrow}{\Pi}\langle K_0 + \hat{x}^i + \hat{x}^j \rangle + \delta \overset{\leftrightarrow}{J}\langle K_0 + \hat{x}^i + \hat{x}^j \rangle$$

$$\geq \overset{\leftrightarrow}{\Pi}\langle K_0 + 2\overset{\leftrightarrow}{x} \rangle + \delta \overset{\leftrightarrow}{J}\langle K_0 + \hat{x}^i + \hat{x}^j \rangle$$

where the second inequality is a consequence of Assumption **P**. Therefore:

$$\delta \overset{\leftrightarrow}{J}\langle K_0 + 2\overset{\leftrightarrow}{x} \rangle \geq \delta \overset{\leftrightarrow}{J}\langle K_0 + \hat{x}^i + \hat{x}^j \rangle \tag{9A.20}$$

Combining (9A.19) and (9A.20), it follows that:

$$g\langle K_0 + 2\overset{\leftrightarrow}{x} \rangle \equiv \overset{\leftrightarrow}{J}\langle K_0 + 2\overset{\leftrightarrow}{x} \rangle - \hat{J}\langle K_0 + 2\overset{\leftrightarrow}{x} \rangle$$

$$\geq \overset{\leftrightarrow}{J}\langle K_0 + \hat{x}^i + \hat{x}^j \rangle - \hat{J}\langle K_0 + \hat{x}^i + \hat{x}^j \rangle \equiv g\langle K_0 + \hat{x}^i + \hat{x}^j \rangle \tag{9A.21}$$

But, recalling (9A.18), it follows from Assumption **G** that:

$$g\langle K_0 + 2\overset{\leftrightarrow}{x}\rangle < g\langle K_0 + \hat{x}^i + \hat{x}^j\rangle$$

which contradicts (9A.21). ∎

Notes

1. Of course, the identification of the process of invention/innovation and the resulting technological knowledge with a process of 'creative destruction' (Schumpeter, 1950) is the best known early advocation of dynamics in this respect. Since then, there has been a voluminous and expanding literature on the subject which has led, on the one hand, to evolutionary economic theories – see, e.g., Nelson and Winter (1982); Dosi (1988); Dosi *et al.* (1988); Nelson (1995) – and, on the other, to more mainstream economic appraisals – see, e.g., the survey studies of Kamien and Schwartz (1982); Stoneman (1983); and various chapters in Schmalensee and Willig (1989). Finally, many valuable insights into the process of technological change have been contributed by the very extensive literature at the intersection of history of technological advance, economics, and industry case studies such as Rosenberg (1982, 1994), Freeman (1982), Mowery and Rosenberg (1989), Mokyr (1990), Utterback (1994), and various studies of Paul David to name only a few.

2. Early attempts to document the widely spreading phenomenon of technology linkages included studies such Berg, Duncan and Friedman (1982) and Mariti and Smiley (1983). Since then, economics and business literature on strategic partnering with significant technological content has been exploding. See, for example, Hladik (1985), Harrigan (1986), Fusfeld and Haklisch (1987), Contractor and Lorange (1988), Hagedoorn and Schakenraad (1990), Brockhoff, Gupta and Rotering (1991), Rothwell and Dodgson (1991), Cairnaca, Colombo and Mariotti (1992), Teece (1992), Hobday (1995), Hagedoorn (1995), Vonortas (1991, 1995a) and Vonortas and Safioleas (1995).

3. De Bondt (1995) has an extensive collection of contributions to this literature. Motta (1992) and Poyago-Theotoky (1994) examine the effect of R&D on product innovation (quality improvement).

4. Interestingly, the trade-off between R&D spillovers and R&D investment cannot be supported in general. While there are examples of industries where the enforcement of stricter intellectual property rights seems to contribute to the incentives for single firm investment in R&D (e.g., chemicals, pharmaceuticals), there are many examples of others where lax intellectual property rights regimes have gone hand in hand with heavy commitments to R&D (e.g., software, electronics, automobiles) (Levin *et al.*, 1987). Cohen and Levinthal (1989) and Papaconstantinou (1990) have shown that the existence of this trade-off is sensitive to changes in the working assumptions of the models including the exogeneity of the spillover parameter and the specific functional forms for the production function of knowledge and production cost function that are utilized.

5. Dynamic analyses of R&D investment are not lacking altogether. See, e.g., Joshi and Vonortas (1995) for an alternating move, dynamic model of R&D

investment where firms compete in both R&D and output. Earlier attempts to approximate dynamics include Benoit and Krishna's (1987) discussion of a model where a precommitment in production capacity in the first time period is followed by a repeated game in prices. Such treatments are limited, however, by the assumption that firms do not alter their precommitments during the course of the game

6. This is in the Bulow *et al.* (1985) sense that an increase in the output of the rival Firm j decreases the marginal revenue of Firm i. It is also referred to as the *Hahn condition* and ensures that the output reaction functions are downward-sloping in the (q^i, q^j)-space.

7. Note that no formal existence result for optimal R&D sequences has been provided. However, existence can be determined as follows. Consider any tuple(K_0^i, K_0^j) and (h_0^i, h_0^j). Under suitable restrictions on Π^m, $m = i, j$, there exists a maximal sequence $\{\Pi_t^*\}$ such that for any sequence $\{(x_t^i, x_t^j)\}$ satisfying the constraints given by (9.16), $\Pi^m(K_t^i, K_t^j, x_t^m) \leq \Pi_t^*$ for all $t \geq 1$ and $\Sigma_1^\infty \delta^{t-1} \Pi_t^* < \infty$. Let all sequences $\{(x_t^i, x_t^j)\}$ satisfying the constraints given by (9.16) be called *feasible*. Then, feasible R&D levels are a sequentially closed subset of $\times_1^\infty \Pi_t^*$ which is compact by Tychonoff's theorem (Debreu, 1959, ch. 1). Since closed subsets of compact sets are also compact, feasible R&D levels belong to a compact set. Next, the function $\Sigma_1^N \delta^{t-1} \Pi^m(K_t^i, K_t^j, x_t^m)$, as the finite sum of continuous functions, is also continuous. By the Monotone Convergence theorem, $\Sigma_1^N \delta^{t-1} \Pi^m(K_t^i, K_t^j, x_t^m) \to \Sigma_1^\infty \delta^{t-1} \Pi^m(K_t^i, K_t^j, x_t^m)$ as $N \to \infty$. Since this convergence is bounded from above by the summable sequence $\{\Pi_t^*\}$, it is uniform in N and, therefore, the function $\Sigma_1^\infty \delta^{t-1} \Pi^m(K_t^i, K_t^j, x_t^m)$, $m = i, j$, is also continuous. The existence of an optimal R&D sequence now follows from the well-known Weierstrass theorem that a continuous function on a compact set achieves a maximum on the set.

8. The terminology has been borrowed from Ouchi (1989) who discusses examples of such organizations. The Semiconductor Research Corporation (SRC) is an example of a secretariat. The Semiconductor Manufacturing and Technology Institute (Sematech) is an example of an operating entity.

9. See Katz (1986) and Katz and Ordover (1990) on the issue of external competition to the RJV.

10. Given the usual assumptions in these models. 'Overshooting' has been often found in tournament models where competitors take part in an innovation race with one winner.

11. Economists anticipated such a result long ago. In his classic paper, for example, Nelson (1959) discussed some reasons why joint ventures may raise the incentives to undertake highly inappropriable research which individual members would not have undertaken on their own. The difference between his analysis and ours is that we analyze a homogeneous product industry whereas he based his qualitative argument on research uncertainty and incentives due to increased product heterogeneity among RJV members. The two arguments are complementary.

12. For a summary of the debate, see, e.g., US Senate (1991). Vonortas (1995b) also discusses the issue.

References

Benoit, J-P. and V. Krishna (1987) 'Dynamic Duopoly: Prices and Quantities', *Review of Economic Studies*, LIV, pp. 23–35.

Berg, S.V., J. Duncan and P. Friedman (1982) *Joint Venture Strategies and Corporate Innovation* (Cambridge, Mass.: Oelgeschlager Gunn and Hain Publisher Inc.)

Brander, J. and B. Spencer (1983) 'Strategic Commitment with R&D: The Symmetric Case', *Bell Journal of Economics*, 14, pp. 225–35.

Brockhoff, K., A.K. Gupta and C. Rotering (1991) 'Inter-firm R&D Co-operations in Germany', *Technovation*, 11(4), pp. 219–28.

Bulow, J., J. Geanakoplos and P. Klemperer (1985) 'Multimarket Oligopoly: Strategic Substitutes and Complements', *Journal of Political Economy*, 93, pp. 488–511.

Cairnaca, G.C., M.G. Colombo and S. Mariotti (1992) 'Agreements Between Firms and the Technological Life Cycle Model: Evidence from Information Technologies', *Research Policy*, 21, pp. 45–62.

Cohen, W.M. and D.A. Levinthal (1989) 'Innovation and Learning: The Two Faces of R&D', *Economic Journal*, Setember, pp. 569–96.

Contractor, F.R. and P. Lorange (eds) (1988) *Cooperative Strategies in International Business* (Lexington: D.C. Heath).

D'Aspremont and Jacquemin (1988) 'Cooperative and Noncooperative R&D in Duopoly with Spillovers', *The American Economic Review*, December, pp. 1133–7.

Dasgupta, P. and J. Stiglitz (1980) 'Industrial Structure and the Nature of Innovative Activity', *Economic Journal*, 90, pp. 266–93.

De Bondt, R. (1995) 'Spillovers and Innovative Activities', *International Journal of Industrial Organization*, forthcoming.

De Bondt, R. and C. Wu (1997) 'Research Joint Venture Cartels and Welfare', Chapter 3 in this volume.

De Bondt, R. and R. Veugelers (1991) 'Strategic Investment with Spillovers', *European Journal of Political Economy*, 7(3) pp. 345–66.

De Bondt, R., P. Slaets and B. Cassiman (1992) 'The Degree of Spillovers and the Number of Rivals for Maximum Effective R&D', *International Journal of Industrial Organization*, 10(1), pp. 35–54.

Debreu, G. (1959) *Theory of Value* (New York: John Wiley & Sons).

Dixit, A.K. and J.E. Stiglitz (1977) 'Monopolistic Competition and Optimum Product Diversity', *The American Economic Review*, 67, pp. 297–308.

Dosi, G. (1988) 'Sources, Procedures, and Microeconomic Effects of Innovation', *Journal of Economic Literature*, 26, pp. 1120–71.

Dosi, G., C. Freeman, R.R. Nelson, G. Silverberg and L. Soete (eds) (1988) *Technical Change and Economic Theory* (London: Pinter Publishers).

Freeman, C. (1982) *The Economics of Industrial Innovation*, 2nd edn (MIT Press).

Fudenberg, D. and J. Tirole (1983) 'Capital as Commitment: Strategic Investment to Deter Mobility', *Journal of Economic Theory*, 31, pp. 227–50.

Fusfeld, H.I. (1986) *The Technical Enterprise* (Cambridge, Mass: Ballinger).

Fusfeld, H.I. (1994) *Industry's Future: Changing Patterns of Industrial Research* (Washington, DC: American Chemical Society).

Fusfeld, H.I. and C.S. Haklisch (1987) 'Collaborative Industrial Research in the U.S.', *Technovation*, 5, pp. 305–15.

Gilbert, R. and R. Harris (1984) 'Competition with Lumpy Investment', *Rand Journal of Economics*, 15, pp. 197–212.

Gugler, P. and J.H. Dunning (1993) 'Technology-Based Cross-Border Alliances', in R. Culpan (ed.), *Multinational Strategic Alliances* (New York: International Business Press).

Hagedoorn, J. (1995) 'Strategic Technology Partnering During the 1980s: Trends, Networks and Corporate Patterns in Non-Core Technologies', *Research Policy*, 24, pp. 207–31.

Hagedoorn, J. and J. Schakenraad (1990) 'Inter-Firm Partnerships and Co-operative Strategies in Core Technologies', in C. Freeman and L. Soete (eds) *New Explorations in the Economics of Technological Change* (London: Pinter Publishers).

Harrigan K.R. (1986) *Managing for Joint Venture Success* (Lexington, Mass.: Lexington).

Hladik K.J. (1985) *International Joint Ventures: An Economic Analysis of U.S. – Foreign Business Partnerships* (Lexington, Mass.: Lexington).

Hobday, M. (1995) 'East Asian Latecomer Firms: Learning the Technology of Electronics', *World Development*, 20(12), pp. 1817–28.

Jorde, T.M. and D.J. Teece (1990) 'Innovation and Cooperation: Implications for Competition and Antitrust', *Journal of Economic Perspectives*, 4(3), pp. 75–96.

Jorde, T.M. and D.J. Teece (1992) *Antitrust, Innovation, and Competitiveness* (New York: Oxford University Press).

Joshi, S. and N.S. Vonortas (1995) 'A Theory of Dynamic Competition in R&D', Discussion Paper, Department of Economics, The George Washington University, Washington, D.C.

Kamien, M.I. and N.L. Schwartz (1982) *Market Structure and Innovation*, (Cambridge University Press).

Kamien, M.I., E. Muller and I. Zang (1992) 'Research Joint Ventures and R&D Cartels', *The American Economic Review*, 82(5), pp. 1293–306.

Katz, M.L. (1986) 'An Analysis of Cooperative Research and Development', *Rand Journal of Economics*, 17(4), pp. 527–43.

Katz, M.L. and J.A. Ordover (1990) 'R&D Cooperation and Competition', *Brookings Papers on Economic Activity: Microeconomics*, pp. 137–91.

Levin, R.C., A.K. Klevorick, R.R. Nelson and S.G. Winter (1987) 'Appropriating the Returns from Industrial Research and Development', *Brookings Papers on Economic Activity: Microeconomics*, 3, pp. 783–820.

Mariti, P. and R.H. Smiley (1983) 'Cooperative Agreements and the Organisation of Industry', *The Journal of Industrial Economics*, 31(4), pp. 437–51.

Mokyr, J. (1990) *The Lever of Riches* (New York: Oxford University Press).

Motta, M. (1992) 'Cooperative R&D and Vertical Product Differentiation', *International Journal of Industrial Organization*, 10, pp. 643–61.

Mowery, D.C. and N. Rosenberg (1989) *Technology and the Pursuit of Economic Growth* (Cambridge: Cambridge University Press).

Nelson, R.R. (1959) 'The Simple Economics of Basic Scientific Research', *Journal of Political Economy*, 67, pp. 297–306.

Nelson, R.R. (1995) 'Recent Evolutionary Theorizing about Economic Change',

Journal of Economic Literature, XXXIII, March, pp. 48–90.

Nelson, R.R. and S.G. Winter (1982) *An Evolutionary Theory of Economic Change* (Cambridge, Mass.: Belknap Press).

Ordover, J.A. and W.J. Baumol (1988) 'Antitrust Policy for High-Technology Industries', *Oxford Review of Economic Policy*, 4, pp. 13–35.

Ouchi, W.G. (1989) 'The New Joint R&D', *Proceedings of the IEEE*, 77(9), pp. 1318–26.

Papaconstantinou, G. (1990) 'Research Spillovers, International Competition and Economic Performance', Ph.D. dissertation, The London School of Economics and Political Science, University of London.

Poyago-Theotoky, Joanna (1994) 'Research Joint Ventures and Product Innovation: Part I', mimeo, Department of Economics, University of Nottingham.

Reinganum, J.F. (1989) 'The Timing of Innovation: Research, Development, and Diffusion', in R. Schmalensee and R.D. Willig (eds), *Handbook of Industrial Organization* (New York: Elsevier Science Publishers).

Rosenberg, N. (1982) *Inside the Black Box: Technology and Economics* (Cambridge: Cambridge University Press).

Rosenberg, N. (1994) *Exploring the Black Box: Technology, Economics, and History* (Cambridge: Cambridge University Press).

Rothwell, R. and M. Dodgson (1991) 'External Linkages and Innovation in Small and Medium-Sized Enterprises', *R&D Management*, 21(2), pp. 125–37.

Schmalensee, R. and R.D. Willig (eds) (1989) *Handbook of Industrial Organization* (New York: Elsevier Science Publishers).

Schumpeter, J.A. (1950) *Capitalism, Socialism, and Democracy*, 3rd edn (New York: Harper & Bros).

Shapiro, C. (1989) 'Theories of Oligopoly Behavior', in R. Schmalensee and R.D. Willig (eds), *Handbook of Industrial Organization* (New York: Elsevier Science Publishers).

Simpson, R.D. and N.S. Vonortas (1994) 'Cournot Equilibrium with Imperfectly Appropriable R&D', *The Journal of Industrial Economics*, XLII(1), pp. 79–92.

Spence, M. (1976) 'Product Selection, Fixed Cost, and Monopolistic Competition', *Review of Economic Studies*, 43, pp. 217–35.

Spence, M. (1979) 'Investment Strategy and Growth in a New Market', *Bell Journal of Economics*, 10, pp. 1–19.

Spence, M. (1984) 'Cost Reduction, Competition, and Industry Performance', *Econometrica*, 52(1), pp. 101–21.

Stoneman, P. (1983) *The Economic Analysis of Technological Change* (New York: Oxford University Press).

Suzumura, K. (1992) 'Cooperative and Noncooperative R&D in an Oligopoly with Spillovers', *The American Economic Review*, 82(5), pp. 1307–20.

Teece, D.J. (1992) 'Competition, Cooperation, and Innovation: Organizational Arrangements for Regimes of Rapid Technological Progress', *Journal of Economic Behavior and Organization*, 18, pp. 1–25.

US Senate (1991) 'The National Cooperative Research Act Extension of 1991', Bill no. 479.

Utterback, J.M. (1994) *Mastering the Dynamics of Innovation* (Boston, Mass.: Harvard Business School Press).

Vonortas, N.S. (1991) *Research Cooperation in R&D-Intensive Industries* (Aldershot: Avebury).

Vonortas, N.S. (1994) 'Inter-firm Cooperation with Imperfectly Appropriable Research', *International Journal of Industrial Organization*, 12(3), pp. 413–35.

Vonortas, N.S. (1995a) 'Research Joint Ventures in the U.S.', Working Paper, Center for International Science and Technology Policy, The George Washington University, Washington, DC.

Vonortas, N.S. (1995b) 'Disconnected: Economics and the Micro-process of Technological Advance', Working Paper, Center for International Science and Technology Policy, The George Washington University, Washington, DC.

Vonortas, N.S. and S. Safioleas (1995) *Inter-firm Strategic Alliances in Information Technology: The Case of Developing Countries*, Report to the Private Sector Development Department, The World Bank, Washington, DC, September.

Index